Safe Assets in the Global Economy

Safe assets constitute an essential component of the contemporary, international financial system and are vital to its stability. As they are perceived as risk-free assets, they are a special type of financial instrument. Although the vast majority of safe assets are issued by governments, due to the increasing interdependence of economies, resulting from the liberalisation of capital flows, financial openness and the ineffectiveness of the international monetary system, issues relating to their significance, creation and allocation are global. This book combines theoretical threads by systematising the concept and characteristics of safe assets against the background of alternative financial instruments with empirical analyses that present trends in shaping demand, supply, price conditions and various interdependencies in the financial markets. It shows the position and role of safe assets in the global financial sector, in the context of ongoing challenges, such as the evolution of forms of money and the processes of currency competition, the outbreak of financial and economic crises, the accumulation of foreign exchange reserves, financial innovations, the scale of securitisation and monetary integration. Although safe assets are not a new category of financial assets, they are inherently connected with the evolution of money. Thus, this book examines the determinants of their creation, motives of holding and the consequences of a shortage – all within the changing nature of the international financial system. Historical, political and institutional backgrounds are taken into account. This book will appeal to researchers, scholars and advanced students of macroeconomics, international finance and economics, investment analysis, financial economics and econometrics.

Joanna Bogołębska is an associate professor in the Department of International Business and Trade, University of Lodz, Poland.

Ewa Feder-Sempach is an assistant professor in the Department of International Finance and Investment, University of Lodz, Poland.

Ewa Stawasz-Grabowska is an assistant professor in the Department of International Finance and Investment, University of Lodz, Poland.

Routledge International Studies in Money and Banking

Financial and Technological Innovation for Sustainability
Edited by Artie Ng and Jatin Nathwani

Digital Transformation and the Economics of Banking
Economic, Institutional, and Social Dimensions
Edited by Piotr Łasak and Jonathan Williams

Behavioral Finance in the Digital Era
Saving and Investment Decisions
Elżbieta Kubińska, Magdalena Adamczyk-Kowalczuk and Anna Macko

International Banking in Global Perspective
Edited by Carmela D'Avino and Mimoza Shabani

Non-Fungible Tokens
Multidisciplinary Perspectives
Edited by Usman W. Chohan

Open Banking
Global Development and Regulation
Francesco De Pascalis and Alan Brener

Banking Reforms in Africa
Implications for Economic Welfare and Poverty Reduction
Agnes Olatokunbo Martins

Safe Assets in the Global Economy
Supply, Demand and Financial Stability
Joanna Bogołębska, Ewa Feder-Sempach and Ewa Stawasz-Grabowska

For more information about this series, please visit: www.routledge.com/Routledge-International-Studies-in-Money-and-Banking/book-series/SE0403

Safe Assets in the Global Economy

Supply, Demand and Financial Stability

Joanna Bogołębska, Ewa Feder-Sempach and Ewa Stawasz-Grabowska

Routledge
Taylor & Francis Group
LONDON AND NEW YORK

First published 2025
by Routledge
4 Park Square, Milton Park, Abingdon, Oxon OX14 4RN

and by Routledge
605 Third Avenue, New York, NY 10158

Routledge is an imprint of the Taylor & Francis Group, an informa business

British Library Cataloguing-in-Publication Data
A catalogue record for this book is available from the British Library

Library of Congress Cataloging-in-Publication Data
Names: Bogołębska, Joanna, author. | Feder-Sempach, Ewa, author. | Stawasz-Grabowska, Ewa, author.
Title: Safe assets in the global economy : supply, demand and financial stability / Joanna Bogołębska, Ewa Feder-Sempach, Ewa Stawasz-Grabowska.
Description: Abingdon, Oxon ; New York, NY Routledge, 2024. | Series: Routledge international studies in money and banking | Includes bibliographical references. |
Identifiers: LCCN 2024007395 (print) | LCCN 2024007396 (ebook) | ISBN 9781032453415 (hardback) | ISBN 9781032453439 (paperback) | ISBN 9781003376538 (ebook)
Subjects: LCSH: Financial instruments. | Financial institutions—Investments. | Investment analysis. | International finance.
Classification: LCC HG4521 .B568 2024 (print) | LCC HG4521 (ebook) | DDC 332.6—dc23/eng/20240422
LC record available at https://lccn.loc.gov/2024007395
LC ebook record available at https://lccn.loc.gov/2024007396

ISBN: 9781032453415 (hbk)
ISBN: 9781032453439 (pbk)
ISBN: 9781003376538 (ebk)

DOI: 10.4324/9781003376538

The Open Access version of this book was funded by University of Lodz.

For Product Safety Concerns and Information please contact our EU representative: GPSR@taylorandfrancis.com. Taylor & Francis Verlag GmbH, Kaufingerstraße 24, 80331 München, Germany.

'To our Families - for being the most valuable asset and letting us feel safe'

Contents

List of figures xi

Introduction 1

1 **Concept, Definitions and Functions of Safe Assets** 4
1.1 The Overall Characteristics of a Safe Asset 4
1.1.1 Definitions, Key Features and Functions 4
1.1.2 The Attributes of a Safe Asset 7
1.1.3 Safe Assets as a Financial Instrument and Money 10
1.2 Safe Assets vs Safe-Haven Assets 13
1.2.1 The Characteristics of Safe Havens 13
1.2.1.1 Gold as a Safe Haven 16
1.2.1.2 Safe-Haven Currencies 21
1.2.1.3 Other Categories of Safe Havens 23
1.2.2 Safe-Haven Assets and Asset Pricing Theory 25
References 30

2 **The Supply of Safe Assets** 36
2.1 Determining Safe Asset Supply in an International Context 36
2.1.1 Global vs Regional Providers of Safe Assets 36
2.1.2 The Exorbitant Privilege Concept 38
2.1.3 Characteristics of a Global Safe Asset Provider 42
2.2 The Structure of the Supply of Safe Assets 44
2.2.1 Safe Asset Provision from a Historical Perspective 44
2.2.2 Contemporary Tendencies in the Supply of Safe Assets 48

2.3 The Role of Debt in Safe Asset Creation 56
2.3.1 Public vs Private Debt in the Provision of Safe Assets 56
2.3.2 The Special Role of Public Debt as a Source of Safe Asset Provision 63
2.3.2.1 The Limitations of Public Debt as Safe Assets – The Laffer Curve 63
2.3.2.2 Economic and Non-economic Determinants of Public Debt Creation in the Role of Safe Assets 66
References 70

3 The Demand for Safe Assets 74
3.1 Demand for Safety 74
3.1.1 Commercial Banks' Demand for Safe Assets 75
3.1.2 Motives Behind Holding Safe Assets 79
3.2 Central Banks' Demand for Safe Assets 84
3.2.1 Foreign Exchange Reserves in the Portfolios of Central Banks 84
3.2.2 Gold in Central Banks' Portfolios 87
3.2.2.1 Gold as a Component of Central Banks' Reserves 87
3.2.2.2 The Changing Sentiment of Central Banks towards Gold 92
3.2.2.3 Central Banks' Gold Fever of 2022 and Its Consequences 97
3.3 Sovereign Wealth Funds' Demand for Safe Assets 100
3.4 Other Market Participants' Demand for Safe Assets 106
3.5 The Role of the Foreign Sector in the Ownership of Domestic Safe Assets – The Case of a Global Provider (USA) 110
References 116

4 Safe Asset Shortages and the Implications for Financial Stability. In Search of New Sources of Supply 121
4.1 Financial Stability and Its Link with the Safe Assets Market 121
4.2 Imbalances in the Demand and Supply of Safe Assets 125
4.2.1 Causes of the Demand–Supply Mismatch of Safe Assets 125

4.2.2 *Consequences of the Demand-Supply Mismatch for Financial Stability* 127

4.3 *The Evolution of Public Debt Levels of Safe Asset Supplier Countries* 130

4.4 *Mechanisms of Safe Asset Creation and the Stability of the International Monetary System* 135

4.5 *Alternative Sources of Safe Asset Supply* 140

4.6 *The EMU* 143

4.6.1 *Fiscal Frameworks within the EMU and Its Evolution* 143

4.6.2 *A Common Safe Asset for the Euro Area. An Overview of Proposals* 149

4.6.3 *The Role of Supranational Debt in Safe Assets Creation. The Case of EU* 154

4.7 *The Role of EMEs in Producing Safe Assets* 157

4.7.1 *The Rising Role of EMEs in the Global Economy* 157

4.7.2 *China* 159

4.7.2.1 *The Dynamics and Determinants of China's Bond Market Development* 159

4.7.2.2 *Segments of the Chinese Bond Market – The Role of Public Sector Issuance* 161

4.7.3 *India* 167

4.8 *Evolution of the Forms of Money and the Supply of Safe Assets* 169

References 174

Conclusion 181

Glossary 185

Index 187

Figures

1.1	Safe assets functions	6
1.2	Gold vs unexpected market turmoil (2001–2023)	16
1.3	Nominal vs real prices of gold	17
1.4	Average annual return of different global assets in USD	18
1.5	Gold vs S&P500 performance (1980–2023)	20
1.6	Currencies vs S&P 500 performance (2000–2023)	23
1.7	Bitcoin vs S&P 500 performance (2014–2023)	25
1.8	The efficient frontier	27
1.9	Security characteristic line	28
1.10	Security market line	29
2.1	Currency composition of international debt securities as of Q42022 (% of total)	38
2.2	Outstanding sovereign debt (as of October 2023)	39
2.3	Safe assets by category (% of total)	49
2.4	Sovereign bond yields of the euro area, AAA countries against the average	50
2.5	Foreign vs domestic holdings of US Treasury securities (share of total)	60
2.6	US asset-backed securities issuance	60
2.7	Classification of assets from the point of view of liquidity and risk	61
2.8	The Laffer curve for safe assets	64
2.9	The Laffer curve for safe assets for different country groups	64
2.10	The Laffer curve for safe assets by the state of the economy	65
3.1	MFIs' holdings of debt securities issued by euro-area general governments – core countries	76
3.2	MFIs' holdings of debt securities issued by euro-area general governments – GIIPS countries	77
3.3	Global holdings of foreign exchange reserves	85
3.4	Top holders of foreign exchange reserves	86
3.5	Composition of gold demand, 2010–2022	88

3.6 World official gold holdings broken down by income group (shares in gold tonnes) 89
3.7 Countries with the largest reserves (including gold) 90
3.8 Periods of net purchases and sales since the 1950s 93
3.9 European gold sales within central bank gold agreements 94
3.10 Top largest gold buyers in 2022 97
3.11 Asset allocation structure of SWFs 102
3.12 SWFs investment objectives 104
3.13 GPFG's allocation by asset class as of 31 December 2022 (%) 105
3.14 General government debt structure of the euro-area countries in 2022 (% of total) 108
3.15 Foreign vs domestic holdings of US Treasury securities (share of total), 1952–2022 111
3.16 Official vs private foreign holdings of US Treasury securities in January 2023 112
3.17 Major foreign holders of US Treasury securities 113
4.1 Selected contagion channels between banks and sovereigns 123
4.2 General government debt of major advanced economies, 2001–2022 (% of GDP) 133
4.3 China's public debt compared to reserve currency issuers in 2001 and 2022 (% of GDP) 133
4.4 World currency composition of official foreign exchange reserves (shares of allocated reserves) 137
4.5 Long-term sovereign bond yields of some euro-area countries 145
4.6 Credit ratings of the selected euro-area economies (according to S&P) 146
4.7 The stock of euro-area sovereign debt securities broken down by credit rating 149
4.8 GDP based on PPP, global share (%) 158
4.9 Chinese onshore bond market structure (% of total bonds outstanding) 164
4.10 The largest bond markets in the world 165
4.11 Types of digital currencies and the main issues surrounding classification 170

Introduction

This book, titled *Safe Assets in the Global Economy: Supply, Demand and Financial Stability*, undeniably offers cutting-edge, innovative and useful perspectives on safe investments. Each chapter outlines a different issue, reflecting the contemporary economic literature to ensure that the content is international in outlook while also introducing some emerging areas. This book provides collective advice for practitioners and considerations for academics, and it outlines directions for research in the years to come.

Safe assets are a relatively 'young' category in the financial literature despite their – historically – 'old' nature, dating back to the origins of money as a means of storing value. Interest in this particular type of financial asset is reflected in the fragmentary discussion of safe assets in the literature and the lack of terminological and definitional coherence. The first extensive attempt to address the concept of safe assets and signal their role in the financial system was made in 2012 by the International Monetary Fund (IMF). Since then, more and more research has been conducted, mainly in the form of detailed empirical analyses.

Safe assets are an important component of the contemporary international financial system. At the same time, they are a determinant of its stability. Although their creation is an intrinsic feature of the financial system, both domestically and internationally, the importance of their special role is particularly evident in the contemporary conditions of increasing interdependence among economies (resulting from financial openness and liberalised capital flows) and inefficiencies in how the international monetary system functions. The main problem with safe assets stems from their asymmetrical supply, which is concentrated in a few advanced economies. This, coupled with a supply-demand imbalance, persists even though they constitute a constant share of financial assets and the financial markets' ability to supplement them when needed. These conditions have serious consequences for financial stability.

The aim of this book is to indicate the place and role of safe assets in the international financial and monetary system in the context of their contemporary frameworks, mechanisms and deficiencies.

DOI: 10.4324/9781003376538-1

In particular, this book attempts to answer the following questions:

- What is a safe asset? What are its features?
- When does an asset gain and lose the status of safe asset?
- Why is government debt the best candidate to fulfil the role of safe asset?
- Why is the government debt of some countries especially desirable to investors? Is there a limit to its creation?
- What are the threats to financial stability that stem from the existence of such a special category of assets, considering their scarcity and asymmetrical creation?

This book views the functioning of safe assets through the prism of both the international monetary system (IMS) and the international financial system (IFS). Reference to the IMS is relevant from the point of view of the mechanisms of international money creation (or, in other words, global liquidity). The relationship between this system and safe assets can best be captured by analysing the functions of this system. As Pierre-Olivier Gourinchas (2017, p. 169) states: "[...] the fundamental function of the IMS is to allocate scarce safe assets between countries". Examining the perception of safe assets through the prism of the mechanisms of the IFS lets us gain insights into the functioning of the safe assets market within a deep, cross-border, contemporary financial market. This market is abundant in many financial instruments, real assets and financial innovations, offering investment alternatives for different categories of actors.

Despite the distinction between the IMS and IFS adopted in this book, some approaches recognise the operation of a single, dual system. For example, the Bank for International Settlements treats the two systems together, using the term 'international monetary and financial system'. This term generally encompasses the rules governing payments in the realm of goods, services and financial instruments between countries (BIS, 2015).

This book consists of four chapters, with each chapter weaving together theoretical threads and empirical elements derived from the statistical analysis conducted on the basis of various databases. Thus, apart from the strictly theoretical Chapter 1, the remaining chapters are both theoretical and empirical.

Chapter 1 provides a conceptual and definitional synthesis of safe assets. It provides an overview of various definitions, functions and attributes, which is essential to understand what makes an asset safe. The main objective of the issues presented is to show the dilemmas of who (i.e. which sector of the economy) is capable of issuing this special kind of assets, as well as when they can do it and under what circumstances.

Chapter 2 focuses on the supply side, providing an analysis of the determinants and limitations of safe assets issuance. The discussion encompasses global and regional providers, along with insights into the exorbitant privilege doctrine. Understanding the special role of the dominant currency in the IMS in safe asset creation is crucial for appreciating its benefits and threats, both for the issuing countries and the broader globalised economy.

Chapter 3 concentrates on the demand side of the safe asset market. This is presented in two ways. The first way is by sector (industry analysis), where an attempt is made to distinguish the motives of demand for such assets. The second way is by source of demand, i.e., from domestic funds or from abroad. The two levels of consideration overlap, which is intentional, indicating the diversity of demand motives in the course of the evolution of the IMS and IFS. Special attention is paid to the United States, as a true global provider. The chapter explains the role and scale of domestic and foreign holdings of its safe assets, and the special role of their treasury securities.

Chapter 4 introduces yet another important analytical element: financial stability. Here, the links between the safe asset market and financial stability are illustrated. The starting point for the considerations adopted in this chapter is the statement, which is derived from the analyses of trends presented in the previous chapters, that the global economy is characterised by a shortage of global safe assets. While this tendency can be temporarily alleviated (as seen after the COVID-19 crisis with policies of fiscal expansion), it is deemed to be an immanent feature of the contemporary IMS and IFS. In identifying the causes and consequences of the supply-demand imbalance, the need to supplement supply beyond existing sources is pointed out.

This book is mainly based on the international literature on safe assets, including publications by authors from the world's major research and academic centres and international institutions, such as the National Bureau of Economic Research, the International Monetary Fund and the Bank for International Settlements, and publications from central banks, including the European Central Bank and the Federal Reserve System. The data come from the IMF, the World Bank and the World Gold Council, as well as Refinitiv EIKON (Thomson Reuters).

1 Concept, Definitions and Functions of Safe Assets

1.1 The Overall Characteristics of a Safe Asset

1.1.1 Definitions, Key Features and Functions

There is no uniform definition of safe assets in the literature. The term first appeared in the 1980s, mostly in speeches given by central bank officials, and was used to describe low-risk investment. First attempts to capture the essence of safe assets date back to the early 2000s and, more specifically, the Global Financial Crisis (henceforth GFC). The definitions of safe assets used vary as they emphasise different sources of creation, functions and attributes of this type of asset. At the same time, there is a consensus that there are no assets that are completely risk-free and, therefore, offer complete safety. Hence, the term safe assets should refer to assets that are safe relative to other asset classes. As Gelpern and Gerding (2016, p. 5) argue, 'safe' in this context does not mean genuinely risk-free but rather 'safe enough' to ignore the risks for some purposes.

Safe asset is a catch-all term that exists mostly in the economic literature to describe low-risk investments. In the simplest terms, it can be stated that they are a secure store of value, that is an unconditional promise of future repayment (cf. Gourinchas and Jeanne, 2012, p. 5; Golec and Perotti, 2017, p. 5). Commonly, safe assets are also defined as any debt that guarantees a fixed value of money in the future without the default risk of the issuer (cf. Golec and Perotti, 2017; Caballero et al., 2017). Gorton (2016, p. 1) states that these assets are (almost always) valued at face value without the expensive collecting of additional information on this asset and, thus, can be traded without fear of adverse selection. According to Caballero et al. (2017, p. 29), a safe asset is a simple debt instrument that provides investors with a guarantee that it will retain its value during adverse economic events. That is why safe assets are defined as any debt instrument that promises a fixed amount of money with no default risk, which is reflected in their top credit ratings. It is also supported by the results of empirical research (e.g. Habib et al., 2020, p. 25), which indicates that there is no correlation between the perception of assets as safe and shocks that generate an increase in the global risk factor, regardless of their nature (monetary, financial and geopolitical shocks).

DOI: 10.4324/9781003376538-2

In the 2012 International Monetary Fund (henceforth IMF) report, which is one of the first publications in this area, safe assets are defined in relation to five features (IMF, 2012, p. 84):

1 Low credit and market risk,
2 High market liquidity,
3 Limited inflationary risk,
4 Low exchange rate risk,
5 Limited unsystematic (idiosyncratic) risk.

The IMF points out that the first feature is the most important, as it is usually combined with a low liquidity risk. High market liquidity ensures that assets can be sold at any time without having a significant impact on their price. Additionally, the advantage of high liquidity is that debt can be easily rolled over, which is beneficial for both the issuer and the buyer (van Riet, 2017, p. 7). Owning liquid assets provides investors with a form of self-insurance, allowing them to avoid the costly search for external funding when facing information asymmetry or moral hazard. When illiquid assets are sold off at fire-sale prices, those entities that have held liquid financial assets in their portfolios are at an advantage. Thus, high demand for liquidity can explain the lower profitability of liquid financial assets (Golec and Perotti, 2017, p. 6). Government debt is the best example of an instrument that combines low credit risk and a deep and liquid market. However, it can be argued that the first two characteristics pointed out in the IMF report do not always go hand in hand. For example, some assets perceived as safe, such as time deposits, may have low liquidity due to their nature.

In addition, the IMF (2012) underscores the significance of maintaining a low and stable inflation environment. When inflation is high and volatile, even short-term, near-cash instruments become risky assets in real terms (unless they are inflation-protected securities). Low inflation and exchange rate risk make an asset a good store of value, as they let it retain value over time.

Furthermore, the relevance of the individual characteristics identified by the IMF depends on the category of investors, their strategy and their investment horizon. For example, investors with long-term liabilities (e.g. pension funds or insurance institutions) attach less importance to liquidity. For them, safe assets are those with longer maturities, which tend to be less liquid than their counterparts (e.g. treasury bonds vs treasury bills). In turn, investors with a demand for foreign currency-denominated assets will take more account of exchange rate risk. Public entities managing foreign exchange reserves (central banks, sovereign wealth funds) will consider all characteristics due to the high share of foreign currency-denominated credit instruments in their portfolios and the need to maintain liquidity. Finally, the demand for non-credit instruments, such as gold, is strongly motivated by their ability to hold value, with less consideration for market risk (IMF, 2012, p. 84).

Safe assets can also be defined by the functions they perform. The IMF (2012, p. 82) distinguishes five principal functions for which these types of assets are in demand:

1 As a store of value and a portfolio capital cushion,
2 As stable collateral in repo transactions, both private and with the central bank, and in the derivatives markets; thus, they act as a substitute for trust in financial transactions,
3 As a benchmark for price formation, hedging and the valuation of other riskier assets; through this function, safe assets can be an indicator of monetary and financial conditions (e.g. an inverted government bond yield curve can signal an expected decline in economic activity in the future),
4 As a tool in monetary policy operations,
5 As part of compliance with solvency and liquidity regulations, they are a key component of prudential regulation, thereby providing a mechanism for banks to increase their capital and liquidity buffers.

This list of functions is not the only taxonomy, and it was supplemented by Gelpern and Gerding (2016), who recognised the transactional and technological functions (Figure 1.1). Safe assets can be quickly turned into cash, to

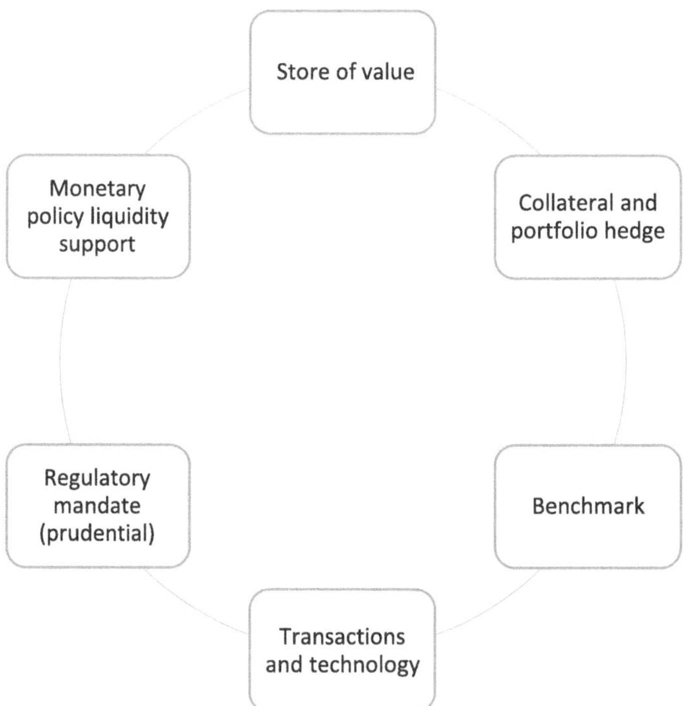

Figure 1.1 Safe assets functions

Source: Own elaboration based on the cited literature.

meet transactional needs, and they can be used as cash substitutes for current transactions. However, some risk-seeking investors might hold safe assets as cash substitutes for ongoing transactions, for example to hedge against transaction risks and maintain access to cash for new investments. On the other hand, when analysing sovereign bonds as risk-free assets, Fisher (2013) identified six functions that are being fulfilled.

Such a vast array of functions mirrors the different risks that safe assets must face and the different purposes they create in the world economy.

Taking into account the wide range of functions performed, it can be argued that safe assets play a key role in the economy and have important implications for transaction and savings efficiency, financial crises, general aggregate macroeconomic activity and monetary policy (Gorton, 2016, p. 1). This is exactly why many economists, following the IMF, describe safe assets as the cornerstone of the global financial system.

1.1.2 The Attributes of a Safe Asset

As the concept of safe assets is multidimensional, various attempts have been made to characterise them by their attributes. A literature review allows the following list to be formulated:

1 Moneyness and liquidity

These are two closely related but not completely overlapping concepts. Full moneyness refers to the ability to convert assets into cash at face value and on demand, regardless of the phase of the business cycle. Meanwhile, liquidity is "[...] a measure of the ability to buy or sell a product in a desired quantity and at a desired price and time without materially impacting the product's price" (IOSCO, 2017, p. 2). In other words, liquidity is understood as the ability to convert tradable assets into money, at face value or not, in all phases of the business cycle. The distinction between the two concepts is introduced to describe assets with a low degree of liquidity, but that have a moneyness feature, such as money market fund shares. An example of safe assets that have both characteristics is short-term government debt instruments (cf. Gabor and Vestergaard, 2018, pp. 143–144). Short-term government debt is a 'near-money' asset; thus, it is a close substitute for cash in providing liquidity (Nagel, 2016). Golec and Perotti (2017) stated that moneyness explains why short-term debt issued by the private financial sector can be a better substitute for short-term debt than long-term government bonds. More specifically, long-term debt cannot be redeemed for cash on demand; thus, in effect, it lacks moneyness. Despite this, in most cases, the terms are used interchangeably. Gorton (2016, p. 9) says that the terms money and liquidity premium are usually used synonymously, as they refer to the no-questions-asked attribute (see below).

2 Information insensitivity

Financial assets are considered safe if new information about their characteristics does not affect the desire to own them. Therefore, they are resistant to costly information acquisition regarding their value (Dang et al., 2012). Thus, there is no benefit in gathering additional information about the value of assets, nor are there concerns about adverse selection in buying or selling them (Gorton, 2016, p. 1). For example, a bond with a near-zero default risk is insensitive to information in the sense that its value depends only on the development of the yield curve to maturity and not on the characteristics of the issuer. Once an instrument is deemed safe (e.g. by a rating agency), investors agree on its value without the need to gather further information on the issuer (Gourinchas and Jeanne, 2012, p. 5) However, as pointed out by Gourinchas and Jeanne (2012, p. 6), for genuine information insensitivity, is also necessary for key market participants, such as the central bank, to behave appropriately, for example, by formulating a promise to purchase an asset when its price falls below a certain ceiling. The information insensitivity implies that assets have money-like features and are good stores of value (Nagel, 2016).

3 The good friend analogy

Metaphorically, safe assets 'are like good friends'; that is they are always there when you need them. These assets retain or even increase their value and liquidity exactly when they need to. This means that they perform their functions regardless of the economic cycle, including, in particular, in times of crisis, so that they are safe across the economic cycle. Since they are a kind of self-insurance, they are desired even at a lower interest rate. Securitised instruments or sovereign bonds issued by peripheral eurozone countries are examples of assets that were perceived as safe before the outbreak of the 2007/2008 financial crisis and lost this property in a slump. According to Brunnermeier and Huang (2018, p. 5), this property explains why safe assets are used as a buffer against risky assets. In fact, holding safe assets allows risky investments to scale up.

4 Flight-to-safety/flight-to-quality

These phenomena are observed when financial market participants withdraw from investments perceived as riskier towards those characterised by greater safety (convergence with the safe-haven asset class). For example, empirical research (e.g. Sène et al., 2021, and the literature cited therein) shows that during the COVID-19-induced shock, flight-to-safety/flight-to-quality phenomena were observed towards US and German government bonds.

5 Safe assets tautology/strategic complementarity

An asset is safe if others expect it to be safe (see, e.g. Caballero et al., 2017). This attribute is strongly related to the history and reputation of the issuer, as is clearly demonstrated by research on the determinants of credit ratings. Starting with the pioneering work of Cantor and Packer (1996), it identifies past defaults as a factor that significantly reduces sovereign creditworthiness (cf. Afonso, 2003; Mellios and Paget-Blanc, 2006; Afonso et al., 2010; Reusens and Croux, 2017; Tennant et al., 2020).

Paradoxically, however, safe assets may appreciate despite a deterioration in the issuers' fundamentals. For example, although the US Congress came close to refusing to raise the US debt ceiling in August 2011, and the Standard & Poor's rating agency downgraded the country's rating, US Treasury prices increased (Brunnermeier and Huang, 2018, p. 5). Similarly, during the Economic and Monetary Union (EMU) debt crisis, German sovereign bonds appreciated in value, even though the development of credit default swap (CDS) spreads indicated an increase in default risk. Thus, safe assets share some features of bubbles or multiple equilibria (Brunnermeier and Huang, 2018, p. 5).

6 No questions asked (NQA)

The costs of collecting information on asset values from an investor's perspective decrease as the issuer's credibility increases (Holmström, 2015). Therefore, the existence of information-insensitive assets is a result of this attribute. Additionally, Gorton (2016, p. 11) states that producing NQA property requires sufficiently credible backing.

7 Convenience yield

The uniqueness of safe assets is associated with a non-monetary (non-pecuniary) return, known as the convenience yield, in the form of liquidity or moneyness and safety; this means that the monetary return to the investor is lower than it would be if these two attributes (liquidity or moneyness and safety) were not present. In other words, yields on safe assets are lower, reflecting investors' willingness to pay a higher price to own assets characterised by liquidity and safety, the convenience yield (Habib et al., 2020). Convenience yield is not a directly observable category. Existing estimates usually relate it to US government bonds. For example, Krishnamurthy and Vissing-Jørgensen (2012a, after Gorton, 2016) show that, over the period 1926–2008, US Treasury bond yields would have been 73 basis points higher on average if not for the moneyness and safety that characterise these assets. These estimates are an approximation of the convenience yield. Jiang et al. (2021) took the spread between 12-month US dollar LIBOR[1] and the yield on 12-month Treasury bonds as a measure of convenience yield.[2]

The above list of attributes underlines that there are, in fact, different economic channels of safe asset creation through which behavioural factors, such as information sensitivity and coordination among investors, could play the premier role.

As a synthesis of a complex list of functions and attributes of safe assets presented above, Bletzinger et al. (2022) formulated a broad and thorough definition of a safe asset. It is characterised by three aspects: quality, robustness and liquidity. This definition seems to be complete, joining fragmented aspects of safe assets mentioned in previous findings and shedding light on their special nature today.

Thus, a safe asset:

- is of the highest credit quality (= low default risk),
- retains its value in bad times (robustness = good friend analogy),
- is traded in liquid markets (liquidity – can be sold at or near current market prices).

1.1.3 Safe Assets as a Financial Instrument and Money

While trying to ascertain which economic entity can create safe assets, a key problem emerges. It stems from the changing, hard-to-grasp nature of safe assets, which makes it difficult to establish a clear definitional boundary. One can distinguish two approaches:

The narrow approach states that genuine safe assets are issued or guaranteed by a 'safe government' (He et al., 2016; Golec and Perotti, 2017, p. 5), while those issued by the private sector can be regarded as 'quasi-safe' at most (Golec and Perotti, 2017). In addition, He et al. (2016) detailed the concept of 'secure government' in their definition, which refers to a country with its own central bank, stable currency and effective protection of property rights.

In the broad approach, there are three sources of safe asset creation:

1 Central bank money,
2 Government debt,
3 Private asset market.

Thus, it is possible to distinguish three categories of potential issuers of safe assets: the central bank, the government and government agencies, and private sector institutions. However, they concluded that claims in the private sector are inherently risky and should remain so to limit moral hazard instances. For this reason, the private sector may not create a good basis for providing safe assets. Apart from central bank money, government debt remains the best candidate for safe asset status (Gourinchas and Jeanne, 2012, p. 36). Defining safe assets from the side of the set of instruments, Gourinchas and Jeanne included cash, guaranteed deposits and any debt that is tradable, liquid or that has the highest credit rating.

The private sector's ability to issue safe assets is initially linked to the credit risk of the instrument. It is determined not only by the solvency risk of the issuer, but also by the structure of the instrument. In addition, short-term debt created by the private sector has the disadvantage of being susceptible to a run unless there is some form of government support, for example, in the form of a deposit guarantee scheme (Gorton, 2016, p. 2). The private sector can provide relatively safe assets in the form of bank deposits, money market fund units, short-term corporate debt securities, repo facilities, short-term interbank lending, high-quality corporate debt and securitised debt (Xiong, 2018, p. 4).

Central banks can expand banking system reserve balances, mainly by open market operations. From a commercial bank's perspective, these funds can be treated as safe assets because:

1 They are liquid (can be used for immediate settlements),
2 They are not subject to market risk,
3 They are free of credit risk (at least in nominal terms, given the central bank's ability to issue fiat money).

However, this means that central bank money is susceptible to inflation risk and is therefore not entirely risk-free (IMF, 2012, p. 110). The central bank also creates cash money, which acts as a medium of exchange that is free of market and credit risk, but not free of inflation risk (Gorton, 2016, p. 1). The central bank can also issue money bills and offer term deposits to financial institutions. These instruments could be considered safe assets in a broader context, since they have zero credit risk and generally low market risk, given their short-term maturity. In addition, they are used to absorb excess liquidity in the banking system and are, therefore, a maturity and liquidity transformation instrument within central bank liabilities (IMF, 2012, p. 110) (Table 1.1).

Table 1.1 Potential safe assets

Public Safe Assets	*Private Safe Assets*
Central banks reserves	Bank deposits
Treasury securities	Corporate debt
Municipal, agency, supranational debt	Commercial papers
Cash	Repurchase agreements

Source: Own elaboration based on the literature.

Taking into account the different mechanisms of safe asset creation, some economists differentiate between 'inside' and 'outside' liquidity. 'Inside' liquidity is created through claims in financial firms and are traded within the financial sector. 'Outside' liquidity refers to assets that represent claims in the real economy, governments, non-financial businesses or households. This distinction describes the phenomenon of safe assets, namely that it may be a simple debt contract or a more complex financial instrument based on securitisation and other forms of private safe asset production.

Taking into account different safe asset categories and the multiple functions they fulfil, one can conclude that (Gelpern and Gerding, 2016, p. 13):

- assets with multiple attributes may fulfil different functions, sometimes in different markets,
- some functions may be accommodated with more than one safe asset.

The set of functions and categories of assets that can be fulfilled is presented in Table 1.2.

Table 1.2 Functions performed by each safe asset class

Features \ *Assets*	*Public Debt*	*Claims on Central Bank*	*Quasi-Public Debt (Agency, Municipal, Supranational)*	*Banks Debt*	*Corporate Debt (AAA Rating)*	*Commercial Paper*	*Money Market Fund Shares*	*ABS (AAA Rating)*	*Repos*
Store of value	✓	✓	✓	✓	✓	✓	✓	✓	
Payments, transactional reserves	✓ (Short-term debt)	✓	✓	✓		✓	✓		✓
Collateral, portfolio hedge	✓	✓	✓	✓	✓	✓	✓	✓	
Benchmark	✓				✓				
Monetary policy, liquidity support	✓	✓	✓	✓		✓ (Crisis facilities)	✓ (Crisis facilities)	✓	✓
Regulatory mandate (prudential regulations)	✓	✓	✓	✓			✓	✓	

Source: Gelpern and Gerding (2016, p. 17).

Table 1.3 Safe asset functions in relation to classical money functions

Money Functions	*Safe Asset Functions*
Store of value	Held in parallel with risk assets Held for the provision of safe assets by the banking system
Unit of account	Benchmark/reference asset
Means of payment (transactional)	Good and stable collateral, which facilitates financial market trading

Source: Own compilation based on Brunnermeier et al. (2016).

Due to money-like attributes and a wide range of functions, to some extent, safe assets fulfil the classical functions of money. For example, the information insensitivity of assets implies that safe assets have money-like features (e.g. they can easily be pledged as collateral) and are a good store of value. However, the question of whether money is a safe asset has not yet been answered unanimously in the literature. For Benigno and Nisticò (2015), money is 'the safe asset par excellence'. Meanwhile, Brunnermeier et al. (2016) call safe assets and money 'close cousins', which illustrates an important characteristic: the terms safety and liquidity may become synonyms in the case of safe assets. This phenomenon is presented in Table 1.3.

Having defined safe assets as a functional category of financial contracts and situated them against money (used as legal tender), it is important to highlight the demand side created by investors. Specifically, investors mainly rely on safe assets to provide collateral in repurchase and derivatives markets, instruments to fulfil prudential requirements and pricing benchmarks (IMF, 2012, pp. 88–116).

1.2 Safe Assets vs Safe-Haven Assets

1.2.1 The Characteristics of Safe Havens

The term safe haven has been used primarily to refer to an asset with low risk and high liquidity (Upper, 2000), making it similar to a safe asset, and although the two terms can be used interchangeably, they are different in nature. The general understanding of safe-haven assets is an investment that can retain or increase in value during times of market crisis. Investors all over the world look for safe havens to reduce their portfolio's risk in the event of market collapse.

In times of global uncertainty, the notion of a safe-haven asset evolved to characterise an asset that investors wish to hold in uncertain times (Kaul and Sapp, 2006). In 2000, this feature became crucial to indicate safe-haven assets (Kaul and Sapp demonstrated that the US dollar during the GFC is a case in point). Hence, the term safe-haven asset emphasises the function of an asset as an effective hedge: one with a return uncorrelated (or negatively related) to that of the reference portfolio. A safe-haven asset moves in the opposite direction to the other assets during market downturns, meaning that it performs well when the reference portfolio suffers significant losses (Ranaldo and Soderlind, 2010).

The attribute of hedging has been perceived in two alternative ways. According to Upper (2000), a safe-haven asset is akin to any hedging asset, as it may provide hedging benefits on average (unconditionally). In Upper's (2000) analysis, German government bonds should be uncorrelated or negatively correlated with their reference asset (stock market index). Alternatively, Baur and Lucey (2010) and Bouri et al. (2020) view a safe-haven asset as one that does not co-move with other assets in times of financial stress (conditionally). This means that the asset would not automatically lose its safe-haven status if the price of the safe-haven asset fell in a non-crisis period. The above formulation of safe-haven assets – the need to decouple safe-haven assets from the prosperity markets – is crucial to differentiate them from safe assets. Defining a safe-haven asset as one that is generally characterised by a negative risk premium, as proposed by Ranaldo and Soderlind (2010), can be interpreted as a compromise between these two alternatives (c.f. Feder-Sempach et al., 2024).

Another difference in defining the two categories of assets is attributed to the role of information. While safe assets are defined as being insensitive to information (Gorton et al., 2012), safe-haven assets, which are defined by their relationship to other assets during specific periods, are dependent on information flows (Baur and McDermott, 2016). This feature is vital, as it indicates that both categories of assets manifest themselves in different time horizons; that is the former is perceived as safe on a continuous basis across the business cycle. In contrast, the occurrence of the safe-haven attribute is short-lived and limited to times of market stress and overall uncertainty (Baur and McDermott, 2016). This was empirically confirmed by Ranaldo and Soderlind (2007), who found that the safe-haven effects are present in hourly as well as weekly data, although it seems to be strongest at frequencies of one to two days. Thus, the concept of a safe-haven asset is clearly different from that of a safe asset (see Table 1.4).

The safe-haven features above helped Baur and McDermott (2010) distinguish between strong and weak safe-haven effects. A strong safe-haven asset is one that is negatively correlated with another asset or portfolio in times of falling stock prices, while a weak safe-haven asset is uncorrelated. These two types are mostly reliable for the length of the effect. The property of a hedge is that, on average, it holds, while the property of the safe haven is that it

Table 1.4 Differences between safe assets and safe-haven assets

No	*Factor*	*Safe Asset*	*Safe-Haven Asset*
1	Time	All the time, regardless of market crisis; a long-lived phenomenon	Only during a market crisis; a short-lived phenomenon
2	Information	Insensitive to information	Dependent on information
3	Correlation	Uncorrelated with other assets' returns on average	Negatively correlated with other asset returns during a market crisis

Source: Own elaboration based on the cited literature.

holds in particular times, for example during a financial crisis. This division is used in ongoing research, and it is the difference between the safe-haven property and the hedge property of financial assets that may have changed recently.

Ultimately, a safe haven is defined as a security that is negatively correlated with stock market returns in the case of a market crash. This feature is contrasted with a hedge property, which is defined as a security that is uncorrelated with the stock market on average (Baur and Lucey, 2009). Therefore, contrary to previous confusion in definitions, Baur and Lucey (2009), followed by Baur and McDermott (2010), introduced precise conceptual distinctions between the terms hedge (formerly considered to be a function of safe haven) and safe haven, adding one more, namely diversifier, which an asset that is positively, but not perfectly correlated with another asset, on average (see Table 1.5).

As far as the theoretical concept of safe haven is concerned, it is usually perceived as a hiding place, meaning that investors can protect wealth in adverse market conditions. It can offer investors the opportunity to hold its value in the event of a crisis. However, the safe-haven effect is generally present in developed financial markets (Baur and McDermott, 2010).

There are several assets that are labelled safe havens in most cases:

- Gold, sometimes silver and other commodities,
- Reserve currencies,
- Public debt,
- Stocks,
- And recently, cryptocurrencies, such as Bitcoin.

As a consequence, portfolio managers look for assets that are negatively correlated or uncorrelated with the main components of the portfolio to limit their exposure to losses in the event of market turmoil (Triki and Ben Maatoug, 2021; Feder-Sempach et al., 2024).

Table 1.5 Strong and weak safe-haven and hedge and diversifier definition

No	*Name of the Feature*	*Definition*
1	Strong safe haven	An asset is a strong safe haven when it is negatively correlated with the stock market during periods of market distress
2	Weak safe haven	An asset is a weak safe haven when it is uncorrelated with the stock market during periods of market distress
3	Diversifier	An asset is a diversifier when it is positively but not perfectly correlated with the stock market on average (not only during times of financial distress)
4	Hedge	An asset is a hedge when it is uncorrelated with the stock market on average (not only during times of financial distress)

Source: Own elaboration based on the cited literature and (Feder-Sempach et al., 2024).

1.2.1.1 *Gold as a Safe Haven*

Gold is still the most popular and most widely used safe-haven commodity. As an unexpected economic situation evolves, gold prices tend to increase as a result of investor decisions driven by its safe-haven status. Before the COVID-19 crisis, the price of gold hovered below 2,000 US dollars, having not made significant progress since GFC. Gold prices tend to reflect changing macroeconomic conditions. It is lined with monetary and fiscal policy, demand from jewellery makers and central banks, and bar and coin demand, driven by saving incentives. The current uncertainty caused by the Russian invasion of Ukraine shows that financial institutions and individual investors are likely to give more consideration to safe-haven assets such as gold by pushing their price above widely recognised levels (see Figure 1.2).

There is no single explanation for why gold is usually treated as a safe-haven asset, but it has always been used as an inflation hedge. It has been recognised as an effective hedge against inflation, including cases of extreme inflation (Bampinas and Panagiotidis, 2015; Valadkhani et al., 2022). Over 50 years, its average annual return amounted to 10.4%, largely exceeding the United States' average annual inflation rate of 4.1%.[3] As can be seen from Table 1.6, which analyses the performance of gold under various inflation conditions since 1971 (the year of the Bretton Woods collapse), on average,

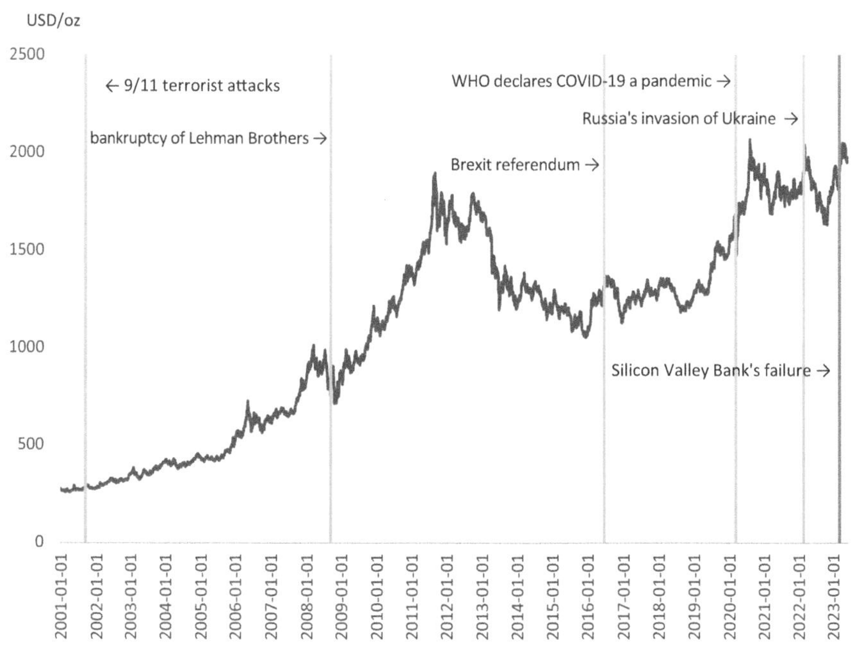

Figure 1.2 Gold vs unexpected market turmoil (2001–2023)

Source: Own elaboration based on Refinitiv EIKON data.

Table 1.6 Average annual nominal gold return in USD (%) against inflationary developments

CPI Inflation	*Average Annual Gold Return (USD, in %)*
Below 0%	4.1
0%–3%	6.2
3%–6%	8.2
Above 6%	25.0

Source: Authors' own calculations based on Refinitiv Eikon data.

Calculations conducted with the Consumer Price Index; all Items for the United States.

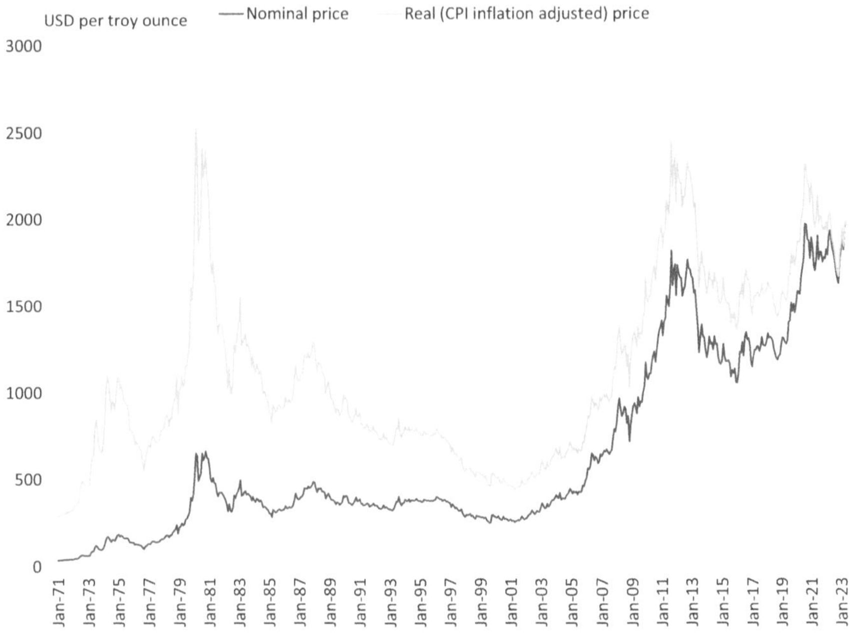

Figure 1.3 Nominal vs real prices of gold

Source: Authors' own calculations based on Refinitiv Eikon and FRED data.

Real prices calculated with the Consumer Price Index; All Items for the United States (June 2023 = 1).

it has effectively protected investors against inflation. In particular, it has proved to be an effective hedge in periods of low inflation (0%–3%), elevated inflation (3%–6%) and the highest inflation (6% and more).

The data also show that gold prices increase in real terms in periods of extreme inflation (cf. Figure 1.3). They reached their highest real price in 1979, during the Great Inflation period, when US CPI inflation rates were nearing their peak of 14.8% (reached in March 1980). Relatively high (per historical standards) real prices of gold were also observed when inflation rose sharply after the COVID-19 pandemic hit.

In the context of inflationary concerns, the supply of gold has been increasing at a steady pace, estimated at 1.7% y/y over the past two decades (World Gold Council Report, 2023, p. 4). This is in sharp contrast to fiat money, whose supply can be arbitrarily adjusted by a domestic central bank to meet its monetary policy goals (as in the case of large-scale quantitative easing launched by the Federal Reserve System in response to the GFC and the COVID-19-induced crisis). The oversupply of fiat currency can reduce its purchasing power over time.

Gold is also sought by investors due to its ability to deliver long-term positive returns, regardless of the business cycle phase. Since 1971, its price in USD has increased by an average of 10.4% y/y,[4] and by 9.9% y/y over the 21st century. Thus, gold compares favourably with many other asset classes. As demonstrated in Figure 1.4, which plots the average annual returns of different asset classes since 2001, gold outperforms most of the assets included. In particular, its return exceeded that of US Treasuries, other commodities and most equities. It was at a similar level to global emerging market equities and was second only to crude oil.

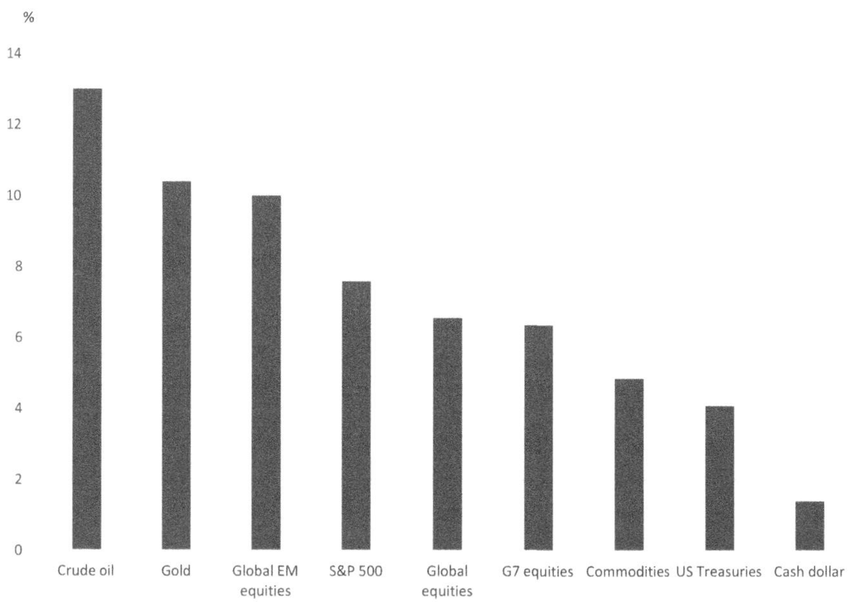

Figure 1.4 Average annual return of different global assets in USD

Source: Authors' own calculations based on Refinitiv Eikon data.

EIKON tickers names: LIGHT CRUDE SE, GOLD, RF GLOB EM, SP 500, RF GLOBAL, RF G7, RF/CC CRB ER, US 10Y GVT BNM, KLIEM.

Returns from 31 December 2001 to 31 December 2022.

The ability to deliver solid returns in various market conditions draws from gold's diverse sources of demand. It is thanks to this characteristic that it is called an all-weather asset. In periods of turbulence in the financial markets, gold has proved to exert negative correlations with equities and other risky assets, which are susceptible to uncontrollable selloffs. Moreover, it is considered a highly liquid investment, which can easily be converted into cash. It allows investors to meet their liabilities even when markets are stressed and other assets are sold at fire-sale prices, which makes it a particularly effective portfolio diversifier. In turn, in times of prosperity, gold prices are driven by the wealth effect, as it is strongly demanded by consumers as a jewellery or technology component, for example. This was recently the case with Chinese consumers, who reportedly rushed to buy jewellery, bars and coins in the first quarter of 2023 after the country's zero-COVID policy was lifted (Sharma, 2023).

Moreover, when the economy overheats and inflation expectations rise, gold is sought-after by investors eager to preserve their purchasing powers. This is because it tends to negatively correlate with equities, especially in times of high uncertainty and extreme market selloff (World Gold Council Report, 2023). Additionally, gold is said to be uncorrelated with other types of financial assets, such as conventional stocks or bonds, which are a crucial feature of safe havens. According to Baur and Lucey (2010), gold is a safe haven for stock markets in the United States, the United Kingdom and Germany. Similarly, gold can also be a hedge for stock investments in the United States and the United Kingdom but not for bonds (see Figure 1.5).

For more evidence, the following empirical analysis was carried out. Parameters of the AGDCC-GARCH model were estimated to calculate the time-varying correlation coefficients. Rates of return on the S&P 500 and rates of return on the price of gold from January 1978 to June 2023 were calculated. The frequency of data was daily. Next, the whole sample was divided into two subperiods:

1 A crisis period, characterised by rates of return on the S&P 500 lower than the sample mean by more than three standard deviations,
2 A stable period, characterised by rates of return on the S&P 500 larger than the sample mean minus three standard deviations.

After dividing the sample into two subperiods and calculating the time-varying correlation coefficients, the hypothesis about the equality of correlation coefficients in both subperiods was tested. Table 1.7 presents the values of the average correlation coefficients, as well as the results of testing the validity of the hypothesis.

The results indicate that correlation in times of (relative) stability is significantly higher than in times of crisis. Based on the analysis of rates of return on the S&P 500 and correlation coefficients on different days, a few

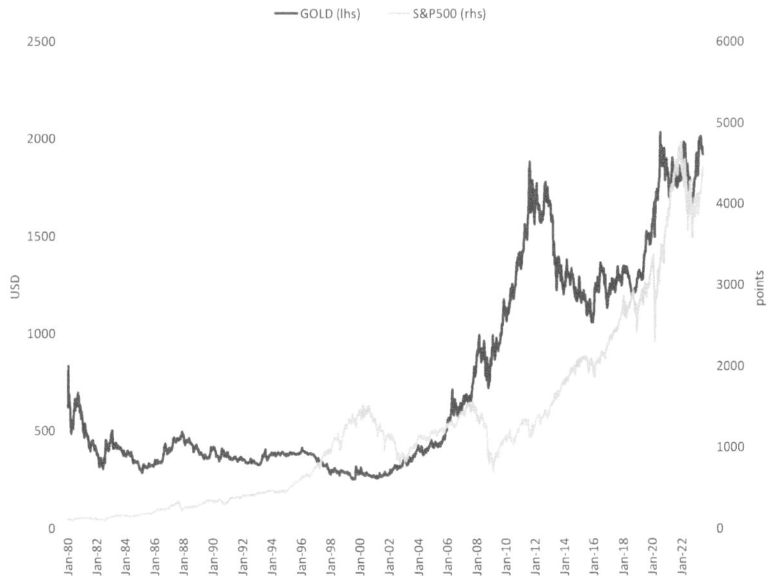

Figure 1.5 Gold vs S&P500 performance (1980–2023)

Source: Own elaboration based on Refinitiv EIKON data.

Table 1.7 Testing the equality of correlations between stable and crisis periods

Sub Period	*Mean*	*Standard Deviation*	*p-Value of Testing Equality of Correlation Coefficients*
Stable	-0.014	0.085	0.000
Crisis	-0.076	0.095	

Source: Authors' own calculations based on WGC and Refinitiv Eikon data.

characteristic short periods were distinguished (Table 1.8). These periods are characterised by large (in absolute value) and negative correlations between rates of return on the S&P 500 and rates of return on gold obtained based on the AGDCC-GARCH model.

As can be seen from Table 1.8, short periods of the highest cumulative plunges in the S&P 500 have been identified. Chronologically, they were:

- The stock market downturn at the turn of 1987/1988, including the infamous black Monday (19 October 1987),
- The stock market downturn of 2002,
- The GFC,
- The August 2011 stock markets fall (amid the height of the sovereign debt crisis in the euro area),

Table 1.8 Identification of short periods of strong negative correlation between rates of return on S&P 500 and gold

Short Period	*Cumulative Rate of Return on S&P 500 (%)*	*Cumulative Rate of Return on Gold (%)*	*Average Correlation between Rates of Return on S&P 500 and rate of return on Gold*
1987-10-16–1988-01-20	-20.6	+2.3	-0.274
2002-07-10–2002-09-24	-15.1	+3.9	-0.153
2008-08-01–2009-01-30	-42.8	+0.1	-0.082
2011-08-02–2011-09-20	-6.8	+10.3	-0.137
2020-02-06–2020-03-12	-29.6	+1.1	-0.169
2022-03-23–2022-04-22	-5.5	+1.4	-0.144

Source: Authors' own calculations based on WGC and Refinitiv Eikon data.

- The 2020 stock market crash (amid the global spillover of COVID-19 and worldwide recession triggered by lockdowns),
- The 2022 stock market decline.

In all of these periods of extreme market selloffs, cumulative rates of return on gold were positive, ranging from 0.1% (the GFC) to 10.3% (the August 2011 stock markets fall). Throughout all periods of the highest risk, gold delivered a negative correlation with equities. Hence, our results provide further evidence that in times of uncertainty, gold may effectively protect investors' portfolios when other, that is more risky assets, tumble in value.

1.2.1.2 Safe-Haven Currencies

Safe-haven currencies are expected to remain or increase in value when turbulence hits the global economy. The four major safe-haven currencies are the US dollar, the Japanese yen, the Swiss franc and the euro. The list of safe-haven currencies is compatible with the list of main reserve currencies with a quasi-monopolistic position of the US dollar followed by the euro. However, the global structure of foreign exchange reserves does not explain the strong representation of the yen and franc as safe-haven assets, and it overestimates the role of the euro.

Therefore, the determinants of safe-haven currency status are largely compatible with the determinants of international currencies (Bogołębska et al., 2019). These determinants are based on the structural features of the economy (Habib and Stracca, 2012). Based on monthly data on 52 currencies over a quarter of a century, they showed that only a few country-specific factors, such as the net foreign asset position and the size of the stock market, and in the case of advanced countries, the interest spread compared to the United States, are systematic drivers of safe-haven currency behaviour. Masujima (2019) indicated that drivers are not permanent; they tend to change dynamically. The results of the panel regression suggested that determinants of safe havens changed from external sustainability factors (current account surplus) to market-driven factors (carrying trade opportunity and high liquidity) during and after the GFC. Furthermore, the results highlighted the increasing effects that changes in the monetary policy position and market risk appetites have on a currency's safe-haven status.

An important property of safe-haven currencies is that they serve as the funding currency in carry-trade transactions (Ranaldo and Soderlind, 2007). Empirical research confirms that as a result of the unwinding of carry trade transactions, safe-haven currencies have nonlinear appreciations with increasing foreign exchange risk (Ranaldo and Soderlind, 2007). However, as pointed out by McCauley and McGuire (2009), this contradicts the theory of interest rate parity, which holds that what investors gain on an interest rate differential, they lose over some horizon to currency depreciations. Searching for the properties of currencies that make them serve as funding currencies in carry trades, based on the experiences of the franc and the yen, shows that low yields play the primary role. The structural characteristics of the economy, as highlighted in the traditional literature, are crucial to fulfilling the role of safe-haven currencies. These characteristics encompass the political, institutional, social and financial stability of the country, low inflation, comfortable official foreign reserves, high savings, net foreign asset position (as empirically confirmed by Habib and Stracca (2012, 2020)) and confidence in the central bank (as confirmed later by Jansen and Studer (2017)).

However, low yields played the main role when using the yen and the franc as funding currencies. This characteristic of Swiss interest rates has been evident for many decades (Baltensperger and Kugler, 2016). Funding carry trade currencies (mainly the yen and the franc) experiences yet another pressure on appreciation, in addition to the one that arises from the demand for currencies that are perceived as safe havens, in effect delivering a 'safety premium'. The latter source of appreciation is sometimes quoted as the key attribute of a safe-haven currency (e.g. Masujima, 2019).

The empirical research confirms the different paths of safe-haven currency behaviour. For example, Ranaldo and Soderlind (2007, 2010) confirmed that the Swiss franc, along with the yen and, to a smaller extent, the euro, has significant safe-haven characteristics and moves inversely with international equity markets and foreign exchange volatility. Meanwhile, based on daily data analysis of the 26 currencies issued by both advanced and emerging economies between 1999 and 2013, Coudert et al. (2014) found that only the yen and the US dollar exhibited safe-haven properties. The yen's safe-haven status was documented by De Bock and de Carvalho Filho (2013), who showed that the yen appreciates against the US dollar during risk-off episodes. Hossfeld

Figure 1.6 Currencies vs S&P 500 performance (2000–2023)

*JPY/USD exchange rate was multiplied by 100.

Source: Own elaboration based on Refinitiv EIKON data.

and McDonald (2015) found in their monthly frequency analysis of data spanning more than 26 years that the dollar and, even more so, the franc qualify as safe-haven currencies. Grisse and Nitschka (2015) pointed out that the currency's safe-haven status has changed over time and that the Swiss franc appreciates against the euro in response to increases in global risk but depreciates against the dollar, the yen and the British pound. Using daily data, Fatum and Yamamoto's (2016) empirical analysis indicated that during the GFC, the yen exhibited the most profound safe-haven behaviour. They also demonstrated that safe-haven currency behaviour is time-dependent, confirming the theoretical predictions of Baur and Lucey (2010). The US dollar is still considered the best safe-haven currency for short- and medium-term investments, followed by the yen and the Swiss franc (see Figure 1.6).

1.2.1.3 *Other Categories of Safe Havens*

Debt instruments issued by the public sector are considered safe havens because they provide high-quality income regardless of economic uncertainty. Usually, international investors tend to have more confidence in debt instruments issued by governments of advanced economies, starting with the US treasuries issued by the global reserve currency issuer. Government bonds are the best example of safe-haven assets because of their lower volatility and the high expected creditworthiness of their issuers. Debt instruments issued by the US (T-bills), UK (Gilts), German (Bunds) and Japanese (JGBs) governments can act as safe-haven assets because of the high-quality returns and risk-free label.[5]

Contrary to popular belief, some stocks can play the role of safe-haven assets. Investors interested in reducing their risk during economic downturns can also choose defensive stocks to provide stable earnings and consistent returns. Typically, defensive stocks provide dividends regardless of economic prosperity when they are issued by well-established companies. It may be explained by their low correlation with the overall stock market, which results in a beta parameter lower than one. Yousaf et al. (2023) investigated FAANA (Facebook, Apple, Amazon, Netflix and Alphabet) stocks acting as a hedge, diversifier and safe haven against four alternative assets, that is gold, US treasury bonds, the US dollar and Bitcoin. They showed that FAANA stocks acted as weak or strong safe havens against gold, bonds, Bitcoin and the US dollar. Ultimately, this study is different from the existing literature because it examined the FAANA stock as safe havens, and filled the gap in international research by changing the commonly used patterns.

Bitcoin is a decentralised digital currency, independent of any political centres, neither governments nor central banks. For that reason, Bitcoin and other cryptocurrencies can be considered a potential safe-haven asset. Nonetheless, the literature suggests that Bitcoin fulfilled this role to a limited extent at most. The empirical results presented by Bouri et al. (2017) indicate that it is a poor hedge and is suitable only for diversification purposes. They also indicated that its safe-haven properties vary between horizons, and it appears to be strikingly positively associated with equity markets (Rashid et al., 2022).

Meanwhile, Choi and Shin (2022) and Będowska-Sójka and Kliber (2021) showed that, unlike gold, Bitcoin prices decline in response to financial uncertainty shocks, which is in contrast to a safe-haven property. This complex economic phenomenon could be explained by Bitcoin prices and their responses to economic shocks; this response is different from gold, but similar to commodities such as crude oil (Gronwald, 2019). Interestingly, after policy uncertainty shocks, Bitcoin prices do not decrease, showing that it is independent of selected government decisions.

There is also an asymmetry in the drivers of Bitcoin prices between bullish and bearish markets. Shazad et al. (2019) reached similar conclusions. They showed that while gold is an effective safe-haven asset for all G7 stock indices, Bitcoin offers a safe-haven role for the Canadian stock index only. According to some researchers, Bitcoin should not even be considered a potentially safe-haven asset given its lack of liquidity, high volatility and high transactional costs. The market for all cryptocurrencies, including Bitcoin, is highly speculative and unregulated (Smales, 2019), which is why, during the COVID-19 crisis, cryptocurrencies were not used as safe-haven assets

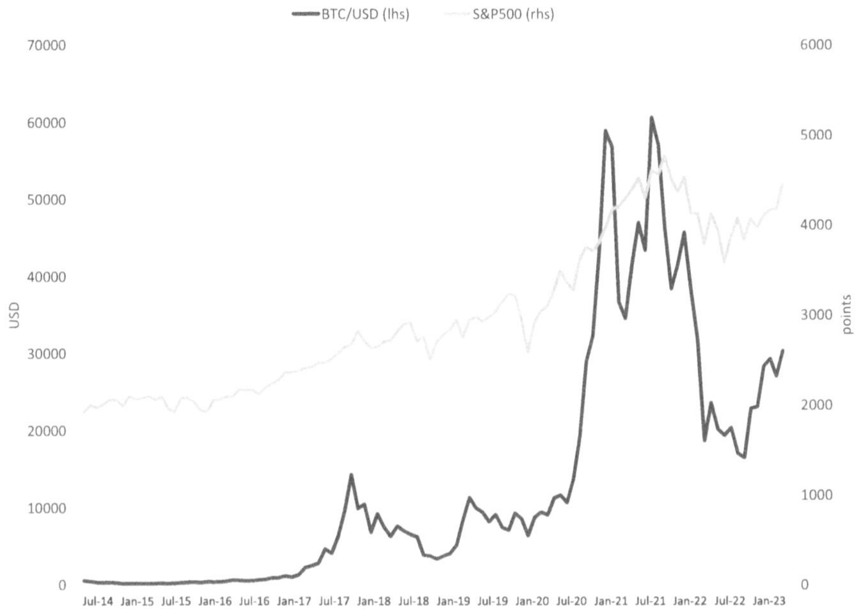

Figure 1.7 Bitcoin vs S&P 500 performance (2014–2023)

Source: Own elaboration based on Refinitiv EIKON data.

(Cheema and Szulczuk, 2020). Nedved and Kristoufek (2023) showed that Bitcoin moves with the stock markets, but commodities like oil and gold can have safe-haven properties. Contrary to previous research (Bouri et al., 2020; Shahzad et al., 2020), gold was identified as a strong safe-haven asset for Bitcoin. However, the role of Bitcoin as a safe-haven asset is still under discussion (see Figure 1.7).

Finally, the search for alternatives to the safe-haven assets mentioned above is far from over. The 'exotic' safe-haven candidates include rare coins, precious metals (other than gold), as well as industrial metals, wine, real estate, commodities and crude oil (cf., Batten et al., 2010; Dimitriou et al., 2020). However, as suggested by many empirical studies, their potential to fulfil the role as a safe haven largely depends on the nature of the crisis (Echaust and Just, 2022) and is country-specific (Ali et al., 2020).

1.2.2 *Safe-Haven Assets and Asset Pricing Theory*

Portfolio diversification is widely used in international investments. The goal is to create a pool of different assets with weak or negative correlations, allowing investors to minimise their losses if unforeseen events occur. Nowadays, widespread advanced technological improvements help international investors build a portfolio with minimum risk (Bhuiyan et al., 2023).

Markowitz (1952) pioneered modern portfolio theory with the idea of creating the most efficient portfolio by reducing volatility and the risk of losses by choosing assets that are potentially negatively correlated. He advocates that the way to choose a portfolio and reduce risk is to diversify, which can be described as spreading the risks across multiple assets from different industries instead of building a portfolio of one or two assets. He proposed how investors should combine assets into a portfolio that would provide the best possible combination of risk and return, that is the highest potential rate of return for a given level of risk or that would minimise the risk for a given level of return (Miziołek et al., 2020).

Investors should first consider the relationship between different investment opportunities, including all types of assets and all international markets. It is vital to consider the entire spectrum of investments because the returns of all these investments interact. Second, portfolio theory assumes that investors are risk averse, meaning that when given a choice between two assets with equal rates of return, they will choose the one with the lower level of risk. Therefore, the relationship between the return and risk is expected to be positive. For that reason, investors require a higher rate of return to accept the higher risk (Reilly and Brown, 1997). Markowitz proposed a basic portfolio model, showing that the variance of the rate of return was a significant measure of portfolio risk. He derived the portfolio risk formula using the portfolio variance, and this formula indicates the importance of diversification in reducing the total portfolio's risk (Miziołek et al., 2020).

Knowing that investors are risk-averse and would prefer more return to less, and less risk to more, it is advisable to find a portfolio that offers a greater return for the same risk, or a lower risk for the same return. Therefore, there is an efficient set of different financial assets that consists of an envelope curve of all portfolios that lie between the global minimum variance portfolio and the maximum return portfolio. This specific set of portfolios is called the efficient frontier (Elton and Gruber, 1995, pp. 82–83). The efficient frontier contains the best of all possible combinations. It represents the set of portfolios that have the maximum rate of return for every given level of risk or the minimum risk for every level of return. Figure 1.8 depicts the efficient frontier.

An investor can potentially choose a point along the efficient frontier based on his utility function and risk awareness. It is essential that no portfolio on the efficient frontier can dominate any other portfolio on the efficient frontier; hence, all of them have different rates of return and risk characteristics. Because each investor's risk-return utility function differs, an individual investor's portfolio choice will be different from that of someone else (Miziolek et al., 2020).

The most widely used simplification of portfolio theory is the single-index model proposed by Sharpe (1964). According to this model, returns on a security can be represented by the performance of a single factor-market index.

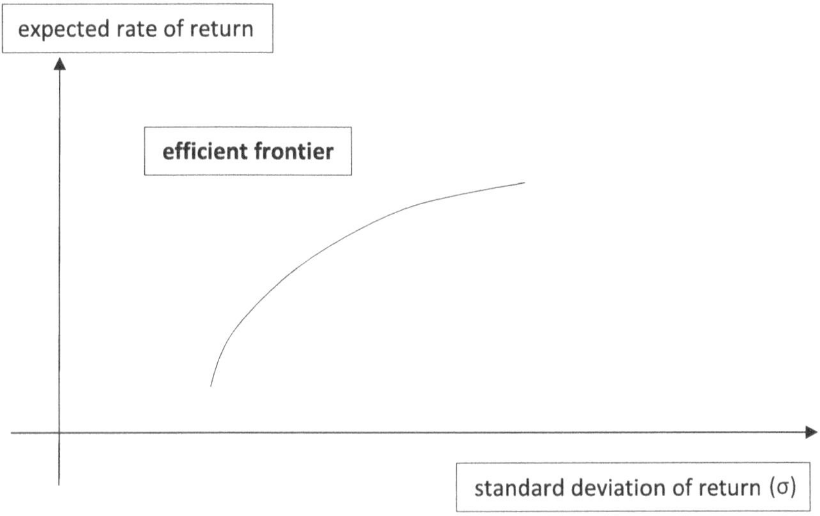

Figure 1.8 The efficient frontier
Source: Reilly and Brown (1997, p. 271).

The formula of the model can be written as follows (Elton and Gruber, 1995, pp. 130–131):

$$R_i = \alpha_i + \beta_i R_m + \varepsilon_i;$$

Where:
R_i – the rate of return for asset i,
α_i – the component of the i-th security return that is independent of the market index,
β_i – the slope coefficient that relates the return of the i-th security to the return of the market index,
R_m – the rate of return for the aggregate market index,
ε_i – random variable, $E(\varepsilon_i) = 0$.

In Sharpe's model, the crucial measure is beta, which shows the sensitivity of individual assets to market movements. The use of a single index market model calls for estimates of the beta parameter for individual financial assets that could potentially be included in a portfolio. The single index market model is used to estimate beta parameters, which can be used to assess risk. To estimate the risk measured by beta, investors use the regression model. This regression line is called the security characteristic line. It is defined as the best-fit regression line through a scatter plot of the rate of return for individual risky assets and for the market portfolio over a designated period (see Figure 1.9).

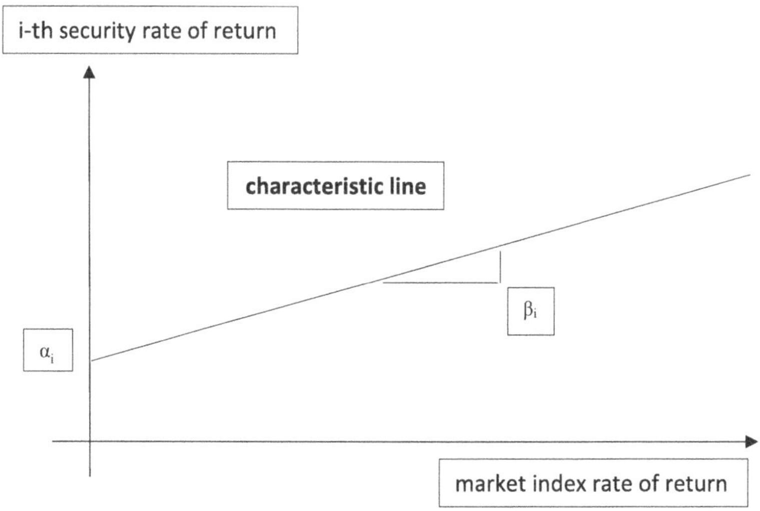

Figure 1.9 Security characteristic line
Source: Elton and Gruber (1995, p. 138).

Figure 1.6 shows that the intercept of the regression line is the alpha, while the slope of the line is the beta. Beta is a measure of volatility relative to the general market. The beta parameter is treated as an indicator of risk, and its value can be used as a risk measure:

$\beta < 0$ – a beta of less than zero indicates that an asset has an inverse relationship with the market. Those assets tend to increase in price when the general market prices fall, and they are potential safe-haven assets.

$0 < \beta < 1$ – a beta of less than one indicates that an asset return moves less than the market return; there is a lower systematic risk than the market. Defensive stocks have a beta of less than one.

$\beta = 1$ – a beta equal to one indicates that an asset's return is the same as the market return.

$\beta > 1$ – a beta greater than one indicates that the asset's return moves higher than the market return; there is a higher systematic risk than the market. Aggressive stocks have a beta greater than one (Miziołek et al., 2020).

Theoretically, a safe-haven asset is negatively correlated with another asset during market distress; hence, these assets have negative beta parameters to hold their value during market turbulence, and they can reduce risk (see Table 1.9).

Following the classification presented in Table 1.9, the correlation of different assets can be replaced by the beta parameter that determines whether diversification works. The beta parameter shows how one asset moves compared to another, which, in this case, is used to depict the different properties of a financial asset.[6] A potential problem may arise when investors would like

Table 1.9 Beta parameter and asset's properties

No	*Asset Properties*	*Beta*
1	Safe haven	Negative or 0 beta in times of financial distress or bear market conditions
2	Diversifier	Beta over 0 but not equal to 1 on average, bull and bear market conditions
3	Hedge	Negative or 0 beta on average, bull and bear market conditions

Source: Own elaboration based on the cited literature.

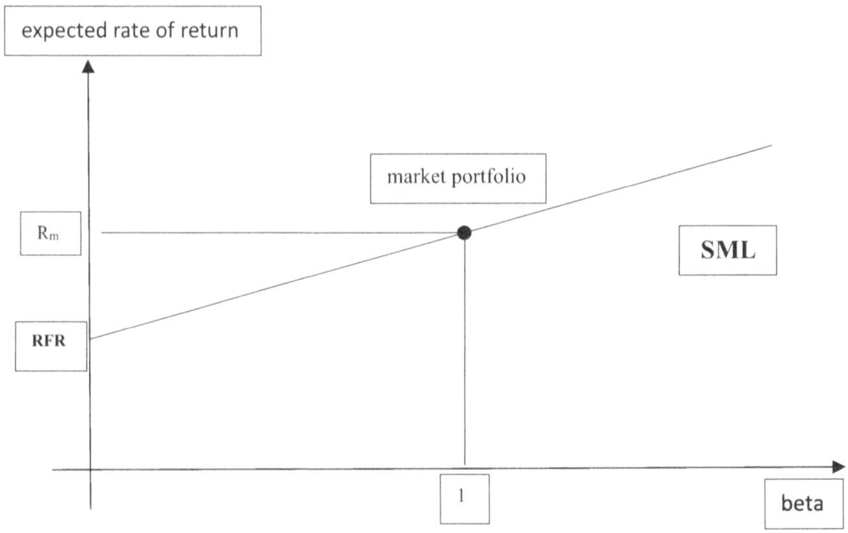

Figure 1.10 Security market line

Source: Reilly and Brown (1997, p. 283).

to assess beta only for times of financial distress, which is hard to capture and short-lived. Sometimes, beta is calculated separately for bull and bear market conditions (Levy, 1974; Fabozzi and Francis, 1977; Dębski et al., 2016), and this might be helpful in defining the safe-haven properties of any asset in a portfolio.[7]

The aforementioned beta parameter is a relevant risk measure; however, it is vital to determine an appropriate expected rate of return on a risky asset according to the Capital Asset Pricing Model (Sharpe, 1964; Lintner, 1965). The visual representation of the relation between risk and the required rate of return of an asset is the security market line (SML) (see Figure 1.10).

The SML equation shows that the expected rate of return for a risky asset is determined by the risk-free rate (RFR) plus a risk premium for the individual asset. The risk premium is defined as a product of the systematic risk of an asset (beta parameter) and the market risk premium (Reilly and Brown, 1997, p. 288). A direct implication of Capital Asset Pricing Model (CAPM) is that the equilibrium expected return of an asset should be equal to the risk-free rate plus a risk premium that is proportional to the covariance of the asset return with the return on the market portfolio, which is the commonly used measure of the systematic risk (Miziolek et al., 2020).

The idea of a risk-free rate is explained as the interest rate an investor can expect to earn on an investment that has no risk, that is a safe asset investment (short-term government debt). This is a theoretical measure of an investment with zero risk over a specified period. The RFR is usually a government short-term security rate because it has no default or interest rate risk, for example three-month US treasury bills.

All issues regarding portfolio diversification, hedge and safe-haven properties of different financial assets are deeply rooted in portfolio theory (Markowitz's model of portfolio selection and the CAPM model of asset pricing). The diversification ability of financial assets is also addressed in the financial literature by He et al. (2018), Blose (2010), Baur and McDermott (2010) and Reboredo (2013). They typically analyse whether the beta of financial assets (usually gold) is zero or negative, as often assumed. Furthermore, liquidity preference theory emphasises its reliance on liquidity. Investors prefer to keep some 'risk-free' financial instruments so that they can quickly turn them into cash to meet transactional needs and pursue investment opportunities.

Notes

1 London Interbank Offer Rate.
2 Jiang et al. (2021) developed the convenience yield theory of exchange rate formation. It recognises the central role of international monetary flows associated with the demand for government debt and related US dollar safe-haven asset markets in determining the USD exchange rate. According to this theoretical-empirical approach (research on the evolution of the USD exchange rate between 1970 and 2011), the current exchange rate of safe assets denominated in that currency reflects the cumulative values of future convenience yields.
3 Calculated for the period January 1971–June 2023 using The Consumer Price Index.
4 Calculations for January 1971–June 2023.
5 Debt instruments are discussed broadly in the following chapters.
6 For more, cf. Melin and Pettersson (2022).
7 The problem of beta stability is well acknowledged, see more: Dębski et al. (2021) and Feder-Sempach et al. (2023).

References

Afonso, A. (2003). Understanding the determinants of sovereign debt ratings: Evidence for the two leading agencies. *Journal of Economics and Finance*, *27*(1), 56–74. doi:10.1007/bf02751590

Afonso, A., Gomes, P., & Rother, P. (2010). Short- and long-run determinants of sovereign debt credit ratings. *International Journal of Finance & Economics*, *16*(1), 1–15. doi:10.1002/ijfe.416

Ahir, H., Bloom, N., & Furceri, D. (2022). The world uncertainty index. *NBER Working Paper*, no 29763. doi:10.3386/w29763

Baltensperger, E., & Kugler, P. (2016). *The historical origins of the safe haven status of the Swiss franc*, Aussenwirtschaft, University of St. Gallen, School of Economics and Political Science, Swiss Institute for International Economics and Applied Economics Research, 67(02), 1–30, August.

Bampinas, G., & Panagiotidis, T. (2015). Are gold and silver a hedge against inflation? A two century perspective. *International Review of Financial Analysis*, *41*, 267–276. doi:10.1016/j.irfa.2015.02.007

Batten, J. A., Ciner, C., & Lucey, B. M. (2010). The macroeconomic determinants of volatility in precious metals markets. *Resources Policy*, *35*(2), 65–71.

Baur, D. G., & McDermott, T. K. (2010). Is gold a safe haven? International evidence. *Journal of Banking & Finance*, *34*(8), 1886–1898. doi:10.1016/j.jbankfin.2009.12.008

Baur, D. G., & McDermott, T. K. J. (2009). Is gold a safe haven? International evidence. *SSRN Electronic Journal*. doi:10.2139/ssrn.1516838

Baur, D. G., & McDermott, T. K.J. (2016). Why is gold a safe haven? (presentation slides). *SSRN Electronic Journal*. doi:10.2139/ssrn.2773395

Baur, D. G., & Lucey, B. M. (2010). *Is Gold a Hedge or a Safe Haven? An Analysis of Stocks, Bonds and Gold*. doi:10.1111/j.1540-6288.2010.00244.x

Będowska-Sójka, B., & Kliber, A. (2021). Is there one safe-haven for various turbulences? The evidence from gold, bitcoin and ether. *The North American Journal of Economics and Finance*, *56*, 101390. doi:10.1016/j.najef.2021.101390

Benigno, P., & Nisticò, S. (2015). Non-neutrality of open-market operations. *CEPR Discussion Paper*, no DP10594. Available at: https://ssrn.com/abstract=2608052

Bhuiyan, R. A., Husain, A., & Zhang, C. (2023). Diversification evidence of bitcoin and gold from wavelet analysis. *Financial Innovation*, *9*(1). doi:10.1186/s40854-023-00495-1

Bletzinger, T., Greif, W., & Schwaab, B. (2022). Can EU bonds serve as euro-denominated safe assets? *Journal of Risk and Financial Management*, *15*(11), 530. doi:10.3390/jrfm15110530

Blose, L. E. (2010). Gold prices, cost of carry, and expected inflation. *Journal of Economics and Business*, *62*(1), 35–47. doi:10.1016/j.jeconbus.2009.07.001

Bogołębska, J., Feder-Sempach, E., & Stawasz-Grabowska, E. (2019). Reserve currency status as a safe asset determinant. Empirical evidence from main public issuers in the period 2005–2017. *Comparative Economic Research. Central and Eastern Europe*, *22*(3), 65–81. doi:10.2478/cer-2019-0023

Bouri, E., Molnár, P., Azzi, G., Roubaud, D., & Hagfors, L. I. (2017). On the hedge and safe haven properties of bitcoin: Is it really more than a diversifier? *Finance Research Letters*, *20*, 192–198. doi:10.1016/j.frl.2016.09.025

Bouri, E., Shahzad, S. J., Roubaud, D., Kristoufek, L., & Lucey, B. (2020). Bitcoin, gold, and commodities as safe havens for stocks: New insight through wavelet analysis. *The Quarterly Review of Economics and Finance*, *77*, 156–164. doi:10.1016/j.qref.2020.03.004

Brunnermeier, M., & Huang, L. (2018). A global safe asset for and from emerging market economies. *NBER Working Paper, no 25373*. doi:10.3386/w25373

Brunnermeier, M. K., Garicano, L., Lane, P. R., Pagano, M., Reis, R., Santos, T., ... Vayanos, D. (2016). The sovereign-bank diabolic loop and Esbies. *American Economic Review*, *106*(5), 508–512. doi:10.1257/aer.p20161107

Caballero, R. J., Farhi, E., & Gourinchas, P.-O. (2017). The safe assets shortage conundrum. *Journal of Economic Perspectives*, *31*(3), 29–46. doi:10.1257/jep.31.3.29

Cantor, R. M., & Packer, F. (1996). Determinants and impact of sovereign credit ratings. *SSRN Electronic Journal*. doi:10.2139/ssrn.1028774

Cheema, M. A., & Szulczuk, K. (2020). Covid-19 pandemic and its influence on safe havens: An examination of gold, T-bills, T-bonds, U.S. dollar, and stablecoin. *SSRN Electronic Journal*. doi:10.2139/ssrn.3590015

Choi, S., & Shin, J. (2022). Bitcoin: An inflation hedge but not a safe haven. *Finance Research Letters*, *46*, 102379. doi:10.1016/j.frl.2021.102379

Coudert, V., Guillaumin, C., & Raymond, H. (2014). Looking at the other side of carry trades: Are there any safe haven currencies? Working Papers 2014-03, CEPII research center.

Dang, T., Gorton, G., & Holmstrom, B. (2012). Ignorance, debt and financial crisis. *Working Paper Yale University*. Available at: http://www.columbia.edu/~td2332/Paper_Ignorance.pdf

De Bock, R., & de Carvalho Filho, I. (2013). *The behavior of currencies during riskoff episodes*, IMF Working Paper 13/08.

Dębski, W., Feder-Sempach, E., & Świderski, B. (2016). Beta stability over bull and bear market on the Warsaw stock exchange. *Folia Oeconomica Stetinensia*, *16*(1), 75–92. doi:10.1515/foli-2016-0006

Dębski, W., Feder-Sempach, E., & Szczepocki, P. (2021). Time-varying beta—The case study of the largest companies from the Polish, Czech, and Hungarian stock exchange. *Emerging Markets Finance and Trade*, *57*(13), 3855–3877.

Dimitriou, D., Kenourgios, D., & Simos, T. (2020). Are there any other safe haven assets? Evidence for "exotic" and alternative assets. *International Review of Economics & Finance*, *69*, 614–628. doi:10.1016/j.iref.2020.07.002

Elton, E., & Gruber, M. (1995). *Modern portfolio theory and investment analysis*. New York: Wiley & Sons.

Fabozzi, F. J., & Francis, J. C. (1977). Stability tests for alphas and betas over bull and bear market conditions. *The Journal of Finance*, *32*(4), 1093–1099. doi:10.1111/j.1540-6261.1977.tb03312.x

Fatum, R., & Yamamoto, Y. (2016). Intra-safe haven currency behavior during the global financial crisis. *Journal of International Money and Finance*, *66*(C), 49–64.

Feder-Sempach, E., Szczepocki, P., & Bogołębska, J. (2024). Global uncertainty and potential shelters: Gold, bitcoin, and currencies as weak and strong safe havens for main world stock markets. *Financial Innovation*. doi:10.1186/s40854-023-00589-w

Feder-Sempach, E., Szczepocki, P., & Dębski, W. (2023). What if beta is not stable? Applying the Kalman filter to risk estimates of top US companies over the long time horizon. *Bank i Kredyt*, National Bank of Poland, *54*(1), 25–44.

Fisher, P. R. (2013). Reflections on the meaning of "risk-free". In Bank for Int'l Settlements (Ed.), *Sovereign risk: A world without risk-free assets?* 65. Available at: http://www.bis.org/publ/bppdf/bispap72.pdf

Gabor, D., & Vestergaard, J. (2018). Chasing unicorns: The European single safe asset project. *Competition & Change*, *22*(2), 139–164. doi:10.1177/1024529418759638

Gelpern, A., & Gerding, F. (2016). Inside safe assets. *Yale Journal on Regulation*, Forthcoming. Available at SSRN: https://ssrn.com/abstract=2843986

Golec, P., & Perotti, E. (2017). Safe assets: A review. *Working Paper Series*, no 2035. European Central Bank.

Gorton, G. (2016). The history and economics of safe assets. *NBER Working Paper*, no 22210.

Gorton, G., Lewellen, S., & Metrick, A. (2012). The safe-asset share. *American Economic Review*, *102*(3), 101–106. doi:10.1257/aer.102.3.101

Gourinchas, P. O., & Jeanne, O. (2012). Global safe assets. *BIS Working Paper*, no 399. Available at SSRN: https://ssrn.com/abstract=2247974

Grisse, C., & Nitschka, T. (2015). On financial risk and the safe haven characteristics of Swiss franc exchange rates. *Journal of Empirical Finance*, *32*(C), 153–164.

Gronwald, M. (2019). Is bitcoin a commodity? On price jumps, demand shocks, and certainty of supply. *Journal of International Money and Finance*, *97*, 86–92. doi:10.1016/j.jimonfin.2019.06.006

Habib, M. M., & Stracca, L. (2012). Getting beyond carry trade: What makes a safe haven currency? *Journal of International Economics*, 87(1), 50–64.

Habib, M., Stracca, L., & Venditti, F. (2020). The fundamentals of safe assets. *ECB Working Paper Series*, no 2355: 2, 25.

He, Z., Krishnamurthy, A., & Milbradt, K. (2016). A model of safe asset determination. *NBER Working Paper*, no 22272.

He, Z., O'Connor, F., & Thijssen, J. (2018). Is gold a sometime safe haven or an always hedge for equity investors? A Markov-switching CAPM approach for US and UK stock indices. *International Review of Financial Analysis*, *60*, 30–37. doi:10.1016/j.irfa.2018.08.010

Holmström, B. (2015). Understanding the role of debt in the financial system. *BIS Working Paper*, no 479.

Hossfeld, O., & MacDonald, R. (2015). Carry funding and safe haven currencies: A threshold regression approach. *Journal of International Money and Finance*, *59*(C), 185–202.

IMF. (2012). Safe assets: Financial system cornerstone? *Global financial stability report*, Global financial stability report – Washington, DC. Available at: https://www.imf.org/external/pubs/ft/gfsr/2012/01/

IOSCO. (2017). *Annual report 2017*. Available at: https://www.iosco.org/annual_reports/2017/pdf/CompleteAnnualReport2017.pdf

Jiang, Z., Krishnamurthy, A., & Lustig, H. (2021). Foreign safe asset demand and the dollar exchange rate. *The Journal of Finance*, *76*(3), 1049–1089. doi:10.1111/jofi.13003

Kaul, A., & Sapp, S. (2006). Y2K fears and safe haven trading of the U.S. dollar. *Journal of International Money and Finance*, *25*(5), 760–779. doi:10.1016/j.jimonfin.2006.04.003

Levy, R. A. (1974). Beta coefficients as predictors of return. *Financial Analysts Journal*, *30*(1), 61–69. doi:10.2469/faj.v30.n1.61

Lintner, J. (1965). The valuation of risk assets and the selection of risky investments in stock portfolios and capital budgets. *The Review of Economics and Statistics*, *47*(1), 13. doi:10.2307/1924119

McCauley, R. N., & McGuire, P. (2009). Dollar appreciation in 2008: Safe haven, carry trades, dollar shortage and overhedging. *BIS Quarterly Review*, Bank for International Settlements, December.

Markowitz, H. (1952). Portfolio selection. *The Journal of Finance*, 7(1), 77–91.

Melin, E., & Pettersson, A. (2022). Safe haven assets during the COVID-19 pandemic: A study of safe haven aspects of gold and Bitcoin in U.S. financial markets.

Available at: https://www.divaportal.org/smash/get/diva2:1666036/FULLTEXT01.pdf

Mellios, C., & Paget-Blanc, E. (2006). Which factors determine sovereign credit ratings? *The European Journal of Finance*, *12*(4), 361–377. doi:10.1080/13518470500377406

Miziołek, T., Feder-Sempach, E., & Zaremba, A. (2020). *International equity exchange-traded funds. Navigating global ETF market opportunities and risks*. Cham: Palgrave Macmillan, ISBN: 978-3-030-53863-7.

Nagel, S. (2016). The liquidity premium of near-money assets. *The Quarterly Journal of Economics*, *131*(4), 1927–1971. doi:10.1093/qje/qjw028

Nedved, M., & Kristoufek, L. (2023). Safe havens for bitcoin. *Finance Research Letters*, *51*, 103436. doi:10.1016/j.frl.2022.103436

Ranaldo, A., & Soderlind, P. (2007). Safe haven currencies. *Swiss National Bank Working Papers*, no 17, 14 September.

Ranaldo, A., & Soderlind, P. (2010). Safe haven currencies. *Review of Finance*, *10*, 385–407, University of St. Gallen Economics Discussion Paper No. 2007-22. Available at SSRN: https://ssrn.com/abstract=999382 or doi:10.2139/ssrn.999382

Rashid, A., Bakry, W., & Al-Mohamad, S. (2022). Are cryptocurrencies a future safe haven for investors? The case of bitcoin. *Economic Research-Ekonomska Istraživanja*, *36*(2). doi:10.1080/1331677x.2022.2140443

Reboredo, J. C. (2013). Is gold a hedge or safe haven against oil price movements? *Resources Policy*, *38*(2), 130–137. doi:10.1016/j.resourpol.2013.02.003

Reilly, F., & Brown, K. (1997). *Investment analysis and portfolio management*. Fifth Ed., The Dryden Press. https://www.amazon.com/Investment-Analysis-Portfolio-Management-Finance/dp/0030186838

Reusens, P., & Croux, C. (2017). Sovereign credit rating determinants: A comparison before and after the European Debt Crisis. *Journal of Banking & Finance*, *77*, 108–121. doi:10.1016/j.jbankfin.2017.01.006

Sène, B., Mbengue, M. L., & Allaya, M. M. (2021). Overshooting of sovereign emerging eurobond yields in the context of COVID-19. *Finance Research Letters*, *38*, 101746. doi:10.1016/j.frl.2020.101746

Shahzad, S. J. H., Bouri, E., Roubaud, D., Kristoufek, L., & Lucey, B. (2019). Is Bitcoin a better safe-haven investment than gold and commodities? *International Review of Financial Analysis*, *63*(C), 322–330.

Shahzad, S. J. H., Bouri, E., Roubaud, D., & Kristoufek, L. (2020). Safe haven, hedge and diversification for G7 stock markets: Gold versus bitcoin. *Economic Modelling*, *87*, 212–224. doi:10.1016/j.econmod.2019.07.023

Sharma, R. (2023, April 23). What strong gold says about the weak dollar. *Financial Times*. Available at: https://www.ft.com/content/e9c78b99-8a29-47e2-b5bf-9f7542608cf6 (Accessed 23 April 2023)

Sharpe, W. F. (1964). Capital-asset prices - a theory of market equilibrium under conditions of risk. *Journal of Finance*, *19*, 425–442.

Smales, L. A. (2019). Bitcoin as a safe haven: Is it even worth considering? *Finance Research Letters*, *30*, 385–393. doi:10.1016/j.frl.2018.11.002

Tennant, D. F., Tracey, M. R., & King, D. W. (2020). Sovereign credit rating: Evidence of bias against poor countries. *The North American Journal of Economics and Finance*, *51*, 100877. doi:10.1016/j.najef.2018.11.006

Triki, M. B., & Ben Maatoug, A. (2021). The gold market as a safe haven against the stock market uncertainty: Evidence from geopolitical risk. *Resources Policy*, *70*, 101872. doi:10.1016/j.resourpol.2020.101872

Upper, C. (2000). How safe was the "Safe Haven"? Financial market liquidity during the 1998 turbulences. BIS Papers chapters. In Bank for International Settlements (Ed.), *Market liquidity: Proceedings of a workshop held at the BIS*, volume 2, 241–266. Deutsche Bundesbank, Frankfurt am Main. Available at: https://www.bundesbank.de/resource/blob/703002/13b62d9ac7220b7dddf2ffe9a70ffb27/mL/2000-02-01-dkp-01-data.pdf

Valadkhani, A., Nguyen, J., & Chiah, M. (2022). When is gold an effective hedge against inflation? *Resources Policy*, 79. doi:10.1016/j.resourpol.2022.103009.

Van Riet, A. (2017). Addressing the safety trilemma: A safe sovereign asset for the eurozone. *ESRB Working Paper Series*, no 35.

World Gold Council Report. (2022), (2023).

Xiong, Q. (2018). The liquidity premium of safe assets: The role of government debt supply. Available at: https://ssrn.com/abstract=2977458 or doi:10.2139/ssrn.2977458

Yousaf, I., Plakandaras, V., Bouri, E., & Gupta, R. (2023). Hedge and safe-haven properties of FAANA against gold, US treasury, bitcoin, and US dollar/CHF during the pandemic period. *The North American Journal of Economics and Finance*, 64, 101844. doi:10.1016/j.najef.2022.101844

2 The Supply of Safe Assets

2.1 Determining Safe Asset Supply in an International Context

2.1.1 Global vs Regional Providers of Safe Assets

In considering the supply-side aspects of safe assets, the literature divides countries into:

- Global providers,
- Regional providers.

According to the majority of the literature, the United States is the only global safe assets provider, but this issue is under discussion. Most studies find that the United States, as an issuer of the dominant currency, has a monopolistic position as a global supplier of safe assets (cf. Farhi and Maggiori, 2018). Gourinchas et al. (2019, p. 38) stated that the 'true' global providers are currently the United States and Japan, and, to a lesser extent, Switzerland, Germany and the United Kingdom (which can also be classified as regional providers). Japan's role as a global provider was acknowledged by Ilzetzki et al. (2022, p. 98), who argued that although the dominant currency tends to be a global safe asset, it is by no means always the safest asset among internationally issued bonds, at least not in the sense of being consistently the lowest yielding. They give the example of the Japanese yen, which provided yields lower than the US dollar in recent years.

On the other hand, a much broader category of global providers was highlighted by Aizenman et al. (2019). The issuers of the 'big four' currencies, that is the United States, the euro area, Japan and Great Britain, are considered to be global safe asset (GSA) providers. GSAs are defined as debt instruments of the 'big four' countries. At the same time, Aizenman et al. accept He's (2016a, 2016b) definition of GSA as any debt issued or guaranteed by a 'safe' government, implying any country with its own central bank, stable currency, and effective protection of property rights. In practice, GSAs are usually safe and liquid assets denominated in the currency of major advanced countries – particularly in US dollars and the debt of the euro area's core.

DOI: 10.4324/9781003376538-3

As one can conclude, the problem with differentiating between two categories of safe asset providers stems from the fact that there is no unanimity on how to define one that is global, that is whether it is a country that issues international currency, a high level of safe debt, or if it is a hegemon (or dominant country) in the International Monetary System (IMS).

The problem with the above classification has not only a practical dimension, disputing the scope of the US dollar, but also the US dollar's central position in the system. It is also the mirror image of the considerations on the optimal structure of the IMS on a theoretical level. In theory, the discussion on whether there can be just one global provider or a few has not been unanimously resolved. It is also strongly related to issues of the hierarchy of determinants of providing global liquidity and structure to the IMS. The key question is whether the IMS should be based on the hegemonic position of one country or the co-existence of international currencies issued by a few countries (the multi-currency system) to make it stable. As Farhi and Maggiori (2018) stated, in theoretical disputes, there have been contrary views regarding the stability of hegemonic vs multi-currency IMS. Theories were based on observations of how the international monetary systems function (i.e. the gold standard, the Bretton Woods system and the multi-currency system; cf. Table 2.1).

Notwithstanding the doubts signalled above about the optimal design of the IMS, the United States seems to be the only country that currently meets all the criteria to call it a true global safe asset provider. The US dollar's dominance in the international financial and monetary system is evident in its ability to fulfil all of the functions of an international currency. The multiple dimensions of its dominance in trade (dominant currency pricing) and

Table 2.1 Some economic thoughts on the stability of the hegemonic vs multi-currency international monetary system

Keynes (1923)	A scarcity of reserve assets under a gold standard or at a zero lower bound is recessionary.
Nurkse (1944)	A multipolar IMS is unstable as investors try to coordinate which country (the UK or USA) will be the ultimate safe asset provider.
Triffin (1961)	An IMS based on the hegemonic position of the USA is unstable as the hegemon is unable to simultaneously meet the demand for reserves and guarantee credible convertibility of USD for gold.
Kindleberger (1967)	An IMS based on the hegemonic position of the USA is stable. The hegemon is the banker of the world; liabilities are covered by assets, and a growing current deficit is natural for providing global liquidity.
Eichengreen (2011)	A multi-currency system (based on the USD, EUR and RMB) is stable as it results in the growth of reserve assets and reduces seigniorage.

Source: Own elaboration based on Farhi and Maggiori (2018).

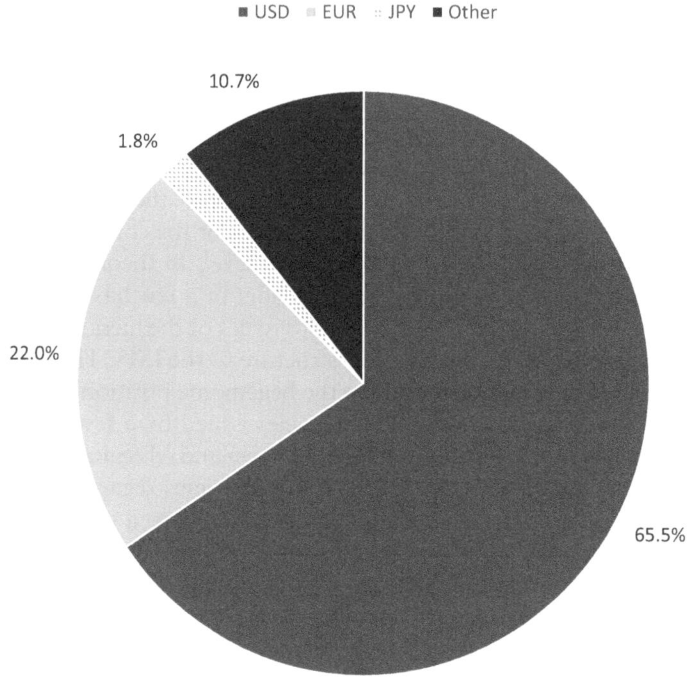

Figure 2.1 Currency composition of international debt securities as of Q42022 (% of total)

Source: Authors' own compilation based on ECB (2023).

finance (dominant currency financing) are particularly visible in trade invoicing, international debt issuance, as well as cross-border loans. Furthermore, as Miranda-Agrippino and Rey (2020) found, due to the dominant role of the US dollar in the global financial cycle and as a global safe asset provider, it is an attractive exchange rate anchor. Interestingly, no currency is pegged to the Japanese yen (Ilzetzki et al., 2022, p. 111).

The dominance of the USD is large in the pricing of financial assets. It is the main currency of international debt denomination (with corporate bonds on top), as illustrated in Figure 2.1. It also dominates in the issuance of sovereign bonds, as illustrated in Figure 2.2. Japan and other regional (global?) providers trail the United States.

2.1.2 *The Exorbitant Privilege Concept*

There is one decisive factor that enables some countries to create global and regional safe assets, that is being the issuer of a reserve currency. A global safe asset provider is one that has exorbitant privilege from the issuance of international currency, with special emphasis put on its function as a reserve currency.

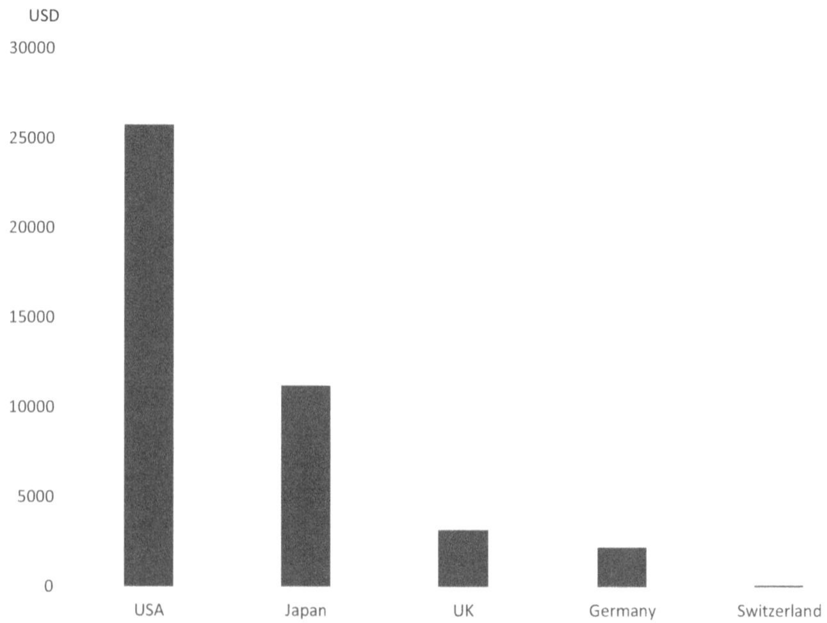

Figure 2.2 Outstanding sovereign debt (as of October 2023)
Source: Authors' own compilation based on ECB (2023).

There are many ways of defining exorbitant privilege in the literature, resulting in various ways of measuring it. The term originally referred to the willingness of foreigners to hold large amounts of US government debt at extremely low interest rates due to the status of the dollar as a world reserve currency under the postwar Bretton Woods system of fixed exchange rates. In recent years, however, the concept has expanded to explain why the United States appears to be enjoying an excess return from its external assets over liabilities across all asset classes, including foreign direct investment, equities, and other forms of portfolio investments (Rogoff and Tashiro, 2015). Thus, this approach extends exorbitant privilege to a broader class of assets than just government bonds. Put simply, the current economic system provides the US government with exorbitant privilege, meaning that it gives the USD an advantage because it is the reserve currency of the world.

The term exorbitant privilege denotes the benefits associated with global currency status. This status is created by official investors' demand for safe and liquid foreign currency assets to accumulate foreign exchange reserves. At the same time, it reduces the financing costs for governments in reserve currency countries. As a result of the evolution of the concept of exorbitant privilege, it can be acknowledged that countries other than the United States can enjoy it, provided they have a cost advantage in any kind of borrowing or investment instrument. According to Curcuru et al. (2013), exorbitant privilege can be explained through the income puzzle and the position puzzle. The income puzzle of positive net income flows to the United States exists even when its net international investment position (IIP) is negative (i.e. the income balance is positive). The position puzzle pertains to a sizeable gap between the reported US net international position and cumulated current account deficits (i.e. the IIP is less negative than the cumulated current account deficits) (Curcuru et al., 2013).

Gourinchas and Rey (2007) empirically demonstrated the effect of exorbitant privilege as the presence of an excess return from holding US net foreign assets and an associated valuation channel as an adjustment mechanism that simultaneously facilitates it. They found that the United States has enjoyed a sizable excess return on its external assets over external liabilities for a long period across all asset classes. By introducing the assumption that the United States has a balanced net IIP, with foreign assets and liabilities amounting to 100% of the country's GDP, Gourinchas showed that an excess return (a higher yield on foreign assets than the cost of financing them) of 2% per year allows the United States to maintain a current account deficit of 2% of GDP on average, without affecting the country's net IIP (Gourinchas, 2017).

However, this concept of exorbitant privilege is not free of controversy, for example, the question of composition effect, specifically, how a country's foreign assets and liabilities are structured and how they impact excess returns. This situation is illustrated by the US's composition of net IIP, with a high share of equity and direct foreign investments (about 55%) in foreign assets and a relatively high share of foreign holdings of US debt (about 70%) in foreign liabilities. Another controversial issue, as seen in Japan, is the practice of debt maturity transformation, where debt liabilities have considerably shorter durations than debt assets. This practice makes the country sensitive to maturity transformation risk (Rogoff and Tashiro, 2015).

Among other definitions, exorbitant privilege is narrowly defined as:

- The occurrence of a liquidity premium due to the issuance of reserve currency,
- A deviation from uncovered interest rate parity,
- The ease of access to capital markets.

The diversity in definitions stems from the fact that it encompasses different effects. In the United States, two elements are highlighted – the ease of external financing (a benefit highlighted in the literature dating from the 1960s) and the positive differential in the return on foreign assets relative to foreign liabilities (which results from the peculiarities of the US's net investment position and based on risk-sharing mechanisms; this benefit is accentuated in the contemporary literature). Together, these factors contribute to the relaxation of fiscal constraints.

Thus, the ability to issue debt cheaply in one's own currency to finance deficits (payment and budget) is most commonly considered an exorbitant privilege. Issuing public debt in one's own currency instead of in foreign currency is a form of insurance against shocks, as there is then no currency mismatch between budget receipts and debt repayments. Additionally, monetary and exchange rate policies can be adjusted to reduce the real burden of the debt, for example, through inflation. Historical experience confirms that sovereign debt crises more often affect countries with higher foreign currency debt levels (Mitchener and Trebesch, 2021, p. 33).

Reducing the cost of external financing is also a consequence of providing foreign (official) investors with 'insurance' against volatility in capital flows and exchange rate risk, precisely in the form of debt creation. According to this approach, the global provider of safe assets acts as an 'insurance' provider for the foreign country. Gourinchas et al. (2010) added a rare-disasters model to the exorbitant privilege literature, acknowledging that it provides insurance against global disasters. Thus, a country enjoys exorbitant privilege because it can provide global investors with 'safer' assets. In exchange for insurance against global 'rare disasters', exorbitant privilege allows for assets to pay lower rates of return.

That is why demand for safe debt is characterised by a relatively low-price elasticity. Regardless of the price (yield) of public securities, demand remains stable (ECB, 2019). Following this interpretation of exorbitant privilege, the European Central Bank (ECB) takes as its best measure the share of foreign official sector holdings of issued public debt with the highest credit quality. According to the ECB's estimates, the exorbitant privilege experienced by the United States, as well as by some euro-area countries that enjoy the highest ratings from credit rating agencies, is economically significant. In particular, holding official reserve assets in the form of debt securities of these economies has contributed to a reduction in term premia of around 160 basis points for US long-term yields and around 110 basis points for their euro-area counterparts (ECB, 2019, pp. 51–54).

According to Gopinath and Stein (2018), the United States, as the issuer of the dominant currency, can benefit from being much more isolated from exchange rate fluctuations than other countries. In fact, a consequence of the United States acting as a global provider of safe assets is the transmission of dollar monetary and credit conditions to the rest of the world (Bruno and Shi, 2012). In this way, foreign demand for safe assets, which affects the value of liquid assets, creates spillover effects from US monetary policy and influences the global financial cycle. Due to the role of the USD and the US's assets in the IMS, returns on risky assets have become increasingly correlated across markets, responding significantly to US monetary policy shocks (Miranda-Agrippino and Rey, 2020). As emerging market government bonds compete for safe asset status with those from advanced economies, they are highly susceptible to spillover from US monetary policy (Brunnermeier et al., 2021).

2.1.3 Characteristics of a Global Safe Asset Provider

The ability to create safe assets is closely linked to the internationalisation of the currency and the exorbitant privilege achieved from its issuance. This privileged position refers to a country that is sufficiently large, with a relatively stable fiscal position, issuing a wide range of debt instruments, in addition to having military power (Gourinchas and Jeanne, 2012; van Riet, 2017). The role of military power, as an additional factor to economic size, was mentioned by Eichengreen (2019). It is pointed out that the United States has had this 'privilege' since the late 1920s, and the United Kingdom before that (Eichengreen and Flandreau, 2009; van Riet, 2017). He et al. (2015) found that the relative size of the market, alongside fundamental factors, plays a key role, thus 'favouring' the currencies of large countries (such as the United States) over smaller ones (such as Switzerland). For assets issued in the currencies of large countries (in US dollars), they introduce the term 'dominant safe assets' (as an analogy to the term much more rooted in the literature, 'dominant currency'). Dominant safe assets act as a safe haven during periods of heightened financial instability, when there is a global flight to quality assets.

The premier role of the size of the economy was mentioned by Ogawa and Muto (2019), who argued that only large economies have deep and liquid markets open to the rest of the world that render their currencies attractive international reserves. As He et al. (2019) stated, market size increases liquidity, with lower premia creating a feedback loop to larger market size. However, they argued that the feedback loop from size to liquidity premia is positive only when there is a strong demand for safe assets. Otherwise, risk premia may rise due to concerns about sustainability. Frankel (2023) stated that 'the economies of Japan, the United Kingdom, and Switzerland are not big enough to sustain the number one (as providers of global liquidity) role'.[1]

The link between fulfilling the role of an international currency and being able to create safe assets was demonstrated empirically by Gopinath and Stein (2018). The novelty of their research stems from the fact that they analysed another function of international currency, namely trade invoicing. This differs from the more commonly examined reserve function concerning the creation of safe assets. They pointed to the complementarity of a currency's role as a safe store of value with its role as a unit of account for invoicing and trade settlement. They showed that the dominant currency in the invoicing function can create demand for safe assets denominated in that currency. The two functions are interdependent and reinforce each other. The large scale of trade invoicing in US dollars (including by non-US exporters) generates increased demand for US dollar safe deposits, thereby conferring an exorbitant privilege on the United States that stems from reduced borrowing costs.

In turn, reduced financing costs increase the attractiveness of USD trade invoicing for exporters outside the country of issue, creating cheaper USD financing. The strong feedback loops (or strategic complementarities) present in the trade and financing function performed by the dominant currency explain why global safe assets are denominated in USD (Farhi and Maggiori, 2018; Gopinath and Stein, 2018). The special role of a dominant currency in trade invoicing can explain why the fraction of goods and services invoiced in USD is disproportionately high compared to the role of the US economy in international trade (Goldberg and Tille, 2009). Additionally, the hypothesis that trade invoicing and settlement functions as a stimulus to greater international usage of the currency is verified in the historical context. Historically, currencies first acquired a role in trade invoicing and settlement before also assuming reserve currency status (ECB, 2023).

Among the factors that determine the ability to create safe assets, the role of legal considerations is highlighted. The ability to issue safe assets is primarily determined by the protection of property rights. Therefore, only entities from countries characterised by a stable political and macroeconomic situation and sound institutions can successfully issue safe assets. Moreover, as Golec and Perotti (2017) pointed out, the safety of assets such as debt instruments can be enhanced by contractual provisions, including:

1 Establishing senior debt status, giving priority over other claims,
2 Adopting shorter maturities for which the risks associated with the investment are less likely to materialise,
3 Establishing collateral, significantly reducing credit and counterparty risk.

Central to asset safety is the role of the institutions that make up the financial safety net. For example, in the case of bank deposits, these are the rules for the operation of the deposit guarantee scheme (e.g. the personal and material scope of the guarantee and the amount of the guarantee). The implementation of the lender of last resort function by the national central bank is also important. In this context, Gourinchas and Jeanne (2012) pointed out that the central bank can make any category of assets safe through an implicit or explicit declaration to buy assets when their price falls below a certain threshold.

Based on empirical research on changes in government bond yields in 40 advanced and emerging market countries between 1990 and 2018, Habib et al. (2020) identified fundamental factors that create the potential status of safe assets: inertia (in the sense of the ability of safe assets to play such a role in the past), political risk rating (quality of institutions) and the size of the debt market. The concept of inertia provides a rationale for directing demand for safe assets on the basis of investors' past decisions. The concept has been used in the literature on IMS to describe the persistence of the dominant currency function despite deteriorating economic indicators of the issuer – as evidenced by the long-term supremacy of the GBP in the IMS, subsequently taken over by the USD.

The large absolute debt size is important, as safe asset investors have 'nowhere else to go' in equilibrium (He et al., 2016b). Importantly, He et al. pointed out that the determinants of safe asset status are heterogeneous, depending on whether the issuer is a developed or emerging market country,[2] which confirms the theoretical assumptions presented by Schuknecht (2018). According to above-mentioned literature, political risk rating and the size of the debt market play an important role only for developed countries. For the second group of countries, in addition to inertia, real GDP and external stability (measured by the current account balance) are of importance. At the same time, there is no single main factor that explains the special role of US public safe assets – both the size of the market and the dominance of the USD in global foreign exchange reserves go some way to explaining it in periods of instability (Habib et al., 2020).

2.2 The Structure of the Supply of Safe Assets

2.2.1 *Safe Asset Provision from a Historical Perspective*

Under successive monetary and fiscal regimes, a variety of asset classes have fulfilled the role of safe assets. Historical experience reflects the variability in the perception of assets considered safe, with confidence playing a pivotal role in their creation. From an evolutionary perspective, coins minted from precious metals can be considered the first safe assets. Gold coins were imperfect in performing their function as safe assets due to the debasing of the metal content of the coin relative to its face value. The high degree of uncertainty about the value of coins, coupled with the widespread practice of counterfeiting and clipping, necessitated the costly acquisition of information on their worth through methods such as metal testing and coin weighing. The fundamental weakness concerning the characteristics of safe assets lay in their inability to meet the requirement of being insensitive to information. Gorton (2016) acknowledged that it is difficult to create information-insensitive safe assets. Historically, development has depended on technology, institutions, the legal environment, as well as a contract design that guarantees repayment of liabilities (Gorton, 2016, pp. 3, 30).

Due to the shortage of specie-based coins and the aforementioned problems with them, different forms of privately produced debt emerged. Bank debt took the form of banknotes, bills, and bills of exchange. Among these, bills of exchange were the earliest and primary form of safe assets backed by private debt for centuries. The primary weakness of bills of exchange, as well as other forms of short-term bank debt, was their vulnerability to runs. According to Gorton (2016, p. 6), there was a famous case in 1763 when the collapse of a large banking institution was followed by a massive withdrawal of funds from merchant banks that financed themselves with short-term debt. From around 1750, the private issuance of safe assets took various forms of debt, usually mortgage claims, as land generally has the capacity to retain its value (Gorton, 2016, p. 8).

Since the 17th century, it has been widely acknowledged that debt is the claim best able to play the role of a safe asset, based on its attributes. As it has evolved, secured debt has taken different forms of contracts, depending on the demand from different categories of market participants and the technology (e.g. the development of legal infrastructure) of contract terms.

The genesis of the development of reliable, safe assets in the form of government debt can be traced back to the institutional changes associated with the increased political power of the English Parliament relative to the power of the monarchy. The emergence of the system of power-sharing institutions – the monarchy and parliament – forced the former to commit to honouring payment obligations on government debt. This was after centuries of financial crises triggered by sovereign debt (Gorton, 2016, pp. 7–8). However, it was only following the development of political and economic factors in the 19th century that government debt could be seen as safe. In fact, as Flandreau and Zendjas (2009, after: Gorton, 2016, p. 8) pointed out, between 1820 and 1830, the government had to rely on the reputation of financial intermediaries to issue debt.

In the 1950s, bank demand deposits were widely regarded as safe assets. The declining role of this instrument was the consequence of changes in the financial system, evident since the 1970s, mainly due to phenomena such as securitisation, the rise of money market mutual funds, and the development of money market instruments (commercial paper and repos). They were accompanied by the increasing importance of wholesale markets compared to retail markets. As a consequence of the transformation in the financial architecture, commercial banks became less-profitable entities, creating a need for additional private sector creation of 'safe' debt, which became a driver for securitisation. These transformations were followed by the development of a shadow banking system (Gorton, 2016, pp. 1, 15, 17), which was interested in 'replicating' the safety and liquidity of banks' liabilities through the use of collateralised financial credit (repos, margin in futures contracts) (Golec and Perotti, 2017, p. 18).

The evolution of instruments considered safe assets is also a result of the evolution of how the essence of money is perceived. It went from being considered a commodity with its own value (metallism/classical approach) to being regarded as an agreement or a contract (chartalism/contractual theory). The contemporary view of public debt as an optimal form of safe asset is based on chartalism, which posits that money is a product of the state and it derives its value from its status as a state-guaranteed legal tender.[3] Chartalism argues that money has no intrinsic value. Its value is given by the government, and its widespread acceptance derives not from the fact that it is covered by bullion, but primarily that it is the only way to pay taxes (Gruszecki, 2015, p. 53). The government incurs debt when it issues its own liabilities, which become financial assets for the public sector. Consequently, since the government has the ability to issue its own currency, it is not financially constrained in its spending (Gruszecki, 2015).

Summing up, history tells us that:

- the role of assets classed as safe assets changes in tandem with changes in the international monetary and financial system, in the concept of money, and in technological advances,
- there can be a wide scope of assets that fulfil the role of safe assets, both in the form of debt (private and public) and non-credit instruments,
- confidence is a decisive factor in creating demand for safe assets.

Given the previous considerations, one may wonder which financial instruments can be perceived as global safe assets. Schmelzing (2020) provides insight into global safe assets from a historical perspective, confirming that their appearance corresponded with the financial dominance of the country/region. He identified the Italian city-states of Venice, Florence and Genoa as the earliest issuers of marketable, long-term sovereign debt during the Renaissance. Venice was treated as the most advanced sovereign debt market, while Florence, home of the Medici Bank, was considered the leader in private, commercial banks. The instruments of these three city-states could be pledged as collateral for bank loans, lent to third parties and used as substitutes for money to pay private obligations and taxes. The participation of international investors, including both 'official' (foreign rulers, religious orders) and private (merchants) ones in the market, enhanced turnover, which gave rise to the establishment of both private broker houses and public debt agencies in charge of issuance and liquidity management (Schmelzing, 2020, pp. 18–19). Epstein (2000) argued that these city-states were able to borrow in the long term because they were compact, merchant-dominated polities with a representative institution that monitored the sovereign.

As Spain's financial dominance grew and its public finance system developed, 'Juros' emerged as the preferred long-term public debt instrument among international investors. Meanwhile, the Spanish monarchy, despite being an absolutist government, did not need help from any other institution to provide credible commitments to its bankers or obtain access to important amounts of credit (Schmelzing, 2020, p. 23). In the late 16th century, economic primacy passed to the Dutch financial centres, making them accessible for investment and payment purposes worldwide. It is suggested that sovereign debt, as well as securities issued by cities, were initially marketed to foreigners by the County of Holland in the 16th century (Eichengreen et al., 2018).

The era of the gold standard, which favours monetary convergence, fostered financial integration with growing international capital flows.

Subsequent financial dominance cases are much more apparently correlated with the dominant position of a country in the IMS, that is England (in the gold standard), the United States (in the Bretton Woods system and in contemporary monetary system) and Germany after its unification in the 19th century, with its rising political and monetary power.

Global safe asset provision is closely connected with the mechanisms and stability of the IMS. Interestingly, historical instances of global safe asset provision overlap with historical experiences involving dominant currencies. As Ilzetzki et al. (2022) argued, since the 1500s, only Spain, the Netherlands, Great Britain and the United States have issued currencies that reached dominant status. Strengthening the stability of the IMS by establishing efficient global liquidity provision mechanisms and credible exchange rate anchors promotes the creation of global safe assets. Table 2.2 shows that periods of instability in the IMS are characterised by a lack of such assets. The interwar period (1919–1939), marked by hyperinflation, competitive devaluations of domestic currencies, and economic autarchy, shows what happens when there is a lack of a global safe asset.

Table 2.2 Global safe assets from a historical perspective

Period	*Asset Used*	*Main Characteristics as Regards Issuance, Monetary and Exchange Rate Arrangements*
1311–1508	Venice: Monte Vecchio, Monte Nuovo Genoa: Compere, San Giorgio Bank Florence: Monte Comune	A variety of local coins (ducats, florins, Byzantine hyperpyrons), with different gold and silver contents, trading at market exchange rates.
1509–1598	Spain: Juros	Spanish dollar, with fixed silver content.
1599–1702	Dutch Province of Holland: Renten	Mainly silver standard. The Dutch florin/guilder with fixed silver content circulated internationally, as well as Dutch bills of exchange (backed by florins).
1717–1907	British consol	The silver standard, then the pound-gold standard. Sterling notes circulated and were used internationally.
1908–1913	German Imperial 3% benchmark bond	
1914–1918	British consol	
1943–1947	US long-term bonds (11.5-year maturity)	
1948–1973	US 10-year bond	The gold-dollar standard (the Bretton Woods system)
1973–present	US 10-year bond	The multi-currency IMS. De facto dollar standard.

Source: Authors' compilation based on Schmelzing (2020).

Another important conclusion is that the appearance and popularity of global safe assets were inherently connected with a country's economic power and financial dominance. It created highly liquid secondary markets and fostered the development of financial infrastructure and the establishment of central banks. It is not a coincidence that central banks, which acted as bankers to the government, emerged during periods of the state's financial dominance – the Bank of Amsterdam was established in 1609, and the Bank of England was established in 1694. The role of a credible central bank in facilitating global safe asset provision is especially evident in England. The Bank of England, by implementing a debt-for-equity swap, relieved the state of its debt overhang. It evolved into the fiscal agent of the state, managing the money supply and floating new debt. These institutional arrangements enabled the English government to fund itself at the lowest rates in Europe while accumulating the single largest debt stock (Neal, 1990; after: Eichengreen et al., 2018).

2.2.2 *Contemporary Tendencies in the Supply of Safe Assets*

According to the IMF estimates (IMF, 2012; cf. Figure 2.3),[4] more than half of the global supply of safe assets is made up of government bonds of the OECD (Organisation for Economic Co-operation and Development) countries with the highest credit ratings, that is AAA/AA (45%) and A/BBB (7%). Securitised instruments are next in terms of share (17%), followed by investment-grade corporate debt and gold (11% each). The shares of the remaining asset classes do not exceed 5%. Importantly, the structure stresses the key role of credit ratings in labelling assets safe.

Governments care about the highest possible ratings, as they largely determine the terms and extent of countries' access to international financial markets. This relationship is illustrated in Figure 2.4, using the example of the euro-area countries. As can be seen, yields on ten-year sovereign bonds are clearly lower in Germany, Luxembourg, and the Netherlands, that is issuers of the highest AAA-rated securities. Furthermore, the sovereign credit rating provides a benchmark for the ratings given to various domestic entities such as banks and companies. As empirical research shows, this informal benchmark, described in the literature as the sovereign ceiling policy, is still used despite declarations by the rating agencies themselves that they are moving away from such a practice (cf. Luitel et al., 2016). In addition, sovereign credit ratings are closely monitored by institutional investors, in particular, those who are legally obliged to take asset quality into account when constructing investment portfolios.

Another important group mentioned by the IMF (2012) is covered bonds. They are debt obligations issued by credit institutions and collateralised by a given pool of assets against which bondholders have a claim as senior creditors. At the same time, they may make a claim against the bond issuer as ordinary creditors. This construction, known as the principle of

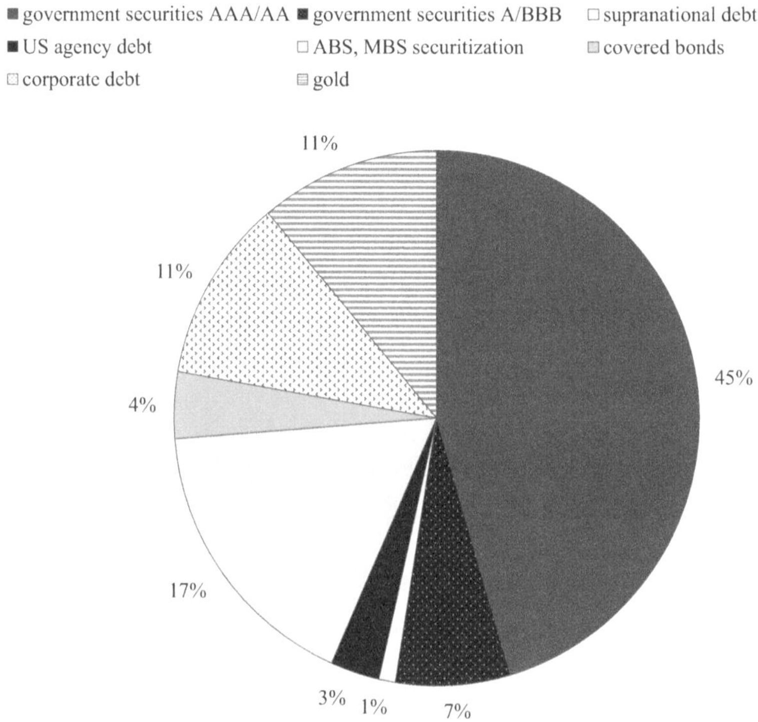

Figure 2.3 Safe assets by category (% of total)

Source: own compilation based on IMF (2012, p. 89).

Note: shares may not add up to 100% due to rounding.

double recourse to the issuer and the collateral provided, makes these assets a low-risk investment. Put simply, covered bonds are secured senior debt issued by banks and perceived by investors as widely used liquid and safe financial instruments. Therefore, covered bonds are safe assets for investors and a stable and cheap source of bank funding, mostly in Europe; they are considered almost as safe as triple-A sovereign debt instruments. However, rapid and strong declines in real estate prices may pose a risk to the covered bonds market because of the dominance of residential mortgages used as collateral.

An instrument that meets the criteria for covered bonds is securities issued by mortgage banks, which are secured by the bank's mortgage claims. The role of covered bonds as instruments that meet the characteristics of safe assets was emphasised by the IMF, noting the strong market potential of German *Pfandbriefe* (IMF, 2012, p. 109). The Pfandbrief system, which supplies credit to landowners, dates back to 18th-century Prussia. It has developed since then as a safe financial instrument. Covered bonds are today a cornerstone of bank funding in Europe. Importantly, over the past two centuries,

Figure 2.4 Sovereign bond yields of the euro area, AAA countries against the average
Source: Eurostat.
* Changing composition.

they have experienced no defaults, and delayed payments to investors have been rare. Nevertheless, as Anand (2016) argued, there may be potential drawbacks to the outlook for this instrument due to new regulations on resolution within the European Banking Union. As banks' incentives to issue covered bonds are closely linked to conditions in the wholesale funding market, they may increase the risk of wholesale bank runs.

Another group of assets under consideration are asset-backed securities (ABS) or mortgage-backed securities (MBS). ABS, which are usually in the form of bonds, generate income in the form of credit card receivables, student loans or consumer loans. Since assets in the form of loan receivables are not sellable, securitisation is used, which offers more opportunities. The issuance of ABS typically begins with a bank initiating a securitisation process by selling a pool of receivables to a *Special Purpose Vehicle* (SPV). After the ABS is issued, the cash flows generated from the segregated assets are used to pay interest and repay the principal owed to the ABS holders. The pool of securitised assets from which the ABS cash flows are generated is called collateral.

ABS have a diversified risk profile because each such security contains only a fraction of the total pool of segregated assets. Whereas ABS are backed by non-mortgage assets, MBS are backed by a pool of mortgages. The agency MBS market is well developed, with an important economic role as collateral for repo financing, and in central banks' monetary policy operations. According to He and Song (2022), the convenience premium for agency MBS (measured as yields spread against AAA corporate bonds) averaged 47 basis points between 1995 and 2021, about half of the long-term Treasury convenience premium. This shows the importance and the potential of agency MBS as safe assets.

From an investor's point of view, ABS/MBS are an interesting investment alternative as they provide higher returns than government bonds. Because the credit risk is spread, that is ABS contain only a fraction of the secured assets, the risk of default is minimised.

In the case of the US financial market, Government-Sponsored Enterprises (GSEs) or Agency securities (commonly referred to as 'agency debt') include securities issued or backed by the Fannie Mae, Freddie Mac, or Ginnie Mae US housing finance agencies. Fannie Mae (Federal National Mortgage Association) and Freddie Mac (Federal Home Loan Mortgage Corporation) were taken over by the US government with the outbreak of the GFC. However, even before the takeover, they were widely perceived as being fully backed by the government.

An important category within safe assets is supranational debt. Supranational issuers (supranationals and multilaterals) are international institutions that provide financing, advisory or other financial services to member countries for the overall goal of improving living standards through sustainable economic growth. Examples of these issuers, the nature of their activities and their ownership structure are presented in Table 2.3.

Supranational issuers are not commercial entities but international institutions generally owned and controlled by governments. They provide them with financial resources, credibility, operational framework and access to liquid capital markets, enabling them to raise the funds necessary to support government policies. According to the credit rating agencies, therefore, the ability of international institutions to repay their financial commitments is not solely determined by their balance sheet but primarily by the ability and willingness of shareholder governments to provide additional support when an institution exhausts its own financial reserves. Strong shareholders are, therefore, a sufficient condition for supranational issuers to receive a high credit rating. When weaker shareholders are behind an institution, its internal strength becomes a necessary condition (Scope Ratings, 2021, p. 4).

Many of the entities are considered by credit rating agencies to be safe asset issuers, often enjoying a higher rating than that given to shareholder countries. This situation may be due to the privileged creditor status of supranational issuers, tax benefits and legal protection from government interference. The data in Table 2.3 confirm the high credit ratings of supranational issuers, ranging from BBB– to AAA on the Fitch Ratings scale. The vast majority of these entities are rated at least double A, with a large proportion considered to have an exceptionally high ability to service their financial obligations, represented by the highest AAA rating.

Table 2.3 Examples and ratings of supranational issuers

Issuer	*Scope of Activities*	*Ownership Structure*	*Rating by Fitch*
Afreximbank (African Export-Import Bank)	African multilateral development bank; focuses on facilitating trade finance in Africa.	As of financial year 2019, there were 156 shareholders: 51 African states and quasi-government entities, 90 African private investors and financial institutions, 14 non-African financial institutions and 1 export credit agency.	BBB
African Development Bank	Multilateral development bank; supports economic development and social progress in Africa, lending to eligible (i.e. creditworthy) countries and, to a lesser extent, private sector entities.	81 member countries: 54 from Africa (60% of subscribed capital) and 27 from outside Africa (40% of subscribed capital).	AAA
Africa Finance Corporation	African multilateral development bank; focuses on infrastructure financing in sub-Saharan Africa.	A total of 27 shareholders: Central Bank Nigeria (42.4%), United Bank of Africa (10.8%), Access Bank (9.6%), First Bank of Nigeria (8.6%), Zenith Bank (%), with the remaining shareholders holding less than 5%.	–
Asian Development Bank	Multilateral development bank; supports the economic and social development of Asia and the Pacific; provides loans to countries and private sector entities.	68 member countries, including 49 from the region. The largest shareholders are Japan (15.6%) and the USA (15.6%).	AAA
Asian Infrastructure Investment Bank	Multilateral development bank; has a mandate to cover the infrastructure financing gap in Asia.	As of August 2020, there were 103 members, with China (30.8%), India (8.6%), Russia (6.8%), Germany (4.6%) and Korea (3.9%) being the most important shareholders.	AAA
Black Sea Trade and Development Bank	Multilateral development bank; supports economic development and regional cooperation in the Black Sea region.	11 member countries; the largest shareholders are Greece, Russia and Turkey (16.5% each), followed by Romania (14%), Bulgaria (13.5%) and Ukraine (13.5%).	–

Caribbean Development Bank	The bank promotes the economic growth and development of Caribbean member countries, as well as their economic cooperation and integration.	28 member countries, of which 23 are from the region and five from outside the region (Canada, Germany, Italy, China and the UK total 35.5%).	AA+
Council of Europe Development Bank	Regional multilateral development bank; lends to European countries for inclusive and sustainable growth, the integration of refugees, displaced persons and migrants, and climate action.	42 member countries of the Council of Europe. Eurozone countries account for 77% of the subscribed capital, with France, Germany and Italy being the largest shareholders (17% each).	AAA
Eurasian Development Bank	Multilateral development bank; promotes economic development, trade and integration among members.	Founders: Russia (65.97%) and Kazakhstan (32.99%); the other members (1.04%) are Armenia, Belarus, Kyrgyzstan and Tajikistan.	BB+
European Bank for Reconstruction and Development (EBRD)	Multilateral development bank; finances the development of market economies in 36 countries in central Europe and central Asia, mainly through private sector financing. Its updated strategy for 2021–2025 aims to increase the share of 'green' investments in total financing to 50%.	70 countries from five continents, plus the EU and the European Investment Bank.	AAA
European Financial Stability Facility (EFSF)	The fund was set up in 2010 as a temporary financial support mechanism for euro-area countries affected by the sovereign debt crisis. Beneficiary countries included Ireland, Portugal and Greece. The assistance was financed by issuing EFSF bonds and other debt instruments on the capital markets. The EFSF was replaced in 2013 by the European Stability Mechanism.	20 euro-area countries; guarantees from non-beneficiary Member States of the programmes, based on the ECB's capital key.	AA-

(*Continued*)

Table 2.3 (Continued)

Issuer	*Scope of Activities*	*Ownership Structure*	*Rating by Fitch*
European Investment Bank (EIB)	EU development bank; focuses mainly on financing infrastructure projects in Community countries. One of the largest issuers of 'green' bonds in the world; committed to developing sustainable finance.	EU Member States.	AAA
European Stability Mechanism (ESM)	Its objective is to ensure financial stability in the euro area by providing financial support to economies that are experiencing or at risk of experiencing severe financial difficulties.	20 euro-area member states; ownership based on the ECB capital key, with the largest share of Germany (27%), France (20%), Italy (18%) and Spain (12%).	AAA
European Union*	The European Union borrows on the capital markets to finance loan programmes (European Financial Stabilisation Mechanism, Balance of Payments Assistance, Macro-Financial Assistance Facility).	European Union Member States.	AAA
Inter-American Development Bank	Multilateral development bank, founded in 1959; lends to countries in the Latin American and Caribbean region.	48 member countries; 26 borrowing members from Latin America and the Caribbean (together 50% of votes); 22 non-borrowing members, including the US (30%), Japan (5%) and Canada (4%).	AAA
International Bank for Reconstruction and Development	The largest part of the World Bank Group. The Bank's main objectives are to end poverty in middle-income countries and in poorer countries with financial capability and promote sustainable economic development. The bank pursues these objectives by providing loans and guarantees to the public sector.	189 member states; the largest shareholders are the US (16.7%), Japan (8.1%), China (4.9%), Germany (4.4%), France (4.1%) and the UK (4.1%).	AAA

International Finance Facility for Immunisation	Accelerates funding for vaccination programmes in developing countries by Gavi, the Vaccine Alliance.	10 donor countries; the UK (49.2%), France (32.8%) and Italy (7.3%) account for the majority of pledges of financial support.	AA-
Islamic Development Bank	Specialised multilateral development bank; supports economic and social development in member countries and among Muslim communities. It finances both public and private sector institutions.	57 member countries of the Organisation of Islamic Cooperation. The largest shareholders are Saudi Arabia (24%), Libya (10%), Iran (8%), Nigeria (8%), the UAE (8%) and Qatar (7%).	AAA
Nordic Investment Bank	Multilateral development bank; finances long-term public and private sector projects in both Scandinavian and Baltic member countries and non-member developing countries.	Five Nordic countries (94.9%) and three Baltic countries (5.1%).	-

Source: Own compilation based on Daiwa Capital Markets, 2021 and the Refinitiv Eikon data as of December 2023.

* While the European Union does have a legal personality, the European Commission acts on its behalf.

An analysis of Table 2.3 allows us to draw the following conclusions. Firstly, supranational issuers are regional in their field of operation and, therefore, belong to the regional providers of safe assets. The exception is supranational debt created within the EU, which aspires to global provider status. European supranational issuers, including the EU, EIB, EBRD and ESM, achieve particularly high credit ratings. The safe asset status of their debt reflects the strength of the shareholders behind them and the soundness of their balance sheets and/or operational framework. They are, therefore, characterised by strong buffers, allowing them to remain resilient to external shocks and strengthen their operations in times of economic difficulties, such as the COVID-19 pandemic and its economic impact. Secondly, supranational debt creators can be divided into two subgroups: RFAs (Regional Financing Arrangements), that is arrangements that provide a financial facility usually (but not always) within an integration grouping (e.g. the ESM), and regional development banks.

Another important financial instrument singled out by the IMF 2012 report is bonds issued by corporations, broadly defined as corporate debt. Corporate debt with the highest rating (AAA) can be classified as a safe asset due to minimal investment risk and a very liquid secondary market, ensuring ease of trading. Corporate debt is mainly issued in the form of corporate bonds, but it includes a whole group of debt instruments issued by companies, including, for example, commercial paper. The corporate debt market is the second-largest market in the world after government securities. Due to the issuer's higher credit risk, investors achieve higher returns in this market than in the public issue market. Bonds issued by corporates have varying maturities (from one year to several decades) and yield varying returns, depending on the issuer's rating. Like government-issued bonds, corporate bonds are also exposed to interest rate risk.

Despite its high price volatility, gold is widely regarded as a safe-haven asset. It gains in value during economic crises and increased financial market uncertainty, which, in the long run, makes it an important category of safe assets. Gold provides safety but is not remunerated and is supplied inelastically. As it is not a debt-based asset, it represents a special case of a safe asset. As a non-credit instrument, it carries no credit risk, and gains the ability to hold value. By being 'no one's liability', it carries no default risk.

2.3 The Role of Debt in Safe Asset Creation

2.3.1 Public vs Private Debt in the Provision of Safe Assets

Debt's ability to be a safe asset derives from the fact that it is a contractual promise, whereby the debtor undertakes to return the face value at maturity (and pay interest), and because it can have all the attributes of such assets. Indeed, debt is the claim least sensitive to fluctuations in value and is immune to adverse selection and moral hazard. The relevance of a particular safe asset attribute and function is also affected by the maturity of the debt. The NQA attribute is more related to short-term debt, as shorter maturities reduce risk. Storing value, on the other hand, is a property of long-term debt (Gorton, 2016, p. 11).

There are two ways to issue safe debt: by securing it in the form of government taxability and through the use of collateral (Gorton, 2016). In discussions on the relationship between public and private debt, different aspects are highlighted. Carapella and Williamson (2015) distinguish public debt from private debt because of its role as collateral. Azzimonti and Yared (2019) stated that whereas government bonds are backed by future tax revenues, 'privately issued safe assets' are backed by the future repayment of pools of defaultable private loans. However, due to the moral hazard that characterises private investors and financial intermediaries, private assets are not able to be as safe as government debt (Xiong, 2018, p. 4). As Gorton (2016, p. 2) stated, privately produced short-term debt is inherently susceptible to runs unless there is some government support, for example deposit insurance. Kacperczyk and Schnabl (2013) stated that money market funds could lack safety because they have strong incentives to take on risk when the opportunity arises and are vulnerable to runs. Finally, one may wonder whether 'private safe assets' can have both a regional and global reach, similar to public assets.

As research in the field of economic history shows, many governments have achieved a state where their debt and guarantees are considered credible, allowing them to enjoy safe asset issuer status. In contrast, for private issuance, the condition for an asset class to be considered safe is that it is backed by credible collateral, for example land, a portfolio of loans or bonds. Mortgages are considered to have fulfilled this condition for almost three centuries, as land does not usually lose value. Another group consists of short-term debt instruments backed by debt, usually long-term debt (debt-on-debt contracts). They are formed by, among others, demand deposits, repos and short-term asset-backed commercial papers, for which the collateral are loan portfolios, bonds and residential mortgages (Gorton, 2016, p. 12).

Recognising the above key differences, the question arises about the role of the private and public sectors in the creation of safe assets. It is based on the assumption that these assets can – in certain situations – be substitutable for each other while also being complementary. It is vital to consider the consequences of safe asset scarcity for financial stability and potential substitutability between public assets and private assets (issued by stable financial institutions, mainly banks and corporations with high credit ratings). According to Azzimonti and Yared (2019), there is a theory of optimal government debt in which publicly issued and 'privately issued safe assets' are substitutes. They state that an increase in public debt crowds out 'private safe assets' less than a one-to-one ratio, decreases interest spreads, and increases deposit rates. Increasing public debt reduces financial market friction and leads to higher inequality. Therefore, the optimal level of public debt is positively correlated with the level of financial market friction.

Krishnamurthy and Vissing-Jørgenesen (2015) observed that, as a consequence of the structural nature of the demand for safe assets, periods of low supply of government debt favour an increase in the creation (crowd-in) of 'private safe assets' like repos and commercial paper. Conversely, in periods of sufficient public debt supply, 'privately issued safe assets' are crowded out. The hypothesis of crowding out was empirically demonstrated by He and Song (2022) in relation to MBS issuance. In their research, the economic channels of agency MBS as safe assets were analysed. They found that Treasury supply (measured by the US debt-to-GDP ratio) negatively affects the MBS convenience premium, which is consistent with the substitutability hypothesis between those two assets in satisfying safe asset demand.

Analysing the substitutability of public and private assets, Kacperczyk and Maggio (2017) and Kacperczyk et al. (2021) pointed out that:

1 It is only visible among assets with very short maturities,
2 The use of private assets as a substitute for government security varies depending on market conditions and the quality of the issuer.

This first observation was empirically confirmed by Kacperczyk et al. (2021) on the European market for certificates of deposit (CD). They found that debt securities issued by the private sector only offer a safety premium when the securities have a short maturity, typically up to one week. The fact that only certificates with short maturities are considered safe, while those with longer maturities are of higher risk, is consistent with the view that assets with shorter maturities are less sensitive to the arrival of new information.

Private financial intermediaries respond to changes in convenience yield: when its value increases due to a shortage of Treasury securities, they issue more safe debt and vice versa (Gorton, 2016, p. 20). Krishnamurthy and Vissing-Jørgensen (2012b) showed that the net supply of government debt is strongly negatively correlated with the net supply of private, 'near-riskless' debt. This was confirmed by the empirical research of Krishnamurthy and Vissing-Jørgenesen (2015), which showed that a decrease in the supply of government securities raises convenience yields, to which financial intermediaries respond by creating more 'safe' debt. The two asset classes are, therefore, almost substitutable.

Holmström and Tirole (2011) also showed that when government bonds are in short supply, the liquidity premium increases, creating incentives for the private sector to provide substitutes for safe debt. Meanwhile, using daily data to analyse the ABS/MBS market for 1978–2010, Xie (2012) showed that ABS/MBS are issued when the expected convenience yield is high. This phenomenon is not observed in other private debt markets, such as corporate bond markets. The link between government debt and its private sector substitutes was also confirmed by Gorton et al. (2012). They showed that, taking into account both government debt and private 'near-risk-free' debt, the share of safe assets in the US economy has remained relatively constant in the overall US asset pool since 1952 (the stability of safe assets hypothesis), which at the same time reflects the structural nature of the demand for safety. The constant 'safe asset share' was accompanied by a twofold increase in the ratio of financial assets as a share of the US economy. Throughout the research period, which spanned 1952–2010, the share of safe assets (government and private assets) in total assets was in the 30%–35% range, allowing Gorton et al. to draw conclusions about the elasticity of adjustments in the financial system. The inherent demand for safety indicates a segmentation of the financial market into safe and speculative asset markets (Golec and Perotti, 2017, p. 3).

The surge in demand for safe assets during the 2002–2007 credit boom, driven by massive capital inflows into the United States amid global economic imbalances, serves as an empirical example of the co-existence of public and 'private safe assets' and its consequences. To better understand the phenomena, one has to look back to the late 1990s. After the 1997–1998 currency crisis, many Southeast Asian countries, wanting to protect themselves from the negative effects of destabilising capital flows in the future, began to transform themselves from importers to net capital exporters through the dynamic accumulation of foreign exchange reserves. In practice, it involved mobilising domestic savings and the subsequent purchase of treasury securities issued by highly developed countries, most notably the United States, due to their status as reserve currency issuers. These assets were also in demand from China. Although it was not one of the countries most affected by the Asian crisis, it needed reserves to intervene in foreign exchange markets as part of its export-led growth strategy. According to estimates by Bertaut et al. (2015), in the pre-crisis period (Q1 2003 – Q2 2007), foreign central banks and other public investors absorbed approximately 80% of the increase in the supply of US government debt instruments. The rapid increase of foreign holdings of US treasury securities at the turn of the 20th and 21st centuries is shown in Figure 2.5.

However, the structural supply scarcity of long-term secure government debt issued by the United States, and, to a lesser extent, other advanced economies, provided a strong incentive for the US financial system to create 'safe private assets' in the form of AAA-rated ABS and MBS instruments. As Xie (2012) showed, prior to the crisis, an average of 86.3% of ABS/MBS contracts received the highest credit ratings.

Securitisation not only redistributed credit risk among financial intermediaries but also resulted in a significant increase in the correlations of their returns. This reinforced a systemic run on the part of investors seeking to avoid risk as it materialised, with dramatic consequences as a result of investors underestimating their exposure to systemic factors (Golec and Perotti, 2017, pp. 16, 24). The GFC revealed the fleeting nature of the safety label attached to highly rated private assets created via the securitisation of riskier assets and loans. Consequently, their issuance stopped (Figure 2.6).

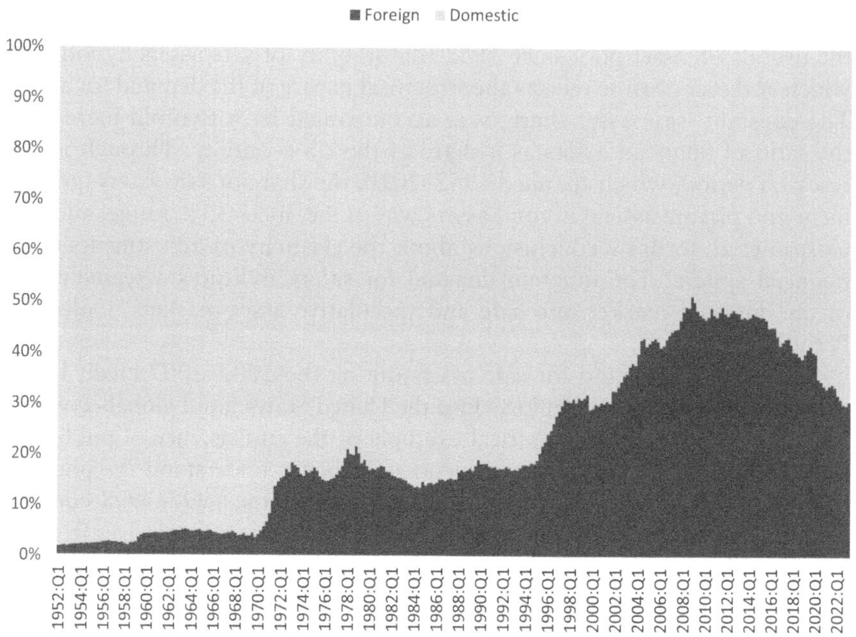

Figure 2.5 Foreign vs domestic holdings of US Treasury securities (share of total)
Source: Authors' own compilation based on the Federal Reserve Board data.

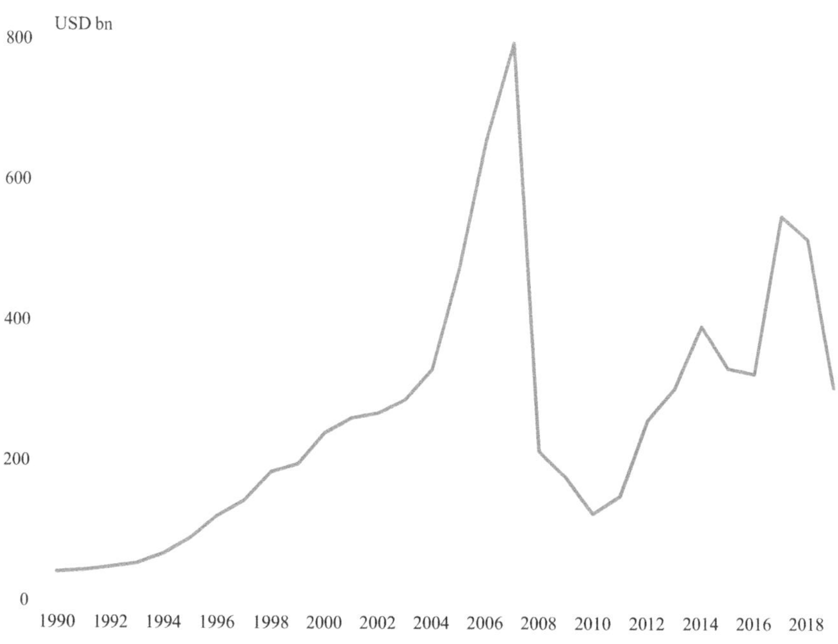

Figure 2.6 US asset-backed securities issuance
Source: US Asset Backed Securities Statistics.

The experience presented here shows that in a systemic crisis, private assets can easily lose their security, thereby contributing to destabilisation in the global economy.

The lack of perfect substitutability between publicly and privately issued assets has also been indicated by empirical research. For example, Kacperczyk et al. (2017) concluded that the issuance of private assets exhibits a high degree of pro-cyclicality, causing them to cease to function as safe assets during periods of financial instability. As they pointed out, this conclusion also applies to private assets with the shortest maturities. Additionally, Gorton (2016, p. 13) stated that during a crisis, 'private sector safe assets' lose their attributes; for example, during the global financial crisis, bank debt lost its NQA attribute.

In other words, the ability of private assets to act as safe assets changes with the credit cycle. This means that safe assets exhibit a cyclical substitution pattern between public and private instruments. In the boom phase, many public and private contracts are considered safe, thus increasing the tendency of investors to view them as close substitutes. Financial crises often erupt after a surge in the supply of 'private safe assets'. During an economic slump, private assets are more vulnerable to price declines compared to public assets (cf. Golec and Perotti, 2017). Therefore, they are considered, at best, quasi-safe, that is devoid of credit risk outside major crises. Figure 2.7 provides a graphical representation of this pattern while also considering liquidity risk.

When considering the prevalence of public assets, or narrowing the gap of public debt over private debt, the question arises as to their origins. The

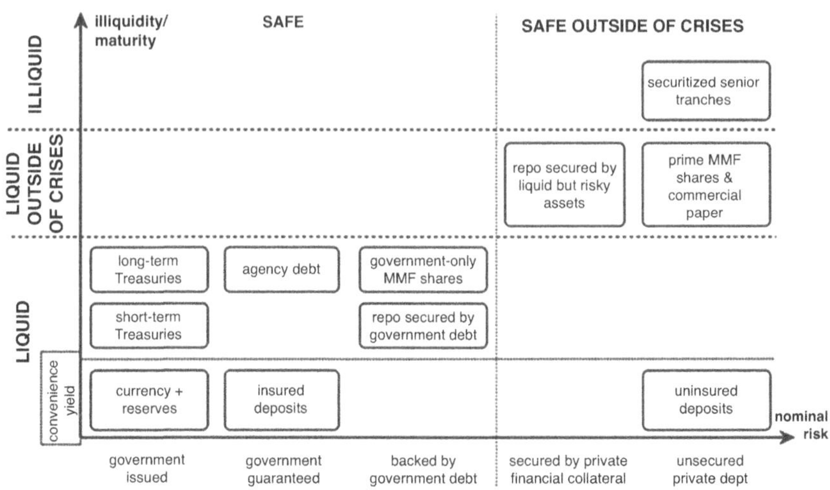

Figure 2.7 Classification of assets from the point of view of liquidity and risk

Source: Golec and Perotti (2017) (the authors acknowledge that they also include the central bank – as a public trust institution – in the category of 'government').

literature points to the following (cf. Gelpern and Gerding, 2016; van Riet, 2017, pp. 8–12, 14–15):

1 The government's ability to tax (power to taxation) and turn to extraordinary measures, such as a one-off tax on deposits. However, this attribute is limited by economic and legal conditions and possible credibility implications. As the experience of the eurozone debt crisis has shown, sovereign bonds of countries with a fragile public finance sector lost their perceived safety, and the attempt to introduce a one-off savings tax in Cyprus in 2013 resulted in a run on the banks there and the introduction of controls on capital flows.
2 The government's ability to borrow bilaterally or from international lenders such as the IMF.
3 The lender-of-last-resort function performed by the national central bank to both the banking and government sectors. It can be argued that the central bank's mere declaration of its ability to conduct (unlimited) interventions in the government bond market has a stabilising effect. As Brunnermeier et al. (2021) argued, the role of the central bank as a market maker of last resort to ensure that the bid-ask spreads remain low makes sense, assuming the good friend analogy as a characteristic of safe assets. This was shown by the ECB's experience with the launch of the Outright Monetary Transactions (OMT) programme in 2012. However, that role is controversial, as it involves moral hazard issues and concerns about the price stability objective, which further affects the credibility of the monetary authority.[5]
4 Legislative and regulatory competencies. Firstly, the state can use these powers to improve the security of the debt instruments it issues. As already mentioned, a prerequisite is the protection of property rights, preventing asset confiscation. Another example is constitutional fiscal rules, introducing quantitative limits on the budget deficit, government spending or public debt to curb fiscal profligacy. In addition, bond issuance can be carried out under a non-domestic legal regime to exclude ex post changes in contractual terms. Secondly, the state can reinforce the perceived safety of assets, which Gelpern and Gerding (2016) referred to as 'labelling'. An example of this is the prudential rules on the risk weights used by banks for government exposures to calculate capital adequacy. Low-risk weights for government bonds are a customary practice that can 'put down' market discipline as it reduces the propensity of investors to continuously monitor the macroeconomic fundamentals of an economy. Thirdly, the law can establish central government guarantees for debt incurred by regional and local authorities and public authority agencies. Thus, the security identified with federal bonds extends to more of the public sector. This may be particularly relevant for countries with a federal system.
5 Opportunities to exert pressure on the financial system. One form is moral suasion, that is government influence on financial sector institutions to

take certain expected actions. For example, during the height of the tensions related to the euro-area sovereign debt crisis, moral suasion played a significant role in encouraging banks from the countries most affected by the crisis to excessively involve themselves in purchasing domestic government bonds. In particular, pressure was exerted on entities that had previously benefited from government support for the banking sector and on state-owned banks; purchases were supposed to limit further increases in the government bond yields of the peripheral EMU countries (cf. Navaretti et al., 2016; Ongena et al., 2019).

6 Greater flexibility in offering instruments with different maturities.

Given these arguments that favour public over private assets as safe assets, government securities should be issued by a country with:

- sound public finances,
- a central bank willing to act as lender of last resort,
- a credible monetary authority, characterised by its ability to maintain the value of money (low inflation and a stable exchange rate),
- a legal system that guarantees the protection of property rights.

2.3.2 The Special Role of Public Debt as a Source of Safe Asset Provision

2.3.2.1 The Limitations of Public Debt as Safe Assets – The Laffer Curve

When considering the creation of public safe assets, the question arises regarding an individual country's potential to issue such assets, taking into account both endogenous and exogenous factors. Schuknecht (2018; cf. Figure 2.8) created the 'safe assets Laffer curve' to analyse this potential. He argues that there is a maximum level of a country's debt at which it is deemed safe. Changes in fiscal policy cause the country to 'move' along the curve – increasing debt causes a movement to the right. It follows that an increase in debt may be beneficial only up to a certain point, where the curve reaches a maximum (point D). Further increases result in the loss of safe asset issuer status, which translates into a lower credit rating.

According to Schuknecht (2018), the safe assets Laffer curve varies depending on the country's level of development, that is the greater the development, the more the curve extends to the right. This means that developed countries have a greater capacity to increase debt without raising doubts about its sustainability. This is particularly true for global and regional providers of safe assets, including the United States, the United Kingdom, Germany and Japan. For these Figure 2.9, the Laffer curve for safe assets for different country groups countries, the curve is shifted most to the right (cf. Figure 2.9).

The position of the safe assets Laffer curve for different countries is determined by a number of endogenous and exogenous factors. First, countries

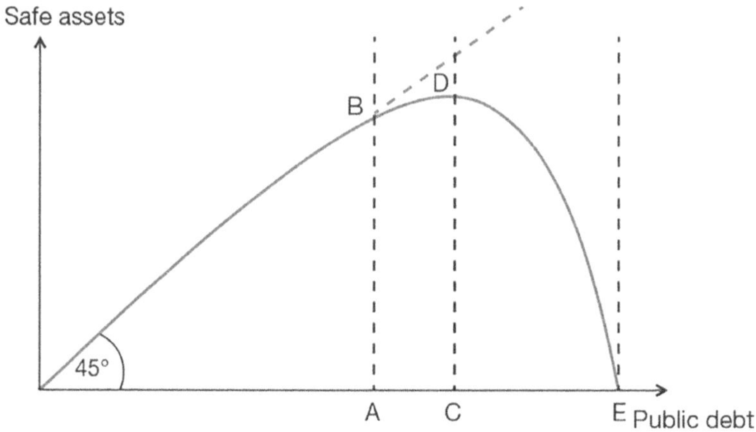

Figure 2.8 The Laffer curve for safe assets
Source: Schuknecht (2018).

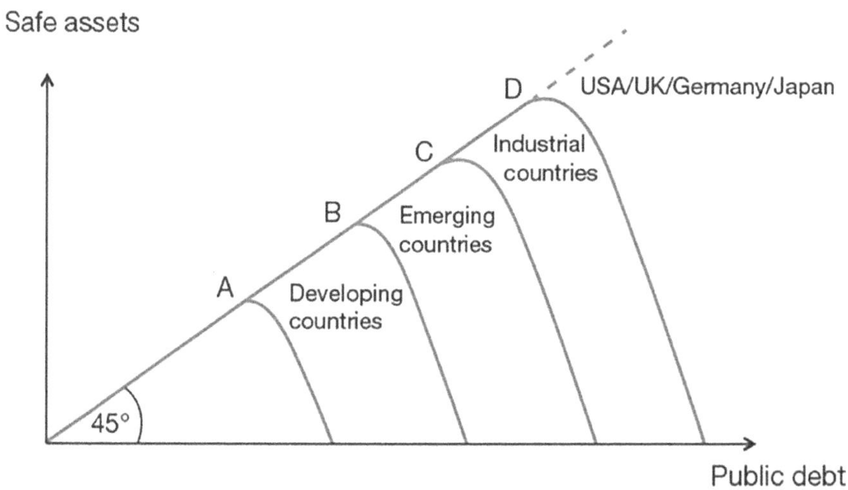

Figure 2.9 The Laffer curve for safe assets for different country groups
Source: Schuknecht (2018).

with a strong fiscal policy have longer curves than countries with unsustainable public finances. Second, countries with independent central banks that maintain stable and low inflation have more credibility than countries with short- or long-term political pressures. Hence, they can safely finance increasing public debt. Third, countries with sound economic growth experience the same positive effects, as the economy can deal easily with high levels of public debt. External factors can also play an important role, in particular, the size and liquidity of the financial market. Market size and successful fiscal and monetary governance are likely to make public debt much safer; for example the United Kingdom and the United States have much higher ratings than many emerging economies with lower debt-to-GDP ratios. Additionally, the home country currency could be a reserve currency, meaning that it can act as a benchmark in international transactions. Again, these factors extend the safe part (from the origin to point C, cf. Figure 2.8) of the safe assets Laffer curve and expand the areas where government debt is less secure (Schuknecht, 2018).

At the same time, the position of the safe assets Laffer curve depends not only on country-specific factors but also on the state of the global economy; that is changes in global uncertainty may impact the perception of assets as safe. As a consequence, countries may face a 'fan' of safe asset curves where the baseline curve is in the middle. More specifically, in times of crisis, when global risk aversion increases, the curve shifts to the left in countries considered less safe, and to the right in countries perceived as safe havens, as was visible during the euro-area sovereign debt crisis. The notable exception is countries that issue reserve currencies. In their case, the curve will be furthest to the right in both good times and in crises (Schuknecht, 2018; Figure 2.10).

The above reasoning shows that there are limits to the supply of safe assets created by government debt, and the maximum amount is not fixed. In general, in times of rising uncertainty, the potential to issue debt is limited compared to economic prosperity. As demand for global safe assets increases dramatically during periods of instability, the issuing country is then subjected to pressures to increase the supply of public safe assets. Consequently, during

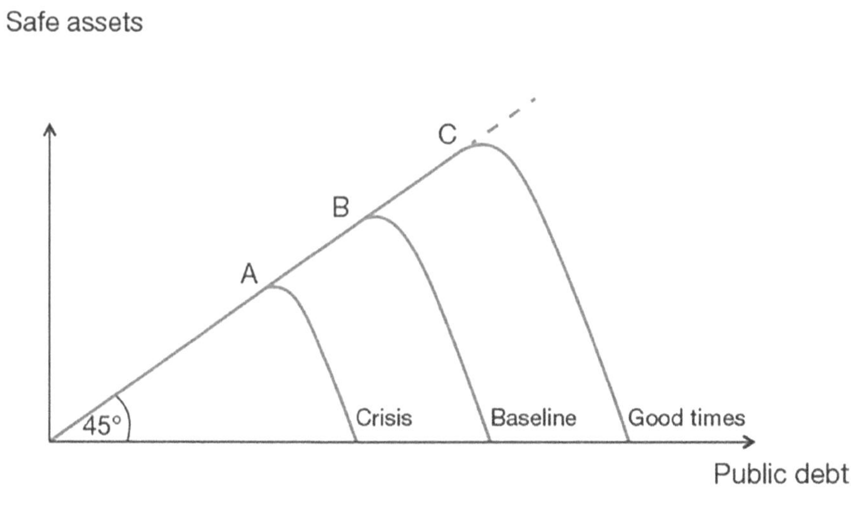

Figure 2.10 The Laffer curve for safe assets by the state of the economy
Source: Schuknecht (2018).

periods of financial instability, the 'exorbitant privilege' achieved is offset by an 'exorbitant duty' on the part of the global provider of safe assets, forcing it to pursue expansionary fiscal policies.

The shortage of safe assets moves from one country to another through international capital flows as investors globally adopt a 'search-for-quality' strategy. In periods of financial instability, the role of global safe assets must be supplemented by their regional providers (the previously mentioned Switzerland, Germany, Japan and the United Kingdom). As a result, when global safe assets are in short supply, increased demand is directed towards regional providers. This demand, which comes from both residents and non-residents, causes the safe asset-issuing country to experience increased capital inflows and, as a result, downward pressure on interest rates and currency appreciation.

Furthermore, He et al. (2016a, pp. 19–20) showed that, in the case of Switzerland, the ongoing policy of limiting the supply of government bonds further stimulated the inflow of funds into the country, as the relatively small stock of debt guaranteed that the issuing country could service its debts. As a result, government bond prices rose, further reducing interest rates to negative levels. In a near-zero or negative interest rate environment, the exchange rate becomes a key adjustment channel, leading to an appreciation of the issuing country's currency for safe-haven assets. Caballero et al. (2015) called this phenomenon the 'paradox of the reserve currency'. The paradox of the reserve currency also implies that reserve currency issuers bear a disproportionately higher cost of the safety trap by absorbing global recession and stagnation (Gourinchas, 2017).

Finally, the reserve currency paradox can be seen as another dimension of 'extraordinary duty', creating dilemmas for national monetary policy (ECB, 2019, p. 39). Such dilemmas, which Gourinchas and Rey (2016) called the 'curse of regional safe asset providers', were felt by Switzerland during the global financial crisis. The increase in the scale of capital inflows, which generated pressure on the appreciation of the Swiss franc, worsening the competitiveness of domestic exports, forced the monetary authorities to introduce an official exchange rate target in monetary policy; they defined a minimum exchange rate of CHF 1.20 per euro. As a result of this modification of the monetary policy framework, Switzerland experienced a costly accumulation of foreign exchange reserves. Between 2009 and 2011, that is during the period of most intense accumulation, the country's reserves increased by 234%. The Swiss National Bank discontinued its exchange rate ceiling on 15 January 2015.

2.3.2.2 *Economic and Non-economic Determinants of Public Debt Creation in the Role of Safe Assets*

The fundamental advantage of a global safe asset provider over a regional one lies in its ability to supply assets irrespective of the economic situation, which is due to the size of the economy and the depth of the financial market. However, its ability to increase the supply of public safe assets is limited by its 'fiscal capacity/space', which can be understood as the ability of a sovereign to borrow without causing (or increasing) investor concerns about its solvency (Rzońca, 2014, p. 362). The importance of fiscal space as a key determinant of the supply of public safe assets was highlighted by He et al. (2015). In their view, its importance is reinforced by the self-fulfilling expectations of investors operating in an environment of strategic complementarity.

The persistent near-zero interest rate environment undoubtedly increases fiscal space. On the one hand, it provides an incentive for fiscal authorities to increase debt, as debt can be rolled over without the need to increase taxes in the future. On the other hand, it sustains heightened uncertainty, including a shortage of confidence in banks, and lowers expected returns on assets other than government securities. This, in turn, shifts economic agents' demand towards government bonds with longer maturities as an asset to provide safety and income (Rzońca, 2014, pp. 361–383; Mitchener and Trebesch, 2021, pp. 6–8). However, the expansion of fiscal space translates into the credibility of the system (the Triffin paradox) and can generate a 'coordinated run on public debt' (Farhi and Maggiori, 2016).

A new version of the Triffin paradox, formulated in the 1960s and commonly referred to as the fiscal version of the paradox, posits that rising budget deficits can undermine investors' confidence in the sustainability of the public debt levels of the country issuing the reserve currency. In other words, the dilemma revolves around the challenge of meeting the global demand for international liquidity (or the global demand for safe assets) while maintaining the solvency of the issuer of such assets, thus ensuring their stable value. Achieving the first objective requires 'secular growth' in the ratio of US government debt to GDP. Meanwhile, for the second objective, which is to maintain the debt as a safe asset, this ratio must be stabilised (cf. Caballero and Krishnamurthy, 2009; Gourinchas and Jeanne, 2012; Caballero and Farhi, 2013). In the hegemonic IMS, the global safe asset provider may be tempted to overextend borrowing because the cost of the crisis (rise in inflation, rather than the risk of default) will be borne not by the hegemon but by the rest of the world (Farhi and Maggiori, 2018). This is an important argument in favour of a multi-currency system, which has many competing global safe asset providers.

An interesting interpretation of the transformation of Triffin's paradox is provided by McCauley (2019, p. 1). In its original form, the paradox revolved around the co-existence of two liquidity resources: the US external liabilities and gold, as implied by the IMS rules that guarantee the convertibility of the USD into gold. When the former exceeds the latter, it leads to a risk of instability in the system, primarily triggered by supply-side forces. In contrast, the Triffin II paradox (which McCauley (2019) explicitly calls the 'safe asset dilemma') focuses on the demand perspective reported on the stock of government liabilities. If their stock exceeds the GDP of the debt-issuing country, it will undermine that country's ability to service the debt. In this version of the paradox, therefore, the focus is on the fiscal risks of the asset-issuing government meeting rapidly growing global demand for these particular liabilities.

The Triffin II paradox, which focuses explicitly on the United States as a global safe asset provider, as well as the analysis proposed by Schuknecht, which broadens the scope to include more developed countries, both suggest that investors exhibit greater tolerance for debt in developed countries than developing ones. He et al. (2016a) also proposed that investors' self-fulfilling expectations can play a role in limiting the creation of public safe assets in the wake of a panic. This raises the question of whether developed countries, who aspire to be global safe asset providers, are immune to default risk and, if so, within what limits.

Mitchener and Trebesch (2021) highlighted the resurgence of the problem of developed countries' 'debt tolerance' and default risk. They pointed out that, since World War II, the debt crisis problem has only affected developing countries. There has been an absence of sovereign debt tensions for developed countries despite high levels of debt – government debt in excess of 100% of GDP was common after the end of World War II. This has led to the consensus that 'advanced countries do not default'. In fact, for more than half a century, there has not been a case of developed country insolvency (Cecchetti et al., 2010, p. 1). In the quest to understand why advanced countries were considered more resilient to the risk of a default crisis, especially in a negative shock situation, attention was drawn to the following (Mitchener and Trebesch, 2021, p. 5):

1 Their economies were more diversified (less dependence on raw material exports),
2 Their institutions were more developed, which also has implications for the ability to conduct crisis management policy (e.g. by the central bank),
3 There are more taxable resources,
4 The size of the state, which translates into the scale of the budget (state capacity),
5 There are traditionally higher levels of debt issuance in domestic currency and under domestic regulation.

At the same time, Mitchener and Trebesch (2021, pp. 5–6) also stated that the currently observed increase in the risk of insolvency of developed countries should, in fact, be seen as a return to trends that have already occurred. They cite, among others, the example of the 19th-century insolvencies of developed countries during the Napoleonic wars, when Austria, France, the Netherlands, Prussia and Sweden suspended foreign debt servicing, or the period after World War I, when public debt was widespread in Europe. The crucial event that triggered a return to treating developed countries as vulnerable to a debt crisis was the crisis that affected the peripheral EMU countries in

2009–2012. According to Mitchener and Trebesch (2021, p. 49), this crisis was paradoxically similar in some respects to the crisis that affected Mexico in 1994–1995. Both episodes, although they involved different groups of countries (developed and emerging ones), revealed the following common features:

1. Debt rollover and the dynamics of a self-fulfilling crisis,
2. Severe debt distress without default,
3. The large-scale 'rescue' credit support (bailouts) from abroad following a sudden stop in private capital inflow,
4. The maturity of treasury securities shortened in times of stress,
5. There was contagion to other government bond markets in the region.

Historical experience and theoretical concepts show that a key problem emerges regarding how to provide a global supply of safe assets while maintaining a balance between the international currency issuer's public debt accumulation and fiscal discipline. In other words, it is necessary to understand the factors that determine (and limit) safe government debt issued by a global reserve currency provider. The literature on the subject does not provide a clear-cut answer, merely pointing out some enabling factors, but without prioritising them.

The factors mentioned earlier in our discussion of the general conditions for creating safe assets, when combined with the determinants of public safe asset creation, can be divided into the following:

- Economic factors (including financial ones): the level of economic development, a stable macroeconomic situation (including low and stable levels of inflation), fiscal space, the use of the non-standard monetary policy instrument of quantitative easing and the extent to which quantitative easing policies are implemented (which can be viewed as a form of debt management – cf. Allen, 2013, p. 216), the size of the economy, and the size and depth of the financial market,
- Non-economic factors (including behavioural and qualitative ones): legal and institutional conditions, regulation of the enforcement of private contracts, political stability, the role of financial safety net institutions (including the role of the central bank in the lender of last resort function), the international appetite for market risk, the credibility and independence of the monetary authority, the extent to which the international currency function (in particular, the reserve function) is performed, and inertia in the IMS.

Notes

1 He distinguishes between the term international currency and 'leading international currency', with the latter indicating the hegemonic position of the country in the IMS, thus being able to create global safe assets.
2 Unlike most authors who address the issue of safe assets, Habib et al. (2020) recognised the potential for developing countries to create safe assets.
3 The forerunner of the state theory of money, from which chartalism emerged and is now often referred to as neo-chartalism, was Georg Friedrich Knapp at the beginning of the 20th century. According to the state theory, money is merely a means of payment, created by the state through formal law; the state also guarantees its monetary functions.
4 The structure might have changed as a result of COVID-19 crisis, c.f. Chapter 4.
5 The ECB's involvement in the OMT operations, which many perceived as a departure from its role as a lender of last resort to the banking system and an encroachment into the domain of being a lender of last resort to governments, may have contributed to undermining the credibility of the central bank.

References

Aizenman, J., Cheung, Y. - W., & Qian, X. (2019). The currency composition of international reserves, demand for international reserves, and global safe assets, *NBER Working Paper,* no 25934. National Bureau of Economic Research, Cambridge.

Allen, B. (2013). *International liquidity and the financial crisis.* Cambridge: Cambridge University Press.

Anand, K. (2016). Covered bonds-safe assets with side effects? *Research Brief*, Deutsche Bundesbank, September.

Azzimonti, M., & Yared, P. (2019). The optimal public and private provision of safe assets. *Journal of Monetary Economics*, *102*, 126–144. doi:10.1016/j.jmoneco.2019.01.012

Bertaut, C., Tabova, A., & Wong, V. (2015). The replacement of safe assets: Evidence from the U.S. bond portfolio. *FRB International Finance Discussion Paper*, no 1123.

Brunnermeier, M., Merkel, S., & Sannikov, Y. (2021). A safe asset perspective for an integrated policy framework. In S. Davis, E. Robinson, & B. Yeung (Eds.), *The Asian monetary policy forum: Insights for central banking*. Chapter 8, pp. 302–332. World Scientific Publishing Co. Pte. Ltd.

Bruno, V., & Shi, H. (2012). Capital flows, cross-border banking and global liquidity. *NBER Working Paper,* no 19038, National Bureau of Economic Research, Cambridge.

Caballero, R., & Krishnamurthy A. (2009). Global imbalances and financial fragility. *American Economic Review*, 99(2), 584–588.

Caballero, R., & Farhi, E. (2013). A model of safe asset mechanism (SAM): Safety traps and economic policy. *NBER Working Paper*, no 18737, National Bureau of Economic Research, Cambridge.

Caballero, R., Farhi, E., & Gourinchas, P.-O. (2015). Global imbalances and currency wars at the ZLB. *NBER Working Paper*, no 21670. National Bureau of Economic Research, Cambridge.

Carapella, F., & Williamson, S. (2015). Credit markets, limited commitment, and government debt. *The Review of Economic Studies*, *82*(3), 963–990. doi:10.1093/restud/rdv006

Cecchetti, S., Mohanty, M., & Zampolli, F. (2010). The future of public debt: Prospects and implications. *BIS Working Paper*, no 300.

Curcuru, S. E., Thomas, C. P., & Warnock, F. E. (2013). On returns differentials. *NBER Working Papers*, no 18866. National Bureau of Economic Research, Inc.

ECB. (2012). Technical features of outright monetary transactions. Available at: https://www.ecb.europa.eu/press/pr/date/2012/html/pr120906_1.en.html (Accessed: 12 October 2021).

ECB. (2019). *The international role of the euro*. Frankfurt am Main.

ECB. (2021) *The international role of the euro*. Frankfurt am Main.

ECB. (2023). *The international role of the euro*. Frankfurt am Main.

Eichengreen, B. (2011). *Exorbitant privilege: The rise and fall of the dollar and the future of the international monetary system*. Oxford University Press.

Eichengreen, B. (2019). *Globalizing capital: A history of international monetary system*, 3rd edition. Princeton: Princeton University Press.

Eichengreen, B., El-Ganainy, A., Esteves, R., & Mitchener, K. (2018). Public debt through the ages, Paper for the IMF Conference on Sovereign debt, 13–14, September.

Eichengreen, B., & Flandreau, M. (2009). The rise and fall of the dollar (or when did the dollar replace sterling as the leading reserve currency?). *European Review of Economic History*, *13*(3), 377–411. doi:10.1017/s1361491609990153

Epstein, S. (2000). Freedom and growth: The rise of states and markets in Europe, 1300-1750. London and New York: Routledge.

Farhi, E., & Maggiori, M. (2016). A model of the international monetary system. *NBER Working Paper*, no 22295, National Bureau of Economic Research, Cambridge.

Farhi, E., & Maggiori, M. (2018). A model of the international monetary system. *The Quarterly Journal of Economics*, *133*(1), 295–355. doi:10.1093/qje/qjx031

Flandreau, M., & Zendejas, J.-F. (2009). Bonds and brands: Foundations of sovereign debt markets, 1820–1830. *The Journal of Economic History*, *69*(3), 646–684. Available at: http://www.jstor.org/stable/40263939

Frankel, J. A. (2023). Dollar rivals. *SSRN Electronic Journal*. doi:10.2139/ssrn.4519229

Gelpern, A., & Gerding, E. (2016). *Inside safe assets*. Georgetown: Georgetown University Law Center. Available at: https://scholarship.law.georgetown.edu/cgi/viewcontent.cgi?article=2845&context=facpub (Accessed: 12 October 2021).

Goldberg, L., & Tille, C. (2009). *Micro, macro, and strategic forces in international trade invoicing*. doi:10.3386/w15470

Golec, P., & Perotti, E. (2017). Safe assets: A review. *Working Paper Series*, no 2035. European Central Bank.

Gopinath, G., & Stein, J. (2018). *Banking, trade, and the making of a dominant currency*. doi:10.3386/w24485

Gorton, G., Lewellen, S., & Metrick, A. (2012). The safe-asset share. *American Economic Review*, *102*(3), 101–106. doi:10.1257/aer.102.3.101

Gorton, G. B. (2016). The history and economics of safe assets. *NBER Working Paper*, no 22210, National Bureau of Economic Research, Cambridge.

Gourinchas, P., & Rey, H. (2007). International financial adjustment. *Journal of Political Economy*, *115*(4), 665–703. doi:10.1086/521966

Gourinchas, P.-O. (2017). The fundamental structure of the international monetary system. In M. D. Bordo & J. B. Taylor (Eds.), *Rules for international*

monetary stability. Past, present, and future. Stanford, CA: Hoover Institution Press, pp. 169–203.
Gourinchas, P.-O., & Rey, H. (2016). *Real interest rates, imbalances and the curse of regional safe asset providers at the zero lower bound.* doi:10.3386/w22618
Gourinchas, P.-O., Rey, H., & Govillot, N. (2010). Exorbitant privilege and exorbitant duty. *IMES Discussion Paper Series 10-E-20.* Institute for Monetary and Economic Studies, Bank of Japan.
Gourinchas, P.-O., & Jeanne O. (2012). Global safe assets. *BIS Working Papers*, no 399.
Gourinchas, P.-O., Rey, H., & Sauzet, M. (2019). The international monetary and financial system. *NBER Working Paper*, no 25782. National Bureau of Economic Research, Cambridge.
Gruszecki, T. (2015). Problemy z rozumieniem współczesnego pieniądza, Acta Universitatis Lodziensis. *Folia Oeconomica.* DOI:10.18778/0208-6018.317.05
Habib, M. M., Stracca, L., & Venditti, F. (2020). The fundamentals of safe assets. *SSRN Electronic Journal.* doi:10.2139/ssrn.3515302
He, Z., Krishnamurthy, A., & Milbradt, K. (2015). A model of reserve asset. *Working Paper,* no 3279, Stanford Business.
He, Z., Krishnamurthy, A., & Milbradt, K. (2016a). A model of safe asset determination. *NBER Working Paper,* no 22271, National Bureau of Economic Research. doi:10.3386/w22271
He, Z., Krishnamurthy A., & Milbradt K. (2016b). What makes us government bonds safe assets? *American Economic Review*, 106, 519–523.
He, Z., & Song, Z. (2022). Agency MBS as safe assets. *NBER Working Paper*, no 29899. National Bureau of Economic Research, Cambridge.
Holmström, B., & Tirole, J. (2011). *Inside and outside liquidity.* Cambridge; Londres: The MIT Press.
Ilzetzki, E., Reinhart, C., & Rogoff, K. (2020). Why is the euro punching below its weight? *Economic Policy*, *35*(103). doi:10.1093/epolic/eiaa018
Ilzetzki, E., Reinhart, C., & Rogoff, K. (2022). Rethinking exchange rate regimes. In G. Gopinath, E. Helpma, & K. Rogoff (Eds.), *Handbook of international economics*, Volume 6. Elsevier, pp. 91–145. doi:10.1016/bs.hesint.2022.02.010
IMF. (2012). Safe assets: Financial system cornerstone? In *Global Financial Stability Report*, Washington, DC.
Kacperczyk, M., & Schnabl, P. (2013). How safe are money market funds? *The Quarterly Journal of Economics*, *128*(3), 1073–1122. https://www.jstor.org/stable/26372519
Kacperczyk, M., & Maggio, M. (2017). The unintended consequences of the zero lower bound policy. *Journal of Financial Economics*, *123*(1). doi:10.1016/j.jfineco.2016.09.006
Kacperczyk, M., Perignon, C., & Vuillemey, G. (2021). The private production of safe assets. *The Journal of Finance*, *LXXVI*(2), April.
Keynes, J. (1923). *A tract on monetary reform.* London: Macmillan.
Kindleberger, C. (1967). The politics of international money and world language. *Essays in International Finance*, no. 61, August, Princeton University.
Krishnamurthy, A., & Vissing-Jørgensen, A. (2012). Short term debt and financial crisis: What we can learn from U.S. treasury supply? *Working Paper.* Northwestern University.
Krishnamurthy, A., & Vissing-Jørgensen, A. (2015). The impact of treasury supply on financial sector lending and stability. *Journal of Financial Economics*, *118*(3), 571–600. doi:10.1016/j.jfineco.2015.08.012

Luitel, P., Vanpée, R., & De Moor, L. (2016). Pernicious effects: How the credit rating agencies disadvantage emerging markets. *Research in International Business and Finance*, *38*, 286–298. doi:10.1016/j.ribaf.2016.04.009

McCauley, R. (2019). Safe assets: Made, not just born. *BIS Working Papers*, no 769.

Miranda-Agrippino, S., & Rey, H. (2020). U.S. monetary policy and the global financial cycle. *The Review of Economic Studies*, *87*(6), 2754–2776. doi:10.1093/restud/rdaa019

Mitchener, K. J., & Trebesch, C. (2021). Sovereign debt in the 21st century: Looking backward, looking forward. *SSRN Electronic Journal*. doi:10.2139/ssrn.3812076

Navaretti, G., Calzolari, G., & Pozzolo, A. (2016). Diabolic loop or incomplete union? Sovereign and banking risk. *European economy. Banks, regulation, and the real sector*, No. 1. Available at: https://european-economy.eu/20161/diabolic-loop-or-incomplete-union-sovereign-and-ban-king-risk/ (Accessed: 12 October 2021).

Neal, L. (1990). *The rise of financial capitalism: International capital markets in the age of reason*. New York: Cambridge University.

Nurkse, R. (1944). *International currency experience: Lessons of the interwar period*. League of Nations.

Ogawa, E., & Muto, M. (2019). What determines utility of international currencies? *Journal of Risk and Financial Management*, *12*(1), 10. doi:10.3390/jrfm12010010

Ongena, S., Popov, A., & Van Horen, N. (2019). The invisible hand of the government: Moral suasion during the European sovereign debt crisis. *American Economic Journal: Macroeconomics*, *11*(4), 346–379. doi:10.1257/mac.20160377

Rogoff, K. S., & Tashiro, T. (2015). Japan's exorbitant privilege. *Journal of the Japanese and International Economies*, *35*, 43–61. doi:10.1016/j.jjie.2014.11.003

Rzońca, A. (2014). Kryzys banków centralnych. Skutki stopy procentowej bliskiej zera, Wydawnictwo C.H. Beck, Warszawa.

Schmelzing, P. (2020). Eight centuries of global real interest rates, R-G, and the 'suprasecular' decline, 1311-2018. *Staff Working Paper*, no 845. Bank of England, January.

Schuknecht, L. (2018). The supply of safe assets and fiscal policy. *Intereconomics*, *53*(2), 94–100. doi:10.1007/s10272-018-0728-5

Scope Ratings. (2021). European Supranational Outlook 2021. Are we moving towards a green safe asset? Available at: http://scoperatings.com/ScopeRatingsApi/downloadstudy?id=790d7a63-ed98-4c73-a928-27e98a24230b

Sunderam, A. (2015). Money creation and the shadow banking system. *Review of Financial Studies*, *28*(4), 939–977.

Triffin, R. (1961). *Gold and the dollar crisis: The future of convertibility*. New Haven, CT: Yale University Press.

van Riet, A. (2017). Addressing the safety trilemma: A safe sovereign asset for the eurozone. *SSRN Electronic Journal*. doi:10.2139/ssrn.3723381

Xie, L. (2012). The seasons of money: ABS/MBS issuance and convenience yield. *Unpublished Working Paper*. Yale University, New Haven.

Xiong, Q. (2018). The liquidity premium of safe assets: The role of government debt supply. *IWH Discussion Papers*, no 11/2017. Halle Institute for Economic Research (IWH).

3 The Demand for Safe Assets

3.1 Demand for Safety

In the literature, the demand for safe assets is based on the money-in-the-utility function. As a result, the convenience premium and the supply of safe assets depend on the demand for them.

Golec and Perotti (2017) distinguished the demand for safety from the traditional demand for liquidity and demand for money. Demand for safety, unlike the demand for liquidity, is not oriented towards access to money as a means of payment. It is more oriented towards preserving asset value. However, as Kacperczyk and Maggio (2017, p. 6) pointed out, it is very difficult to empirically distinguish between the two key components of security demand, namely moneyness (which determines the demand for close money substitutes) and information insensitivity (which determines the ability to preserve wealth).

Demand for safety plays a fundamental role in shaping contract terms[1] and the structure of financial intermediation, with implications for price levels and market segmentation. The demand for safety shapes the behaviour of financial intermediaries, who purchase debt instruments issued by the private sector in good times and debt issued by the public sector (which is the only one that retains the characteristics of safe assets) in times of crisis (Golec and Perotti, 2017, p. 3). An analysis of the determinants of the demand for safety, including components such as information insensitivity, for example, may have important implications for broader empirical research on credit cycles, which need to be differentiated from traditional business cycles. Additionally, the demand for safety may explain phenomena such as the degree of maturity mismatch between assets and liabilities or the level of aggregate risk (Golec and Perotti, 2017, p. 24).

To ascertain the optimal assets that fulfil the safe-asset functions presented in Table 1.1, the relationships between the safe-asset functions performed by different categories of instruments should be juxtaposed with the demand creation motives of different investor groups.

Detailing the motives and their importance for specific economic agents already varies at the country level. In addition, these motives and the role of specific agents have changed as a consequence of the GFC. For example,

DOI: 10.4324/9781003376538-4

as a result of monetary stabilisation in the wake of the GFC, the role of the US Federal Reserve System as a holder of government debt has increased. In the United Kingdom, where institutional investors were traditionally the key holders of government debt, the central bank and foreign investors began to play a more important role (IMF, 2012, p. 90).

When economic entities experience differential access to safe assets, safety-seeking flows begin. This is especially evident for investors from emerging markets who exhibit a heightened demand for such assets due to scarcity in domestic markets. This scarcity is primarily attributed to a less-developed regulatory framework, which hampers the enforcement of property rights. An underdeveloped market that cannot protect investors and depresses the value of local investments and asset prices.

Golec and Perotti (2017, p. 15) also distinguished between individual and institutional demand for safety. An example of institutional demand is central banks' accumulation of foreign exchange reserves, mainly in emerging market countries. Such demand leads to a reduction in the supply of debt instruments issued by the public sector to private investors. As a consequence, individual demand for security is crowded out and becomes channelled into (quasi-) safe private assets.

3.1.1 Commercial Banks' Demand for Safe Assets

Commercial banks are among the largest safe asset holders. According to the IMF estimates, at the end of 2010, they held 34% of outstanding sovereign debt (IMF, 2012, p. 89). Much recent study show that they hold on average 28% of the sovereign debt (Fang et al., 2023). The role of commercial banks in safe asset holdings is particularly pronounced in Japan, followed by the United States, China and France. Banks in these countries jointly account for about 55% of the government debt held by banks globally. The scale of government bond holdings in the portfolios of each country's banks varies. In general – with the exception of Japan – government debt plays a more important role in the portfolios of emerging markets banks than in developed countries. In some, the share of government debt securities in banking sector assets is significant – up to 30% in Turkey and over 20% in Brazil, Mexico and Japan (IMF, 2012, p. 91; Bouis Romain, 2019).

Figures 3.1 and 3.2 show the holdings of debt securities issued by euro-area general governments as a percentage of the total assets of monetary financial institutions (MFIs), excluding the Eurosystem, for the chosen 'core' countries and the GIIPS EMU countries,[2] respectively. The analysed shares may differ not only between large aggregates (e.g. emerging vs developed economies) but also within closely integrated economies, like those that constitute the single European currency area.

Purchases of government debt securities show a cyclical pattern that runs counter to that of short-term market interest rates. It usually implies a rebalancing of MFIs' total assets, with shifts from private to public sector

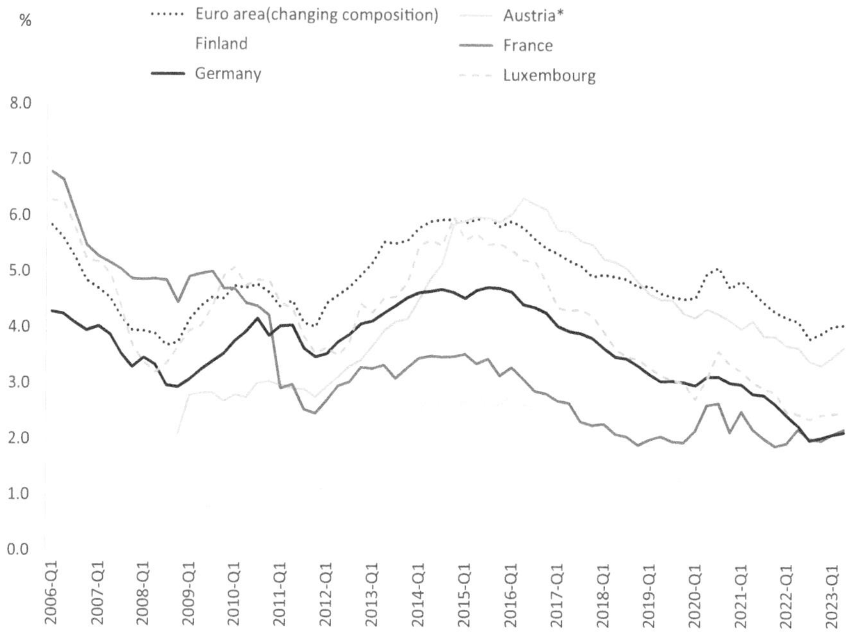

Figure 3.1 MFIs' holdings of debt securities issued by euro-area general governments – core countries

Source: Authors' own compilation based on ECB data. * Data for Austria starts in Q4 2008.

credit (ECB, 2009). However, the MFI's holdings of debt securities issued by euro-area general governments are different in core European countries compared to GIIPS countries. In the former, they are much lower than in the latter. The decline in the portfolio of cross-border banking may also reflect the reduced financial globalisation and financial integration after the GFC. In fact, gross foreign assets relative to GDP rose sharply from 1990 to 2007, when the phase of modern financial de-globalisation has started. In case of monetary union, it took the form of financial fragmentation, as banks have become less active internationally. A return to home bias can be detected – a fall in international bank lending relative to domestic lending in advanced countries compared to the pre-crisis boom in international bank lending.

The banking sector's demand for these assets is driven by the following:

1 The need to manage maturity mismatches between assets and liabilities,
2 They act as primary dealers and market makers,
3 They are used as collateral in repo and derivative transactions,
4 It is possible to obtain preferential regulatory treatment (capital and liquidity requirements) due to holding Treasury debt instruments.

Maintaining safe assets is mainly related to liquidity management and insolvency risk. These assets, especially short-term treasury securities, play a

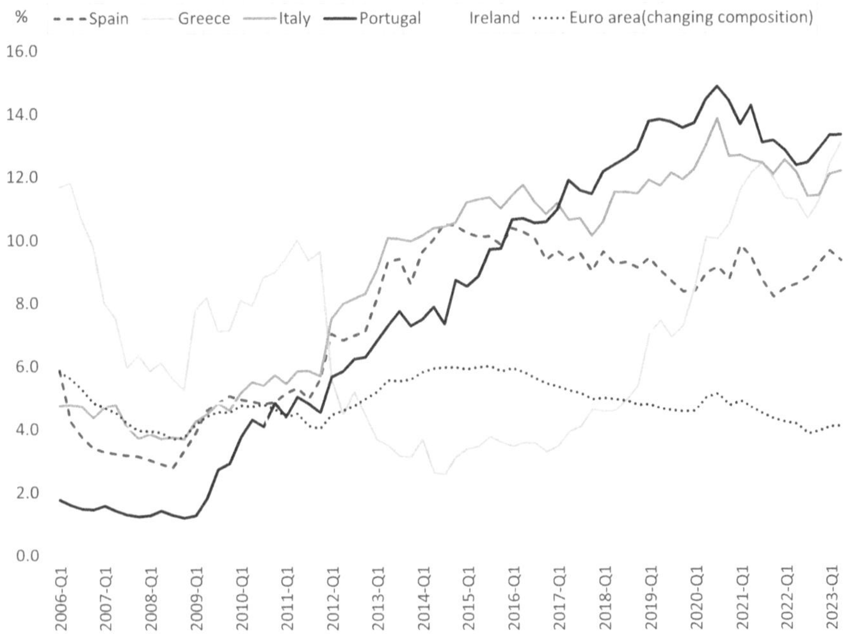

Figure 3.2 MFIs' holdings of debt securities issued by euro-area general governments – GIIPS countries

Source: Authors' own compilation based on ECB data.

key role in liquidity management. Highly liquid and stable income assets are essential due to the term mismatches that characterise banks' balance sheets. During periods of stress, banks can temporarily increase the level of safe assets they hold in order to do the following (IMF, 2012, p. 91):

1 Raise capital ratios via exchange for riskier assets,
2 Gain access to secured funding markets,
3 Counterbalance trading book losses to stabilise income.

The degree of technical and infrastructural links between banks and the government also influences the holding of government debt securities. In countries where banks play the role of dealers and market makers for the government bond market and support secondary market liquidity, actively participating in transactions in financial instruments, these securities play a more important role in banking sector assets (e.g. in the EU, Canada, Japan and the United States). Empirical research shows that holdings by banks are relatively insensitive to yields (Fang et al., 2023).

Banks are also a key player (alongside entities such as hedge funds) in the demand for safe assets for use as collateral in transactions. In the United States and Europe, in particular, government debt instruments dominate as collateral in private repo markets. Over the past decade, the share of

US Treasury and agency debt securities used as collateral in tri-party repo transactions has remained high, hovering around 80%. The category is dominated by US Treasury securities, whose share increased from around 35% in 2011 to around 70% in 2021. By contrast, the share of MBS assets issued by government agencies declined from around 30% to around 20%. In Europe, government debt accounted for 79% of EU-originated collateral for repo transactions. Tri-party repo transactions, which account for only about 11% of total repo transactions in Europe, are based on a greater diversification of collateral, comprising government securities (45%). Other collateral includes corporate bonds, covered bonds and equities (IMF, 2012, p. 95).

Safe assets are also used as key collateral in central bank transactions. The privileged role of government debt instruments in secured transactions with the central bank is related to the historically lower volatility and greater liquidity of these instruments, especially during periods of stress. However, in periods of volatility, as evidenced by the GFC, the central bank may expand its list of assets that are eligible for use as collateral. The relaxation of collateral standards in October 2008 by the ECB, when it lowered the credit threshold for marketable and non-marketable assets from A- to BBB- (with the exception of ABS), may be a case in point (ECB, 2008).

Zero-risk weighting when calculating the capital adequacy ratio has become the regulatory factor that creates a high demand for safe assets from banks. The widespread use of zero risk weighting for sovereign debt, irrespective of the country of issuance and associated risk factors (for banks operating in the euro area, zero risk weighting applied to sovereign debt issued by each Member State) creates a perception of safety detached from underlying economic risks (IMF, 2012, p. 82; cf. also European Parliament Briefings, 2019). Moreover, the accumulation of these assets not only requires additional capital from them but also protects them against liquidity loss, as they are easily tradable and can act as collateral for central bank facilities. Sovereign asset purchases allow banks to alleviate problems of low-quality credit portfolios, insufficient capital and high demand for liquidity (Rzońca, 2014, pp. 370–371). However, the application of a zero-risk weighting on sovereigns' debt leads to harmful effects on bank resilience and intermediation. It encourages more leverage on safe assets and leads to potential overinvestment in the market for higher-risk treasury assets with favourable risk-return characteristics, creating the possibility of undercapitalisation of banks in periods of instability (IMF, 2012, p. 113).

The near-zero interest rate environment is a factor that has significantly increased the scale of banks' purchases of safe assets. Historical experience shows that the share of treasury securities in banks' assets can reach very high levels at low interest rates; for example, in the 1950s, it reached 60%–70% in highly developed countries (Taylor, 2012). However, the cost of increasing the share of sovereign securities in banks' assets is its rising dependence on fiscal authorities. This may encourage the authorities to put direct pressure on the banks to support over-indebted entities (Rzońca, 2014, p. 371).

As predicted by the IMF, banks' high demand for government debt is expected to continue. Prior to the GFC, bank regulation did not have explicit quantitative liquidity requirements on banks. The introduction of new regulations in 2010 (mainly liquidity coverage ratio (LCR) within the Basel III post-crisis reforms) should force banks to hold even more safe assets. The LCR is designed to ensure that banks hold a sufficient reserve of high-quality liquid assets (HQLA) to allow them to survive a period of significant liquidity stress lasting 30 calendar days.

HQLAs are comprised of Level 1 and Level 2 assets. Level 1 assets generally include cash, central bank reserves, and certain marketable securities backed by sovereigns and central banks. These assets are typically of the highest quality and are the most liquid, and there is no limit on the extent to which a bank can hold these assets to meet the LCR. Level 2 assets include certain government securities, covered bonds, corporate debt securities, as well as lower-rated corporate bonds, residential mortgage-backed securities and equities that meet relevant criteria. There are specific thresholds that dictate the proportion of Level 2 assets in a bank's total stock of HQLA.

LCR requirements may, therefore, provide an additional channel for global demand for safe assets, mainly for government debt. Additionally, an increase in the risk weights of riskier treasuries may increase demand for the 'safest' sovereign assets (IMF, 2012, p. 99).

3.1.2 Motives Behind Holding Safe Assets

For central banks, safe assets are an indispensable instrument for implementing monetary policy, including currency interventions and Quantitative Easing (QE).

As part of conventional monetary policy, central banks commonly use safe assets. Based on these assets, they conduct collateralised open market operations (in the form of repos) and outright purchases. They also provide collateralised credit within the framework of a credit window/facility. Central banks generally do not engage in unsecured transactions, thereby protecting themselves (and taxpayers in the event of a need to recapitalise the central bank) from financial losses related to counterparty insolvency (counterparty risk). Therefore, eligible collateral for transactions with the central bank in open market operations and the credit window must be limited to high-quality assets. Domestic treasury securities and, to a lesser extent, central bank bills most often fulfil this function. The types and extent of collateral assets used vary considerably across central banks due to country-specific characteristics, such as banking and financial market structures, the number and diversity of counterparties and statutory requirements (IMF, 2012, p. 110).

Unconventional monetary policy is a broad concept with different tools letting central banks achieve various goals. These tools embrace forward guidance, asset purchases, term funding facilities, adjustments to market operations and negative interest rates.[3] Today, there is a tendency to use the terms Quantitative Easing and Credit Easing (CE) interchangeably for the policy of central banks' purchases of certain assets to stimulate growth; however, one should bear in mind the differentiating aspects. CE focuses on the quality of central bank assets held (therefore, qualitative easing is a synonym), while QE looks at the quantity. The main difference between the two, according to van den End (2019), lies in the effect of the programme on tradable safe asset supply. In the case of a CE programme, there is no reduction in the supply of tradable safe assets.

Unconventional monetary policy, of which Qualitative Easing can be assumed as one of the forms, is implemented to achieve various objectives. In crisis conditions, easing has taken the form of exchanging riskier assets (e.g. those that have lost their safe status) for safe assets of the central bank (central bank money or term deposits offered by the central bank) (IMF, 2012, pp. 110–112). In this context, in a crisis management environment, qualitative easing policies, by providing liquidity in exchange for less liquid collateral, contributed to a temporary reduction in tensions arising from the shortage of safe assets (IMF, 2012, p. 116). From the central bank's point of view, however, it marked its transformation from a lender-of-last-resort function to a 'buyer of last resort', generating effects on government bond yields and government market access (cf. Mitchener and Trebesch, 2021, p. 41, among others). Thus, one can say the primary goal of CE is to stabilise lending markets by having the central bank act as a buyer of last resort for certain debt securities. A good example of a CE instrument was the Securities Markets Programme (SMP) conducted by the ECB between 2010 and 2012. The SMP targeted stressed market segments – sovereign debt markets of peripheral countries.

The Bank of Japan (BoJ) is considered to be the pioneer of the policy of actively buying government debt. It began its QE policy in 2001 and abandoned it in 2006.[4] The rise in popularity of QE came under the management of the GFC, with the wide programmes adopted particularly by the Federal Reserve System, the ECB and the Bank of England. Although Japan was not hit as severely by the crisis as the United States and some of the European countries, it launched a new programme of asset purchases, known as comprehensive monetary easing (CME).[5] The scale of the purchase of Treasury debt securities under QE during the GFC is illustrated by the fact that between 2008 and 2014, the central bank balance sheet in the United States more than quadrupled. In the euro area, the increase was weaker but still significant (cf. Rzońca, 2014, p. 254). Bertaut et al. (2015) empirically showed that during the GFC, the Federal Reserve's extensive asset purchase programmes absorbed more than half of the increase in US government safe debt.

The next wave of government bond purchases by central banks was announced in March 2020 as a consequence of the global pandemic crisis, further increasing their holdings.[6] However, what differentiated the central banks in their involvement in QE policy was the spare capacity to buy additional government bonds. The amount of government bonds purchased by the BoJ prior to COVID-19 was close to 90% of the country's GDP. This made the BoJ switch the focus of its easing from quantitative to qualitative by buying riskier assets and losing its collateral policies (Kowalewski and Shirai, 2023, p. 359).

As Mitchener and Trebesch (2021) pointed out, the large-scale sovereign bond purchase programs of the past 15 years have turned central banks into the single most important sovereign creditor. For example, the share of government debt held by central banks has increased since 2015 as a result of the Eurosystem purchases under the Public Sector Purchase Programme (PSPP) and the Pandemic Emergency Purchase Program (PEPP). It stood at 20.8% at the euro area level at the end of 2020. Analysing the indirect effects of government bond purchases in a PSPP programme, which was in operation from 2015 to 2018, van den End (2019) identified a safe asset channel. Through this channel, excess liquidity created by the QE programme influences the relative demand and supply of safe assets, as well as sovereign bond spreads. The PSPP was aimed at the euro area as a whole, with government bond purchases in proportion to the capital key of EMU countries. By purchasing AAA government bonds, the programme reduced the supply of tradable safe assets, which stimulated demand for tradable safe assets, most likely by non-banks. They do not have access to central bank reserves and buy risk-free government bonds as an alternative. This additional safe asset demand goes with risk-shedding and a widening of risk spreads in the sovereign bonds market, as the yield on safe bonds falls relative to the yield on risky bonds. The empirical analysis indicates that the safe asset channel dominates the usual portfolio rebalancing channel (van den End, 2019).

An assessment of the consequences of central banks' involvement in purchases of long-term treasuries reveals that they may limit the room for further policy manoeuvres, including reducing flexibility. In addition, such action may lead to a loss of asset safety in real terms and to higher exchange rate risk. The large scale of asset purchases may also have a negative impact on creating policy incentives to improve fiscal discipline, as central bank support keeps interest rates and, thus, financing costs low (IMF, 2012, p. 102). What is more, such vast net purchases of public debt issuance may raise questions about the impact of prospective quantitative tightening policy on spreads and debt sustainability. Arslanalp and Eichengreen (2023, p. 5) gave the example of the Italian central bank as one that has engaged in net purchases of general government debt since 2014. It owns more than 600 billion euros of debt (compared to domestic banks, with less than 50 billion euros).

Another area of central bank safe asset usage is the foreign exchange reserve policy. The increase in demand for government debt securities of countries that issue reserve currencies in central bank reserve portfolios is largely the result of the intentional accumulation of foreign exchange reserves since the mid-1990s. This strategy is often pursued by Asian emerging market countries, as well as Japan. An important group of countries implementing such a strategy of exports of capital through the official sector are oil producers (in both emerging and developed countries, with Norway, Russia and countries in the Middle East in the lead).

Considering the variety of motives for accumulating foreign exchange reserves, as well as the different methods of classifying them, a dichotomous division can be made into:

1 intervention motives, often equated with mercantilism,
2 precautionary (insurance) motives, identified with the countercyclical motive.

The precautionary motive of reserve accumulation is a result of the increased openness of trade and the domestic financial system and the gradual liberalisation of capital flows in emerging market countries. As a result of liberalisation policies, the exposure of these countries to fluctuations in capital flows (especially outflows, but also withholding in inflows) has increased, thereby generating strong pro-cyclical shocks to economies. In addition, the procyclicality of commodity price developments is a factor that increases countries' exposure to balance of payments shocks. The absence of adequate regional and multilateral instruments to safeguard against payment and liquidity crises, coupled with the weakness of IMF liquidity support policies, means that countries must seek alternative measures to reduce their dependence on volatile capital flows. This led them to pursue unilateral actions, such as building up liquidity buffers provided by foreign exchange reserves. The ECB extends the motive for precautionary reserve accumulation beyond absorbing external shocks to the following situations: providing foreign exchange liquidity to banks in situations of higher volatility in the interbank market, avoiding volatility in foreign exchange markets, and covering monetary liabilities in case of countries with no-floating exchange rate regimes (ECB, 2019).

A key feature of the intervention (non-precautionary) motive is the central role of the exchange rate as an instrument of economic policy. In the mercantilist motive, the primary objective of economic policy is to stimulate exports by exploiting the undervalued exchange rate. The accumulation of foreign exchange reserves is, therefore, a by-product of the development strategy pursued, which is why McCauley (2019, p. 2) describes it as a 'by-product motive'.

The difficulty in identifying the motives for reserve accumulation is illustrated by the tripartite classification proposed by Arslan and Cantu (2019). They pointed out that, in addition to the precautionary and mercantilist motives, a third motive should be distinguished, precisely as a result of other economic objectives pursued (e.g. managing inflation and smoothing fluctuations in the business cycle).

Although it is difficult to make a clear distinction between the strength of the two key motives empirically, the prevailing conclusion in analyses of the primacy of a given motive in emerging market countries is that while the mercantilist motive became the dominant one in China, the precautionary motive played a major role in other Asian emerging economies. For example, based on reserve accumulation policies in 49 countries between 1980 and 2000, Aizenman and Lee (2006) showed that both motives were important, but the precautionary one played a greater role. Additionally, a study by Dąbrowski (2009) showed that monetary authorities in Asia are guided by the precautionary motive, not by aiming for a pre-declared level of reserves. Their focus is on not allowing a significant reduction in the undervaluation of the domestic currency. The most obvious interpretation of the motives for reserve accumulation is in Japan. By accumulating foreign exchange reserves, Japan pursued a strategy to fight deflation and weak economic growth through stimulating exports, with currency interventions aimed at preventing the yen from appreciating.

In China and Japan, demographics influence reserve-holding behaviour. These countries will probably run current account deficits as their population age, and building up foreign assets now can be seen as part of a strategy of smoothing consumption over time (Allen, 2013, p. 200).

Fahri et al. (2011) introduced the term 'great convergence', which refers to the declining share of developed countries in favour of developing ones in the creation of global GDP. This is mainly due to the rapid economic development of China and the former Soviet bloc countries, as well as countries such as Brazil and India. In addition, the global trend of an increase in the price of commodities supports the development of countries that export them. The hypothesis of great convergence can help explain the dynamic increase in the demand of emerging market countries, mainly their monetary authorities for safe assets. Fahri et al. noted that for this group of countries:

1 Economic development is outpacing financial development; boosting economic growth leads to increased private demand for stable financial assets,
2 Economic growth leads to an increase in the public sector's demand for safe assets; a factor that reinforces demand is the poor development of these countries' financial markets, offering too few risk-free assets (Fahri et al., 2011, pp. 15–16).

In emerging markets, foreign exchange reserves are an important factor in assessing their creditworthiness. A higher level should translate into lower country risk; thus, it can reduce the costs of funding in the international financial markets. Empirical studies point to the important role of reserves in enhancing a country's creditworthiness, particularly in developing economies. For example, such a relationship was identified by Bissoondoyal-Bheenick (2005), Afonso et al. (2011) and Erdem and Varli (2014) in works on the determinants of credit ratings.

It is also important to highlight the increasing role of central banks in international and regional liquidity arrangements, which allow foreign exchange liquidity to be granted to foreign central banks. These arrangements increasingly take the form of swap lines (bilateral or multilateral), which are an important component of the so-called Global Financial Safety Net

(GFSN). As the collateral for foreign exchange liquidity distributed to the foreign central bank (and often through it to the foreign banking system), treasury securities, most often issued by reserve currency countries, are commonly used. For example, during the GFC, the Swiss National Bank activated swap lines for Poland and Hungary to meet the demand for Swiss francs in their banking systems, setting up euro-denominated treasury securities as collateral. The involvement of central banks in this form of official emergency lending provides another motive for them to become important participants in the sovereign debt market (Bogołębska, 2020, pp. 102–108).

3.2 Central Banks' Demand for Safe Assets

3.2.1 Foreign Exchange Reserves in the Portfolios of Central Banks

A characteristic of a multi-currency IMS and an international financial system based on liberalised capital flows is the growth in foreign exchange reserves held by central banks. The scale of this phenomenon is illustrated by the fact that at the end of 2018, total foreign currency reserves held globally had increased to over USD 11 trillion, a tenfold increase compared with 30 years previously. Additionally, about two-thirds of the global stock of foreign currency reserves is held by emerging markets and developing countries (ECB, 2019).

After the break-up of the Bretton Woods international monetary system, developed countries clearly used the reserve accumulation policy far more than developing countries. This trend was still evident at the turn of the 20th and 21st centuries. Only the first years of the new millennium were characterised by a change in the trend. Since then, there has been a marked increase in the share of reserves from emerging market countries in the global foreign exchange reserves (cf. Figure 3.3). The accumulation of foreign exchange reserves is becoming identified with emerging market countries, considered one of the key determinants of global imbalances.

Despite the co-existence of different motives for the accumulation of reserves in emerging market countries, a common feature of these economies, which determines the demand, is openness (financial and trade), often accompanied by the application of a stabilised exchange rate regime. For developed countries (including reserve currency issuers), the importance of foreign exchange reserves is much weaker. For most of these countries, the exchange rate is not a monetary policy objective; it is an endogenous variable that affects the main target variable(s) of monetary policy, such as inflation expectations (ECB, 2019).

Interestingly, the rate of growth in foreign exchange reserves did not weaken with the GFC (despite a slight decline in 2008). This is explained by the concern of emerging market countries that a potential decline in reserve levels does not send a negative signal about their external sector and thus triggers pressure on the exchange rate. Aizenman and Sun (2009) attributed

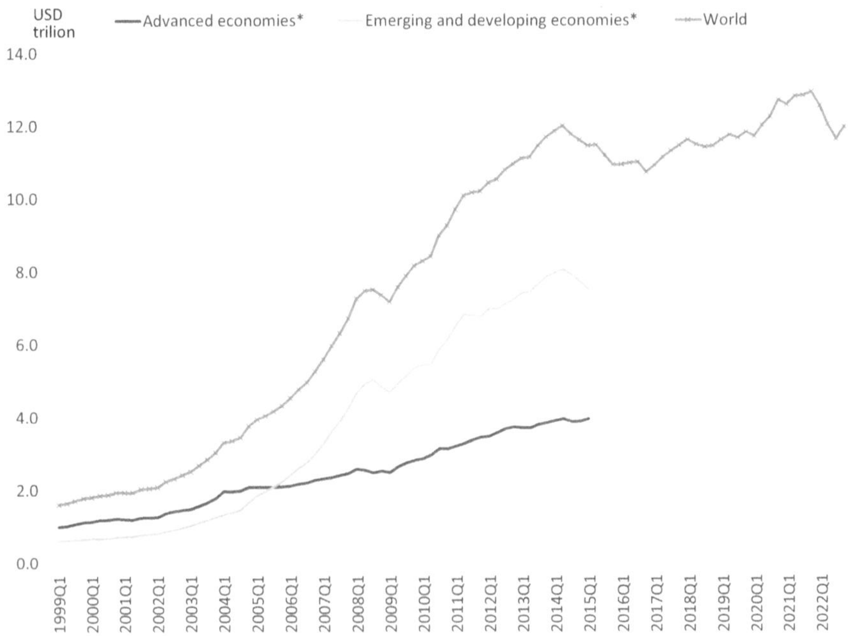

Figure 3.3 Global holdings of foreign exchange reserves.

Source: IMF COFER (access: 10 June 2023).

* Breakdown by advanced, emerging and developing economies available up to Q1 2015.

these countries' limited use of foreign exchange reserves in crisis management to the 'fear of losing reserves', which points to the importance of the psychological factor as a driver of accumulation.

In the post-GFC years, there was a period of a decline in foreign exchange reserves. This was largely attributed to a fall in payment surpluses due to the economic downturn and widely implemented fiscal expansion (a factor that was largely responsible for the decline in reserves in China) and a fall in commodity prices (a factor that was responsible for the decline in reserves in oil-exporting countries). However, after this period, there was a resurgence in global holdings. At the same time, the pace of accumulation was slower than at the beginning of the 21st century, with a noticeable exception that coincided with the COVID-19-induced shock.

Figure 3.4 shows that two countries clearly dominated the reserve accumulation policy: China and Japan. Among the countries taking the next places (also extended to the top 15 holders), a significant representation from Asia is noteworthy. This interesting phenomenon of a regional/neighbourly accumulation policy (or even a 'race' for supremacy in the level of foreign assets held) is explained by a behavioural motive. 'Keeping up with the Joneses' states that a country may fear that having less reserves than its neighbours may result in a worse assessment of its creditworthiness, translating into directing capital

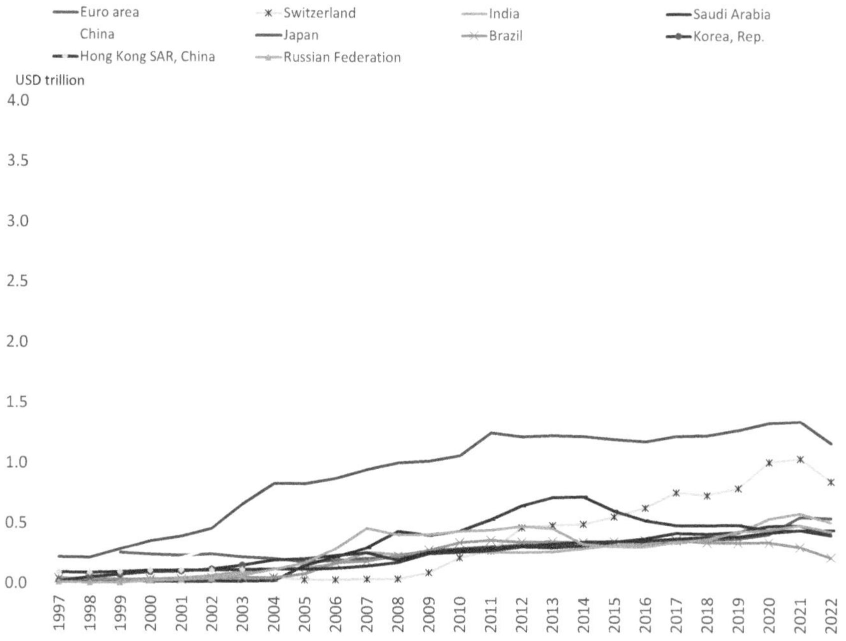

Figure 3.4 Top holders of foreign exchange reserves

Source: World Bank (access: 7 November 2023).

Note: Data for the euro area starts in 1999.

inflows (especially long-term, in the form of foreign direct investment) to countries with a higher rating. Thus, countries compete in accumulation policy. This competing may, in extreme/crisis situations, discourage countries from drawing on their reserves when the need arises (fear of losing reserves). Finally, Brazil, Russia and Saudi Arabia, commodity-exporting countries, are among the leaders in the accumulation of foreign exchange reserves. In these countries, more dynamic accumulation started after 2005, as surging commodity prices contributed to their large balance of payment surpluses. Switzerland is also among the top ten holders, as it was forced to adopt a strategy to counter the appreciation of CHF after the GFC due to its status as a safe-haven currency.

Despite a deceleration observed in the post-GFC period, central bank demand for foreign exchange reserves is expected to continue in the near future. However, in countries where reserve accumulation has exceeded the measures of adequacy[7] and fulfilled the requirements that arise from balance of payments and monetary policy, there is a gradual diversification of the composition of their reserve portfolio. This diversification involves a shift from government debt securities towards higher-yielding instruments. This shift is reflected in actions such as transferring a portion of the stock of foreign assets to special entities or institutions that are categorised as institutional public investors, such as sovereign wealth funds (SWFs).

In addition, factors that favour a gradual easing of the reserve accumulation policy include the following:

1 The presence of an opportunity cost that is associated with the low yield of foreign assets compared to domestic ones; another dimension of the opportunity cost is associated with a shift of resources abroad, thereby forfeiting some domestic investment or consumption. Accumulation policies drain domestic resources, and from the point of view of fiscal conditionality, they reduce domestic fiscal space (Brunnermeier and Huang, 2018, p. 2).
2 A slow change in China's economic development model, that is a shift towards a strategy based on stimulating domestic demand and developing the service sector while moving away from a strategy based on the key role of the export sector.
3 Creating effective liquidity support instruments within the GFSN at bilateral, regional, and global levels (e.g. better access to swap lines, modifying IMF liquidity support facilities and creating RFAs).

3.2.2 *Gold in Central Banks' Portfolios*

3.2.2.1 *Gold as a Component of Central Banks' Reserves*

At the end of 2022, central banks held approximately 20% of the world's gold stocks in their portfolios. Therefore, their decisions to sell or buy, as well as the determinants of their policy actions, such as inflation levels and monetary policy trends, are important price drivers. In a contemporary multi-currency IMS, central banks have become both price-makers in the gold market and price-takers, responding to tendencies in price formation (higher demand during periods of price increases and selling off in periods of price decreases), as well as reinforcing them.

Figure 3.5 presents the main sources of gold demand. It shows a dual demand structure for gold that comprises the following:

- Different categories of investors who use gold as a hedge against tail risks and inflation, as well as a portfolio diversifier,
- Consumers who demand gold for jewellery and industrial use.

For central banks, gold represents both a safe asset and a safe-haven investment, and their investment demand for gold is no different from that of institutional investors or hedge funds (Ghosh, 2016). They purchase gold to diversify their reserve portfolio, although there are other important and unique drivers of central banks' demand for gold, evident in emerging market economies (discussed in detail in Section 3.3.3).

Gold is one of the components of central banks' official reserve assets in developed and emerging market economies. On average, it constitutes 12% of assets in contemporary central banking (as of the end of 2022).

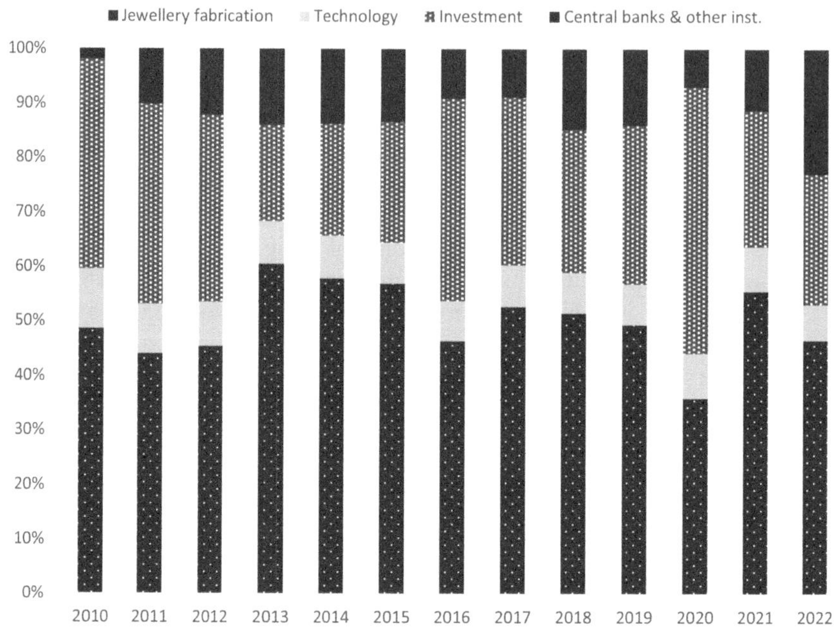

Figure 3.5 Composition of gold demand, 2010–2022

Source: Authors' own compilation based on World Gold Council data.

Figure 3.6 shows the shares of different country groups (distinguished according to the World Bank's income criteria) in world official gold holdings. It is evident that over the 21st century, the proportions between the advanced and developing economies (economies of low to upper-middle income) have been changing to the advantage of the latter. More specifically, at the beginning of the analysed period, advanced economies comprised approximately 76% of the total, while developing economies constituted 11%. However, in 2022 Q4, they stood at 65% and 25%, respectively.[8]

This pattern (and its changing nature) is the outcome of:

- The huge legacy of gold holdings in advanced countries,
- The dynamic accumulation of foreign exchange reserves, mostly in emerging market countries (as indicated previously, cf. Section 3.2).

When discussing gold in the official reserve assets of central banks, one can also look at its role in relation to that of foreign exchange reserves. Figure 3.7 presents the top ten holders of total reserve assets (including gold) between 1997 and 2022. The lower boundary applies to the Asian Financial Crisis that struck many countries of the region in late 1997. In its aftermath, the accumulation of reserves began. The group is heterogeneous, as it comprises both advanced and emerging market economies. In 2022, it accounted for

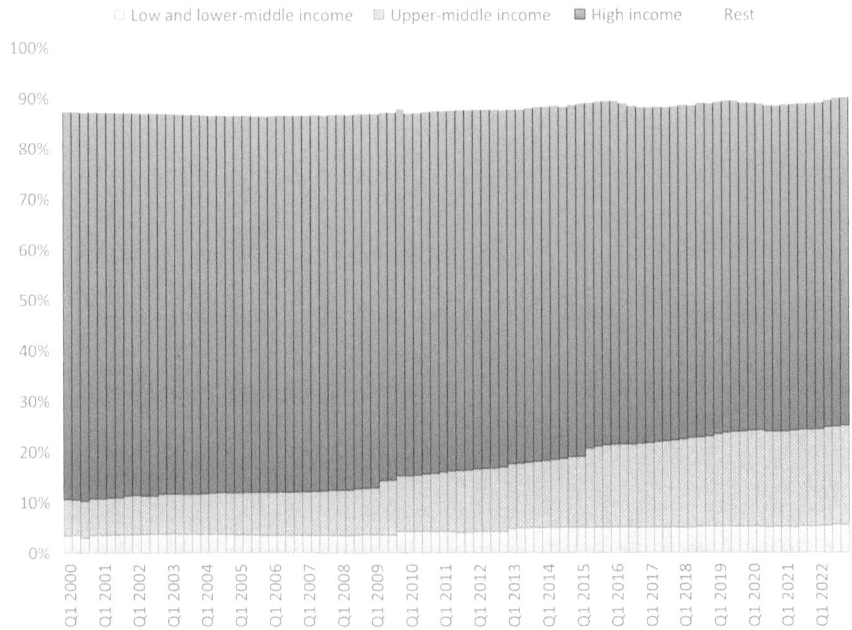

Figure 3.6 World official gold holdings broken down by income group (shares in gold tonnes)

Source: Authors' own compilation based on World Gold Council data.

65% of the total world reserves (as reported in the World Bank database). It shows that foreign reserves are a highly concentrated phenomenon.

In the next step, the shares of gold and reserves excluding gold (the aggregate of special drawing rights, reserves of IMF members held by the IMF, and holdings of foreign exchange) were calculated. The results, presented in Table 3.1, point to a few clear patterns.

1 Reserve currency issuers, that is the United States, the euro area, and Switzerland (up to the GFC), with the noticeable exception of Japan (shares lower than 5%), are characterised by the largest shares of gold. The role of their currencies in IMS allows them to remain on the sidelines of 'the race for reserves' and thus avoid the related cost of accumulating them. Furthermore, of the three issuers, the United States holds the largest share of gold in the total reserves. In fact, it also holds the largest stock of gold reserves, expressed in tonnes. Hence, when assessing the role of gold in the total official reserve assets, one cannot escape the historical context and the central position of bullion in the IMS (the Gold Standard). Back then, the size of gold reserves implied economic activity and the capacity to issue national currency. The balance of payments determines the net stock of gold holdings, with gold inflows affecting the case of net exports.

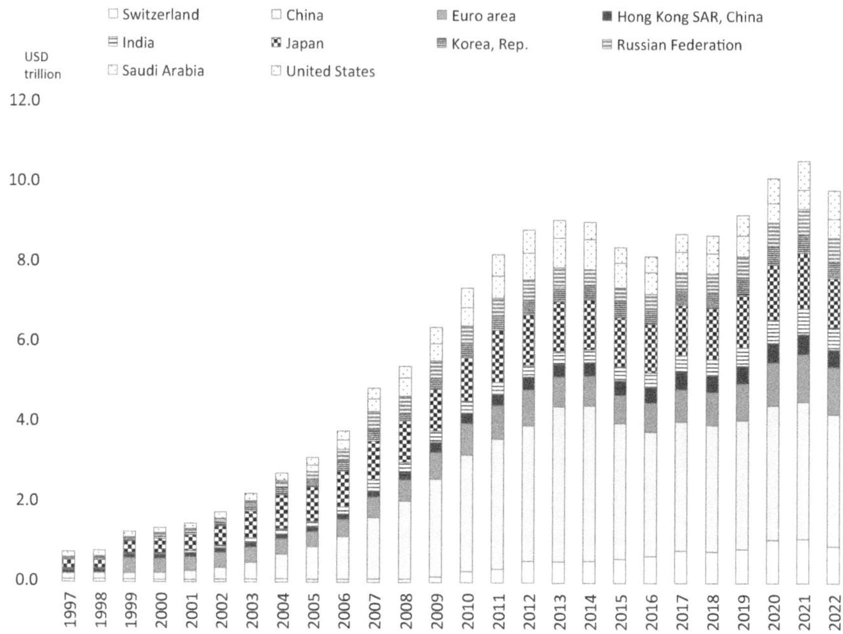

Figure 3.7 Countries with the largest reserves (including gold)

Source: Authors' own compilation based on the World Bank data.

Note: Data for the euro area starts in 1999.

This, in turn, influences the level of national currency issuance due to the obligation to cover the issuance with bullion reserves. Additionally, despite the departure from the above restrictive interdependence and the formal equation of the USD with gold in the monetary functions, the Bretton Woods monetary system favoured the accumulation of gold in central bank reserve portfolios. The primary role of central banks as participants in the gold market is illustrated by the fact that, as late as the 1950s, central banks held 70% of the world's gold stocks. The transition to a multi-currency IMS, which marked a definitive break in the links between monetary policy and central bank gold holdings (gold demonetisation), ended the monetary role of gold (the demonetarisation of gold).

2 The Asian economies in the top ten, including China and Japan, which together account for around 30% of the official world reserves, report substantially lower, single-digit shares of gold. Once again, this can be attributed to the characteristics of the region, that is a strong shift towards foreign exchange reserves triggered by the Asian Crisis.

3 2022 was the year of central banks' 'gold fever', as their annual purchases hit record highs since 1950. The highest demand came from the emerging market economies, including the BRICS countries (Brazil, Russia, India, China and South Africa) and was dictated by geopolitical concerns, among others (cf. Section 3.3.3).

Table 3.1 Composition of total official reserves of top ten holders (in %), 1997–2022

	1997–2001		*2002–2006*		*2007–2011*		*2012–2016*		*2017–2021*		*2022–Gold Fever Year*	
	Gold (%)	*Reserves Excl. Gold (%)*	*Gold (%)*	*Reserves Excl. Gold (%)*	*Gold (%)*	*Reserves Excl. Gold (%)*	*Gold (%)*	*Reserves Excl. Gold (%)*	*Gold (%)*	*Reserves Excl. Gold (%)*	*Gold (%)*	*Reserves Excl. Gold (%)*
China	2.2	97.8	1.6	98.4	1.3	98.7	1.5	98.5	2.9	97.1	3.5	96.5
Japan	2.4	97.6	1.6	98.4	2.6	97.4	2.5	97.5	2.9	97.1	4.0	96.0
Euro area	31.5	68.5	45.6	54.4	59.5	40.5	56.3	43.7	56.2	43.8	53.0	47.0
Switzerland	38.5	61.5	33.9	66.1	28.0	72.0	7.4	92.6	5.6	94.4	6.6	93.4
United States	55.0	45.0	64.6	35.4	75.2	24.8	72.9	27.1	74.4	25.6	67.1	32.9
India	9.5	90.5	4.5	95.5	6.4	93.6	7.0	93.0	6.5	93.5	8.1	91.9
Russia	23.2	76.8	5.2	94.8	5.5	94.5	11.7	88.3	20.2	79.8	23.4	76.6
Hong Kong	0.0	100.0	0.0	100.0	0.0	100.0	0.0	100.0	0.0	100.0	0.0	100.0
Saudi Arabia	7.4	92.6	4.9	95.1	2.4	97.6	2.0	98.0	3.3	96.7	3.9	96.1
Korea	0.3	99.7	0.1	99.9	0.2	99.8	1.1	98.9	1.2	98.8	1.3	98.7

Source: Authors' own calculations based on World Bank data.

For the 1997–2021 subperiod, the averages for the euro area include 1999–2021.

3.2.2.2 *The Changing Sentiment of Central Banks towards Gold*

A special feature of gold holdings in central banks' portfolios is the changing pattern of its role as one of the components of official reserve assets. In fact, periods when central banks are net sellers and buyers of bullion are intertwined. This changing sentiment of central banks towards gold is, in general, the effect of:

- Changing rules within the IMS, together with reserve currency creation mechanisms,
- Tendencies in the price of gold,
- Inflation performance in the global economy.

While tracing the changing sentiment of central banks towards gold since the formation of the Bretton Woods system, one can divide this period into four distinct episodes where demand changed direction (cf. Figure 3.8):

1. The 1950s–1970s – high demand for gold due to the Bretton Woods rules,
2. After the 1970s – 'net neutral'. Subperiods of sales due to the collapse of the Bretton Woods system and the appearance of new investment alternatives twined with subperiods of purchases,
3. After the 1990s – coordinated gold sales,
4. Since approximately 2010 – substantial net purchasing.

The rules of the Bretton Woods system stimulated demand for gold. However, as indicated in Figure 3.8, even under the system, there was a period of net sales. In the late 1960s, when the free market gold price topped 40 USD, the Federal Reserve System and the Bank of England agreed that a significant quantity of gold stored at the Bank of England would be sold to help reduce the demand for US gold reserves. This was an example of a coordinated attempt to influence the price of gold as the private market of gold was flourishing.

From the mid-1970s to the 1990s, central banks generally followed a strategy of selling off gold, as it was no longer at the centre of IMS. By creating an oversupply of gold as a result, they contributed significantly to the low bullion prices of the 1990s.

As a consequence of low gold prices and new investment alternatives, since the 1990s, synchronised sales of gold have been undertaken by central banks. This policy, known as Central Bank Gold Agreements (CBGA), was launched in 1999 as the initiative of 16 European central banks (including the ECB) to protect the gold market from destabilisation. There had been concern that uncoordinated sell-offs would lead to too large price falls. At the time, the agreement covered up to 85% of the total holdings of the central banks involved (Aizenman and Inoue, 2012), illustrating the scale of the agreement. It was often compared to a cartel because of its ability to determine the global

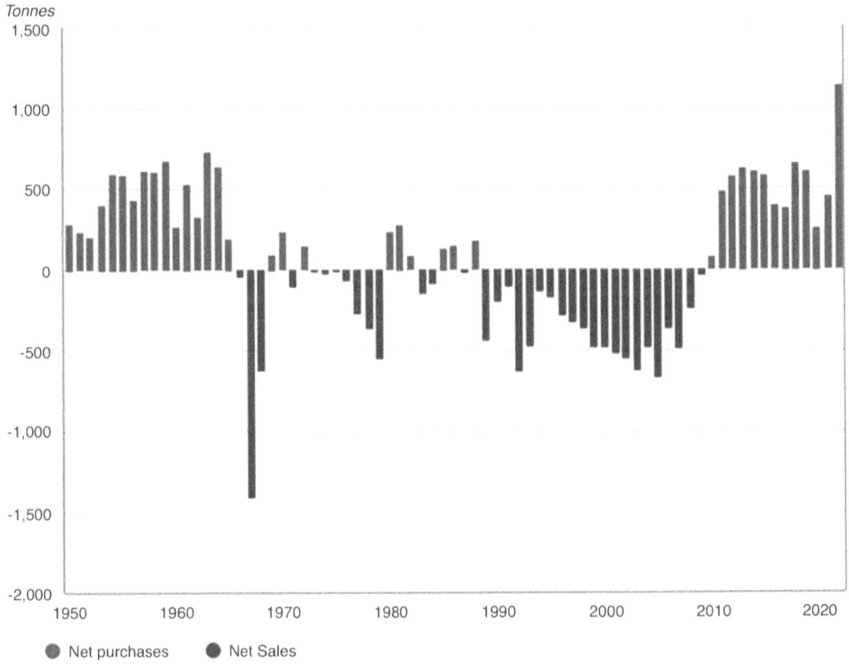

Figure 3.8 Periods of net purchases and sales since the 1950s
Source: World Gold Council.

supply of bullion and thus influence its price. Both the first agreement and subsequent agreements set gold sell-off limits both for the entire agreement period and for individual years within that period. A characteristic feature of the CBGA policy is the decreasing use of sell-off limits, which can be explained by the change in strategy of the central banks, which were interested in acquiring it at the same time. Indeed, over the 20 years of the four successive agreements (CBGA 1, 2, 3 and 4,) the price of gold has increased fivefold.

Figure 3.9 illustrates the sell-off limits set by the signatories and the extent to which they were used in successive five-year CBGAs. Under CBGA 1 (also known as the Washington Agreement on Gold), which ran from 2000 to 2004, the banks used the set limits in full (400 tonnes per annum). The agreement is widely acknowledged to have stabilised price conditions by mitigating the downward trend through factors such as the 'freshness effect' (surprise to participants) and the reduced number of participants in the gold market. Under CBGA 2, which partly coincided with the GFC, banks did not use the entire limit, set at 500 tonnes per year. The last two CBGAs were characterised by an increasing relaxation of the rules, which reflected the improving conditions in the gold market. The change in the terms took the form of an adjustment of the signatories' sale quotas and the loosening of the constraints on the use of derivatives (ECB, 2019).

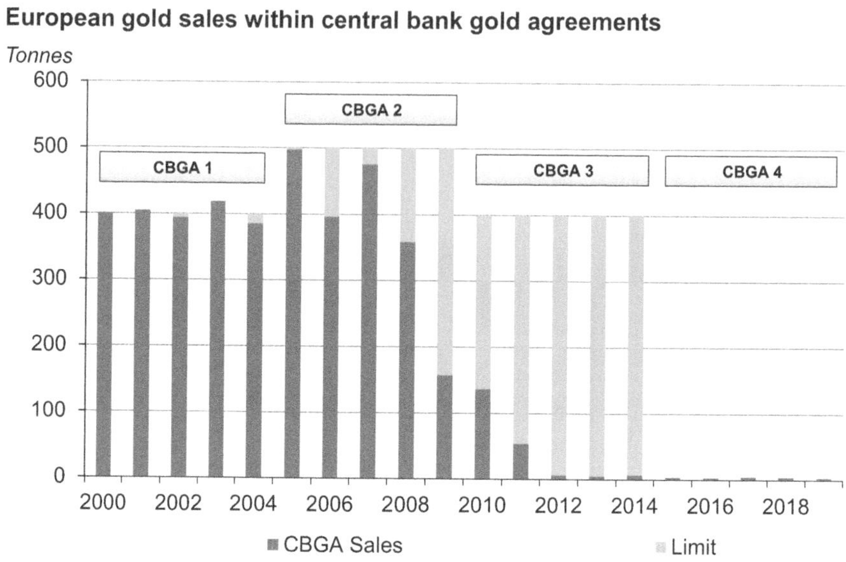

Figure 3.9 European gold sales within central bank gold agreements

Source: World Gold Council.

The last agreement, CBGA 4, expired in 2019, and it seems that this policy will not be continued in the near future. This is due to the agreement's diminishing ability to influence price formation, largely as a result of increased and dispersed sources of demand in the gold market. Market liquidity, and its ability to absorb large volume gold transactions, has improved considerably over the two decades, thereby lowering the need for the CBGA (ECB, 2019). Interestingly, gold sales in this period involved mostly developed countries. The CBGA and London Gold Pool (under the Bretton Woods system) indicate that central banks' gold holding is often coordinated, confirming that gold is recognised as a strategic asset.

There has been a return to gold after the GFC. This shift was the outcome of changing patterns in the management policy of central banks' official reserves. Liquidity and safety remain the overriding goals; however, the rate of return becomes more important as a result of the following:

- When switching to flexible exchange rates, currency pegs become much less popular; thus, foreign exchange interventions become more rarely used as a macroeconomic instrument of monetary policy,
- High levels of reserves as measured by reserve adequacy ratios, especially in emerging market economies,
- Better liquidity provision mechanisms within the GFSN,
- A prolonged low or even negative interest rate environment.

All of these factors provided grounds for diversifying central banks' portfolios. Low interest rates on major reserve currencies diminished the rate of return differentials between securities and gold. While the post-crisis period did not exhibit inflationary tendencies – quite the opposite, deflationary forces emerged – the sheer scale of implementing a QE policy raised concerns about potential inflationary pressures.

Other factors that contributed to changing the sentiment towards gold after the GFC include declining investor confidence in the equity market, a weakening USD, and greater geopolitical risk. The negative correlation of gold with the USD and its low correlation with equities improves risk-adjusted returns, providing impetus for portfolio diversification (Baur and McDermott, 2009).

Importantly, central banks' increase in gold holdings (which made them net buyers in 2009) was largely driven by demand from emerging markets. More specifically, among the top ten countries that added the most to their gold reserves between 2010 and 2022, Poland is the only high-income country (cf. Table 3.2).

Although nearly all central banks' gold buying has come from emerging market economies (EMEs) for the last decade, with its tremendous purchases in 2022, advanced economies (AEs) still dominate the top gold holders. As can be seen from Table 3.3, the United States has the largest gold reserves (8,133.5 t), followed by Germany (3,352.6 t) and Italy (2,451.8 t).[9] The top ten countries with the largest gold reserves are mainly made up of AEs (the United States, Germany, Italy, France, Switzerland and Japan), with a smaller share of EMEs (Russia, China and India).

As a consequence of the trends discussed above, since the beginning of the 21st century, the average share of gold in official reserve assets has been in the range of 10%–15%. The level varies, which is largely due to the different growth of reserves and the reserve management strategy pursued. For example, in Q2 2023, the first quartile of the distribution (0.0%–4.3%) included

Table 3.2 Countries with the largest changes in central bank gold holdings, 2010–2022

Country	*Change in Tonnes*
Russian Federation	1,656.7
China, P.R.: Mainland	956.4
Turkey	425.7
Kazakhstan	278.1
India	229.6
Thailand	160.2
Poland	125.7
Iraq	124.5
Mexico	111.9
Brazil	96.0

Source: Authors' own calculations based on World Gold Council data.

Table 3.3 Top official gold holders (as of July 2023)

Country/Entity	*Tonnes*	*% of Reserves*
United States	8,133.5	68.8
Germany	3,352.6	67.9
IMF	2,814.0	N/A
Italy	2,451.8	65.1
France	2,436.9	66.8
Russian Federation	2,329.6	25.0
China, P.R.: Mainland	2,136.5	4.0
Switzerland	1,040.0	7.4
Japan	846.0	4.3
India	797.7	8.3

Source: World Gold Council data.

countries such as the Czech Republic (0.8%), South Korea (1.5%), Brazil (2.4%), China (3.9%) and Japan (4.3%). In contrast, the fourth quartile (19.5%–84.1%) comprised, among others, Russia (25.1%), Turkey (32.7%), ten countries from the EU-15, the United States (68.9%) and Venezuela (84.1%). In general, no clear differences can be identified across countries by the level of economic development, type of exchange rate regime adopted (which affects the extent of currency interventions used) or geographical location.

As already mentioned, the United States and the euro area are special cases. As a consequence of historical superpowers and the issuance of reserve currencies, they have accumulated and hold a large proportion of their reserves in gold. However, even under EMU frameworks, there is a wide variation in gold's share in total reserves across member countries (Portugal – 69.8%, France – 66.9%, Austria – 56.8%, Spain – 18.2% and Ireland – 5.8%).[10] Within the group of EMU member states, Portugal has the highest share of gold in its reserve portfolio. The main accumulation of gold occurred during the Second World War due to the country's neutrality. Additionally, after the end of the war, the Portuguese government preferred to hold gold reserves rather than invest in the country's economic development (Aizenman and Inoue, 2012, p. 38). In France, on the other hand, the high level of gold reserves is largely linked to the policy of exchanging dollar reserves for gold, initiated by President Charles de Gaule in 1965 with his famous speech that expounded the advantages of gold over the dollar (Pilbeam, 1998, p. 282).[11]

Aizenman and Inoue (2012, p. 13) pointed out that the ratio of reserves to government debt in EMU member states varies, suggesting that both institutional conditions (central bank independence) and international commitments (such as CBGAs) may be regarded as factors that protect governments from the temptation to sell off gold as a means of reducing government debt. This conclusion is of high importance in the face of growing public debt within the EMU.

The stock of gold reserves in the EMU consists of more than those in the portfolios of national central banks. The ECB also has gold in its portfolio, which now accounts for 33.6% of official reserve assets, up from 15% in 1999.[12] The increase in the share, despite the bank's involvement in CBGAs, is explained by the rise in gold prices in the 21st century (ECB, 2019).

3.2.2.3 Central Banks' Gold Fever of 2022 and Its Consequences

2022 was a year of soaring prices (the global rate of inflation was around 9%) and increased geopolitical and economic tensions triggered by the Russian invasion of Ukraine. It was also recognised as a year of 'gold fever' due to record annual central bank purchases of gold since 1950. Altogether, central banks bought 1,136 tons of gold – a 152% increase since 2021.

The highest demand came from EMEs (Figure 3.10). Turkey added 148 t to its gold reserves, while China purchased 62 t, increasing its total gold reserves to over 2,000 t. Strong demand was also reported from the Middle East. Active buyers included Egypt (45 t), Qatar (35 t), Iraq (34 t) and the United Arab Emirates (20 t). These purchases continue the trend of buying gold that has been observed since the end of the GFC.

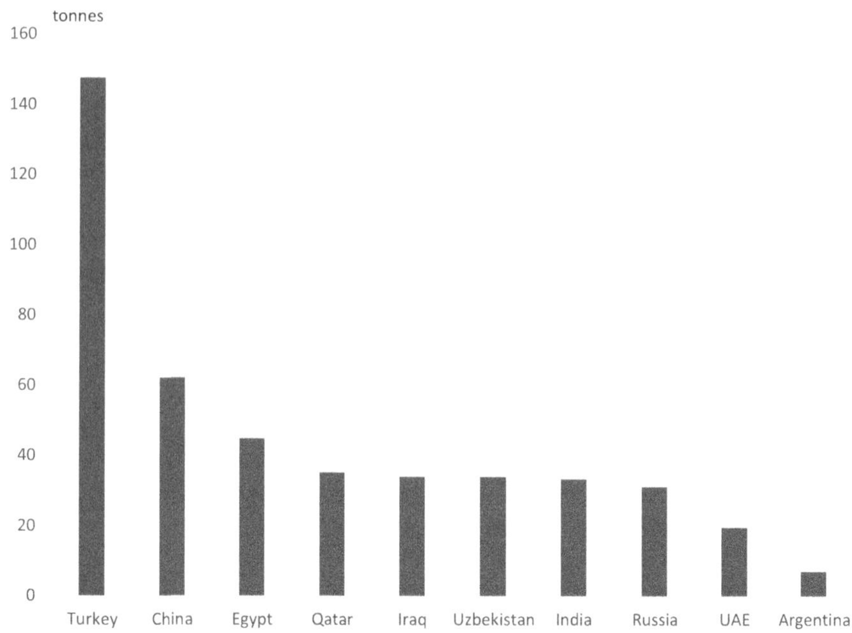

Figure 3.10 Top largest gold buyers in 2022

Source: Authors' own compilation on the basis of World Gold Council data (access: 28 July 2023).

Motivations of demand differ between the developed and developing world. There are indeed motives that are common for those two groups of countries, such as:

- The unique features of gold,
- Monetary conditions in the global economy and the global tendency to diversify portfolios,
- Demonstration effect – foreign reserves may be a component of country risk assessment,
- The dysfunctionality of the current IMS – which may encourage countries to diversify away from the USD as an international currency and attempt to internationalise their, domestic currencies and stimulate currency regionalism.

However, there have been additional motives for gold accumulation in EMEs:

- The signalling effect – foreign reserves may signal a country's economic power (Aizenman and Inoue, 2012)
- The fear/risk of sanctions (McDowell, 2020; Arslanalp et al., 2023).

The dysfunctionality of the IMS, which is overly based on the USD, has given rise to numerous inefficiencies in the system. They include global imbalances, exchange rate volatility, destabilising capital flows and a higher probability of currency crises, and asymmetrical adjustment mechanisms in the external positions of the countries. Together with fears of the macroeconomic position of the dominant currency issuer (mainly the sustainability of its fiscal position, as suggested in the Triffin Dilemma II), they contributed to the loss of confidence in the stability of the system and the search for de-dollarisation strategies. McDowell (2020) stated that introducing sanctions as a toolkit in international economic relations additionally diminishes the attractiveness of the USD as an international currency, stimulating de-dollarisation. In fact, as Drezner (2015) found, the US policy of imposing sanctions is a kind of 'weaponisation' of the dollar, making it an instrument to achieve the country's geopolitical goals.

A high level of central bank gold reserves generally has a positive impact on a country's credit risk assessment, mainly during times of financial market stress. In EMEs, the credit risk factor is of special importance as it influences the cost of funding in the international financial markets.

Rathi and Sahay (2022) analysed whether gold reserves held by central banks enhance a country's resilience to external shocks. They conducted a panel study for 48 countries – both developed and developing – between 2000 and 2020. The explanatory variable was country risk, approximated by CDS credit spreads[13] for five-year government bonds. The set of explanatory variables, in addition to gold reserves, included categories that reflect the country's macroeconomic condition and institutional framework. The results clearly indicate that an increase in gold reserves reduces CDS spreads. In addition, Rathi and Sahay examined the strength of this relationship amidst global risk aversion (the GFC and the COVID-19 pandemic crisis) and for country-specific episodes of debt, inflation and currency crises. On this basis, they showed that during periods of heightened global market stress, a 10% increase in gold reserves leads to a 4% decrease in CDS spreads (vs 3.1% in the absence of these stresses). For domestic episodes, a 10% increase in gold reserves leads to a reduction in CDS spreads of 13.3% (vs 3%) for debt crises and 16% (vs 3.2%) for inflation crises. The effect of gold reserves on CDS spreads was found to be the same during currency crises and beyond. An important conclusion from their study is that by diversifying their reserve portfolio to increase the share of gold, countries can provide protection against potential macroeconomic shocks of different natures (e.g. global, debt or inflationary).

China, India and Russia are excellent examples of countries that have seen their gold reserves increase in recent years. The growth of gold holdings in these countries, which coincides with their rising economic and geopolitical influence, is partly driven by the desire to signal this power through gold reserves (the signalling effect). What is more, in EMEs, the value of gold reserves is a component of assessing a country's credit risk and, therefore, its economic strength in the world.

Aizenman et al. (2019, pp. 14, 40) further point to the role of factors such as the need to diversify the reserve portfolio. They state that in China, this diversification is essential due to the country's high exposure to USD fluctuations as a result of pegging the RMB exchange rate to the USD and insuring against global instability. Diversifying the reserves portfolio as a de-dollarisation strategy is especially evident in China and Russia. The creation of a country's own (non-SWIFT) payment system and diminishing the scale of trade settlements in USD can be symptoms of intentional de-dollarisation policies.

In addition to China, India and Russia, the increased interest in gold accumulation within central bank reserves is also coming from other EMEs, such as Kyrgyzstan, Uzbekistan and Turkey. The share of gold in the official reserve assets of these countries is 49%, 74% and 26%, respectively.

Arslanalp et al. (2023) stated that the imposition of financial sanctions by the United States, the United Kingdom, the EU and Japan (the main reserve-issuing countries) has contributed to the growth in both the volume and value of emerging market central banks' gold holdings. They demonstrated that many of the largest year-on-year increases in individual central banks' gold holdings occur when those central banks are or have reason to think that they may be subject to financial sanctions. Among the ten largest annual increases in the gold share of reserves since 1999, in half of the cases, the countries were subject to sanctions in the same year of the two immediately preceding years. The top example is Turkey in 2020, with a 21% increase in gold share and 29% in gold volume after sanctions imposed by the United States (2018) and the EU (2019). In other cases, increases in gold share of reserves followed irregular political events, such as bomb blasts, coup attempts and financial crises (Arsanalp et al., 2023, p. 24).

There is evidence that the accumulation of gold as an official reserve asset was especially strong in countries that are geopolitically close to China and Russia in an attempt to reduce their risk of exposure to financial sanctions (ECB, 2023a). Ferranti (2023) demonstrated empirically that between 2016 and 2021, countries facing a higher risk of US sanctions increased the share of gold in their international reserves more than countries facing a lower risk (after: Frankel, 2023). What is more, as Arslanalp et al. (2023) indicated, multilateral sanctions have a larger impact on the share of reserves held in gold than unilateral ones. This is attributed to the fact that the latter can force central banks to shift their reserves into the currencies of non-sanctioning countries. In contrast, the former renders foreign exchange reserves a risker class and gold more attractive.

The increased importance of geopolitical factors is also evident in the Central Bank Gold Reserves Survey (2023). According to the report, central banks' demand for gold differs between EMEs and AEs. In particular, the former point to the same three key factors that influence their reserve management decisions: interest rate levels, inflation concerns and geopolitical instability. However, they also pay greater attention to shifts in economic power. The report also highlighted the following points:

- They list concerns about sanctions (the weaponisation of the US dollar) as an important factor in their decisions to hold gold (EME: 25% vs AE: 0%),
- They expect gold to increase as a proportion of total reserves (EME: 64% vs AE: 38%),
- They expect the US dollar to decrease as a proportion of total reserves (EME: 58% vs AE: 46%),
- They intend to increase their gold reserves over the next 12 months (EME: 29% vs AE: 8%).

3.3 Sovereign Wealth Funds' Demand for Safe Assets

As part of a conservative strategy to maintain the value of the portfolio of accumulated wealth, safe assets are a desirable component for both central banks and SWFs, especially stabilisation funds. The investment strategies adopted by central banks and public sector SWFs focus on safety, followed by liquidity and return. From the point of view of currency portfolio management in these entities, liquidity, low credit, and market risk are key elements in the perception of asset safety. Nowadays, SWFs have over $11.5 trillion in assets under management as of February 2023 (Megginson et al., 2023).

Most are located in non-Western countries, and their constant growth has made SWFs important international investors.

There were only 62 funds in 2000; this had increased to 176 by 2023, with further funds due to emerge. New SWFs are being established in sub-Saharan Africa, followed by Asia and Europe. The total assets under management of SWFs have grown each year. SWFs continue to change their policy for private equity and infrastructure allocations, while public equities and fixed income may display a downward trend (Megginson et al., 2023).

An SWF is a state-owned investment fund financed by the government, mainly from the country's surplus reserves, balance of payments or fiscal surpluses, or official foreign currency operations. The origin of SWFs may be derived from commodities (export) or through transfers of assets from official foreign exchange reserves (non-commodities). SWFs are considered to be beneficial for the economy in financing the needs of future generations, although some of them are not as transparent as other institutional investors.

SWFs are willing to invest heavily in safe financial instruments. The demand for safe assets reported by SWFs depends on the type of fund, its risk-return profile and its investment horizon. The SWF type, investment horizon and funding source all affect strategic asset allocation, while the investment horizon is a critical factor. Longer investment horizons are traditionally linked with the ability to take more risks and the ability to benefit from the illiquidity premium. With a short or very uncertain investment horizon, SWFs should have a larger share of their investment portfolios in cash and liquid debt instruments to be able to avoid unexpected losses. Funding sources also affect asset allocation, but only to a certain extent; for example SWFs funded from oil resources should acknowledge the oil-price risk and invest in financial instruments that have a negative or low correlation with the oil market (Das et al., 2010).

There are different classifications of SWFs, but typically, they are categorised as follows:

- Stabilisation funds, which prioritise stabilisation,
- Saving funds – which prioritise capital maximisation,
- Pension reserve funds – which prioritise capital maximisation,
- Reserve investment funds – which prioritise capital maximisation.[14]

Most SWFs are either stabilisation funds or savings funds, and they may have multiple objectives. One feature of the different types of SWFs is the varying share of safe assets in the portfolios, which ranges from 4% to almost 70% (IMF, 2012). As of 2023, almost 60% of SWFs' assets were equity and fixed-income securities, but the level of assets allocated to illiquid alternatives has steadily increased. According to a survey from the International Forum of Sovereign Wealth Funds (IFSWF, 2016), SWFs primarily chose traditional investment categories like equities and bonds, preferring fixed-income securities over stocks. SWFs may shift their portfolio allocation, and in recent years, they have increased their allocations in listed equity, private equity, and real estate. As a rule, SWFs' asset allocation is most likely to be stable, but they may increase their allocations to emerging market issuers (IFSWF, 2016).

Figure 3.11 shows that stabilisation funds used to have the largest number of safe assets, with 69% of the portfolio composition. This is mainly due to their investment policy, which is long term and very similar to that of central banks. The objectives of stabilisation funds are to mitigate the impact of the economic cycle on the economy and countercyclical policies, hence the need for liquid financial assets. They most often invest in highly liquid assets, which are negatively correlated with commodity prices, to neutralise external shocks to the economy. Their investment portfolios are mostly comprised of debt instruments, mainly treasuries with high creditworthiness. Stabilisation SWFs are expected to have a larger share of their portfolios in cash and liquid and highly rated bonds, which is why they are also referred to as 'rainy day funds'. Stabilisation funds' high concentration of investments in safe assets means that these assets are considered close substitutes for foreign exchange reserves. Stabilisation SWFs are sourced from fiscal surpluses, so their investment objectives are likely to be influenced by the dynamics of government debt. When estimating trends in demand for safe assets from stabilisation

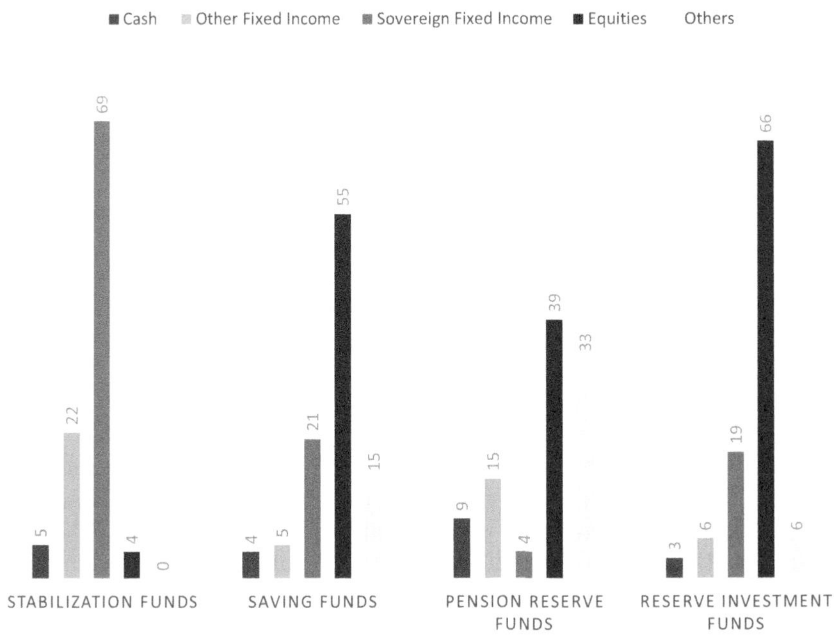

Figure 3.11 Asset allocation structure of SWFs

Source: IMF (2012).

funds, it is important to note that their potential to maintain or even increase demand is driven by:

1 Setting up new funds,
2 The expected assets increase of existing SWFs, especially in emerging markets.

Savings funds are used to collect a much smaller share of safe assets, around 21%. The immediate objective of these types of SWFs is to provide income for future generations by converting non-renewable assets into a diversified investment portfolio. Investment portfolios of this type of fund contain mainly equities, which translates into high risk and potential returns.

Pension reserve funds have the fewest safe assets in their investment portfolios – around 4%. They are established to increase the security of government social benefits and offset the rising cost of paying pensions. In contrast, reserve investment funds are established to reduce the cost of central banks holding reserves; they usually invest in higher-yielding and long-term assets. These funds allocate most of their capital in equities and alternative investments. Around 19% of their portfolio composition is made up of safe assets (Al-Hassan et al., 2013, pp. 5–6).

The investment objectives of SWFs are very diverse. They depend on the country in which they are located and on the amount and type of natural resources that the country possesses. Commonly, they are funded to stabilise the budget from excess volatility in revenues, earn more returns than on foreign exchange reserves, diversify from non-renewable commodity export transactions, and enhance social and economic development by increasing savings for citizens. Their role is very important from a macroeconomic management point of view, and they are, therefore, closely linked to government institutions.

The level of SWFs' revenues affects a country's public finances, monetary policy, and balance of payments (IMF, 2012). International disparities between SWF portfolios could be characterised by region. North American, Asian, and Middle Eastern SWFs are the most diversified in their investment allocations, and they prefer alternative investments and hedge funds. Latin American and African SWFs are relatively risk-averse and centred on fixed-income and public equity instruments, similar to European SWFs, which tend to be relatively conservative and mainly invest in public equity and fixed-income instruments (Wiśniewski, 2017).

The global top three largest SWFs by assets are the Norway Government Pension Fund Global (Europe), which is the largest in the world, the China Investment Corporation (Asia), and the SAFE Investment Company (Asia). They all have different investment objectives (SWFI, 2023; cf. Figure 3.12).

Below, we discuss Norway's Government Pension Fund Global (GPFG) in greater detail as an illustrative example of how an SWF allocates assets. It was established in 1990 and is the largest and most transparent SWF in

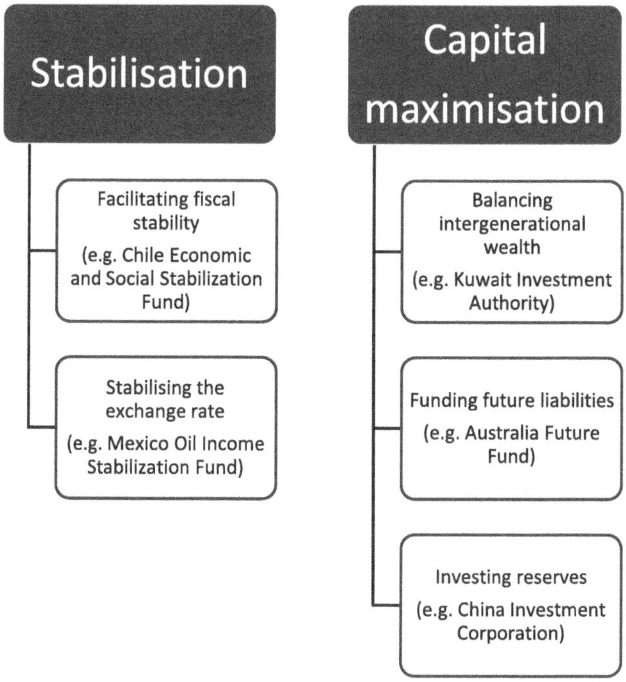

Figure 3.12 SWFs investment objectives.

Source: Own elaboration based on PWC Report (2015) and https://www.toptal.com/finance/market-research-analysts/sovereign-wealth-funds.

the world. One of its benefits is that it allows the government to manage oil assets and revenues to create wealth for future generations. It effectively converts oil assets into an investment portfolio to prevent overheating Norway's economy by including regulations to limit public expenditures. The GPFG's investment goal is to maximise financial returns at moderate risk to provide benefits for future generations.

Compared to other SWFs, the GPFG has a higher risk-bearing capacity by virtue of its long-term investment horizon and the lack of short-term liquidity requirements. Its investment portfolio comprises fixed-income and equity securities and property investments. The market value of the fund has grown steadily; however, its total returns have fluctuated with the global economic trends over the years (Centre for Public Impact, 2019). Figure 3.13 depicts the GPFG's strategic asset allocation.

Incorporated fixed-income instruments are mostly held in USD (50.2%), EUR (28.1), JPY (8%), GBP (4.5%) and CAD (3.8%). The remaining 5.1% are held in other currencies. Government bonds with an AAA credit rating comprise approximately 35.4% of the total portfolio of bonds. The share of government and corporate bonds with the highest rating AAA increased to 49.3% of the total bond portfolio in 2022. Generally, half of the GPFG's bond portfolio comprises safe assets.

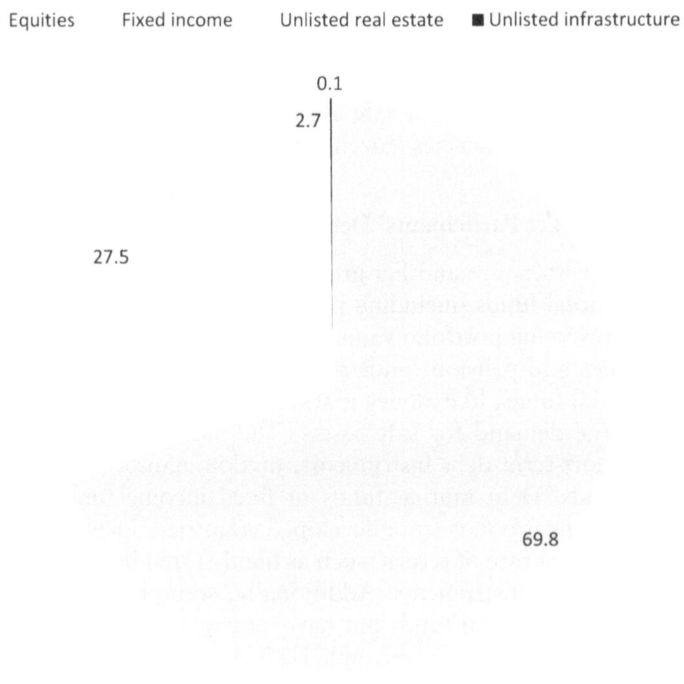

Figure 3.13 GPFG's allocation by asset class as of 31 December 2022 (%).
Source: Government Pension Fund Global Annual Report (2022).

In summary, stabilisation funds have an investment horizon and liquidity objectives similar to central banks' management strategies due to their role in countercyclical fiscal policy. Other types of SWFs show a much more limited demand for safe assets, preferring to invest in riskier asset classes, including real estate. Their investment horizon is much longer due to their objectives and mandate. In particular, they:

1 expect outflows in the future (pension reserve funds),
2 are designed to reduce the cost of holding foreign exchange reserves (funds that invest foreign exchange reserves),
3 are designed to transfer wealth between generations (savings funds).

An interesting implication to international capital flows and asset prices may arise from SWFs' investment decisions. The formation of an SWF signals the wish for greater diversification of the assets controlled by the public sector, thereby impacting the demand for international reserves (Aizenman and Glick, 2009). SWFs can typically play a stabilising role in the global financial markets because they have medium or long-term investment horizons and do not make instant portfolio shifts that impact market stability. Nevertheless, after the GFC, there was an increase in demand for US dollar-denominated assets, mostly government securities (safe assets). However, in the future,

SWF portfolios may change. By favouring regional safe assets providers and emerging market debt instruments, they may lower flows into both US and euro assets (Das et al., 2010). SWFs may be regarded as major players, impacting the demand for global safe assets and, indirectly, international reserve diversification tendencies (Aizenman et al., 2019).

3.4 Other Market Participants' Demand for Safe Assets

Institutional investors are another group that reports a demand for safe assets, that is mutual funds (including ETFs), pension funds and life insurance companies. Preserving portfolio value is particularly important for life insurance companies and pension funds that operate on a defined benefit basis. Low-risk mutual funds, like money market funds or debt mutual funds, may generate a large demand for safe assets. The money market funds consist of safe and short-term debt instruments, predominantly Treasury bills and short-term bonds. Debt mutual funds or fixed income funds traditionally invest in government bonds from developed countries. They focus on investments that pay a set rate of return, such as highly rated bonds or other stable and quite safe debt instruments. Additionally, some types of ETFs, which are not considered mutual funds but have strategies consistent with mutual funds, invest in safe assets, for example US Treasury Bond ETFs.

The asset allocation of a mutual fund can be fixed or variable, comprising a mix of equity and fixed-income securities, depending on the fund's goal and risk appetite. Balanced mutual funds (low and medium risk) usually invest 60% of their portfolio in equity and 40% in fixed-income financial instruments. Their main goal is to preserve capital and generate income. US mutual funds are an important representative group of global private investors that invest in the sovereign debt markets of advanced economies, which are relatively safe financial instruments. This sector of financial market participants has grown rapidly in the last 20 years, which can be best illustrated by the number of total assets managed by the industry. It went from approximately USD 5 trillion at the turn of the century to more than USD 16 trillion at the end of 2022 (ECB, 2023a). The share of highly rated government debt securities in their portfolio is, on average, approximately 15%, with a peak of 30% in 2011.

Empirical evidence shows that this category of global investors tends to reallocate their portfolio of safe assets in response to changes in yields across major currencies. Thus, they implement a strategy of searching for yield within the sovereign debt market of highly rated issuers. The search for a yield strategy is derived from very low levels of safe asset returns over a long period, as in Japan and some European countries. Investors are shifting towards higher-risk assets, such as corporate debt and emerging market debt, or engaging in an increase in carry trade transactions. They are a form of leveraged transaction where funds are borrowed short term at low interest rates and located in higher-yield assets from other countries.

Pension funds' demand for safe assets is linked to the nature of their liabilities and their risk tolerance (e.g. pension funds with inflation-indexed liabilities tend to focus on real returns). Their investment policy is determined by the features of the labour income stream and the investor's life cycle (Bagliano et al., 2009). Different types of safe assets and 'quasi-safe assets' like US Treasuries, ABS, or privately issued investment-grade bonds, are important elements of pension fund investment portfolios. Pension fund asset allocations are dominated by sovereign debt holdings. They accounted for half of the aggregate pension fund assets portfolio. Typically, sovereign bonds, cash, and deposits within pension fund investments represent a larger share of the assets. According to OECD estimates conducted for a group of countries that mainly comprises its members and the BRICS countries (excluding China), bonds and Treasury bills accounted for around 46% of pension fund assets on average in 2018 (OECD, 2019).[15]

For euro-area insurance corporations, debt securities account for more than 40% of their total financial assets, with around 15% of these are issued by the government sector of the monetary union (ECB, 2021, 2023b). As far as pension funds are concerned, the holding of debt securities accounts for around 25% of their total assets, with half of these securities holdings represented by investments in euro-area government bonds. However, clarifying the proportion of these assets held by the aforementioned entities through the prism of their balance sheets is challenging, as they hold substantial amounts of government debt indirectly via investment fund shares.

In the case of euro-area investment funds, the share of debt securities amounts to 37% of their total assets. However, in contrast to insurance corporations and pension funds, their investments in debt markets are geographically more widely distributed. Debt securities of non-euro-area issuers account for more than 50% of their total debt securities holdings (ECB, 2021).

Still, there are factors that favour reducing the demand of these entities for safe assets. A prolonged low interest rate environment, which was stopped by the COVID-19 pandemic crisis, led to a decline in government bond yields and 'pushed' these entities out of their market. At the same time, they may have led them to seek higher returns on capital (the search for yield), which was associated with higher risk (ESRB, 2018). The reduction in the scale of holdings of government debt securities in these institutions' portfolios was also a consequence of the central bank's active participation in the government securities market, including intensive QE operations. However, the shift in portfolio composition towards riskier assets is expected to be a gradual process, given that pension funds are slowly changing their asset allocation strategy (IMF, 2012, p. 93).

The demand from the real sector primarily arises from the inherent incompleteness and frictions within financial markets. These specific characteristics create a precautionary motive for real sector investors, compelling them to accumulate assets in a form that is easily convertible into real resources. If financial markets were not characterised by these features, households and businesses would be able to smooth consumption, finance projects and diversify risk without a particular need to accumulate safe assets (Gourinchas and Jeanne, 2012, p. 5).

The demand for safe assets from non-financial corporations and individual investors is small compared to the investor categories discussed above. It is characterised by a relatively low degree of leverage, so it does not pose a significant risk to global financial stability. For example, according to the SIFMA estimates, in 2022, individuals and other investors, including non-financial corporate institutions, owned 6% and 2% of US Treasury securities, respectively.[16] In the euro area, the average share of households, non-profit institutions serving households, and non-financial corporations in total General Government debt stood at 4% in 2022. Nonetheless, important heterogeneities across the EMU countries are visible. The propensity to hold bonds issued by the GG sector is relatively high in Ireland, Italy, Malta, and Portugal, with shares hovering around 10%–15% (cf. Figure 3.14).

At the same time, the problematic nature of analysing the role of the real sector in financing government debt stems from the fact that it is not easily observable; as it goes beyond direct holding, it requires 'looking through' financial intermediaries (ECB, 2021). In fact, households hold relatively little government debt directly, but indirect holdings via pension and investment funds and insurance corporations are much higher. In the case of the EMU, the share of sovereign debt held directly by households is relatively low,

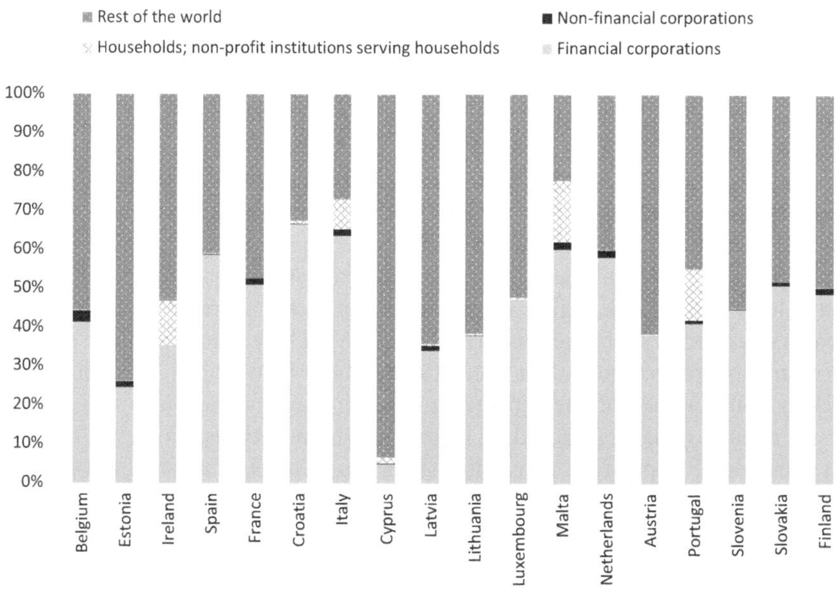

Figure 3.14 General government debt structure of the euro-area countries in 2022 (% of total).

Source: Authors' own compilation based on Eurostat data.
Note: Germany and Greece are excluded due to missing data.

accounting for about 2%. However, when indirect holdings are considered, it rises to almost 16% (ECB, 2021).[17]

The situation is similar in Japan. The share of households in Japanese Government Bonds (JBGs) holdings is estimated at 'only' 1.2% (data as of December 2022). However, life and non-life insurance companies account for 19.1%. When adding shares of public pensions (4.2%) and pension funds (2.8%), one arrives at more than a quarter of JBG holdings. This seems to be a large share, given that the BoJ holds more than half of the outstanding JBGs (52%).[18]

Empirical analysis shows a relatively stable share of safe assets in real sector assets, amounting to around 80% of the national GDP in the United States (Gourinchas and Jeanne, 2012, p. 7).[19] It is possible to identify two periods in which this demand increased: 1981–1988 (the savings and loan crisis) and 2002–2007 (the real estate bubble). However, even during these periods, the increase in safe assets held represented, at most, 20% of domestic product. This increased demand was met mainly through the purchase of Treasury debt securities and safe claims on the financial sector, primarily in the form of bank deposits, as well as money market mutual funds. Stable real sector demand for this asset class is also noted for other developed countries.

Gourinchas and Jeanne (2012) pointed to the fact that Japan stands out from other developed countries, both in terms of its high demand for safe assets (126% of GDP in 1979) and that this demand increased (236% of GDP in 2010). Most of this is attributed to the household sector, which is characterised by a more conservative investment strategy than households in other developed countries. A large part of it is the demand for current and term deposits (which, together with cash, account for half of the financial assets of this category of entities). As of March 2023, banking deposits amounted to 54.2% of household's financial assets, while debt securities amounted to 1.3%. Japanese households' high demand for safe assets is empirically confirmed and considered to be due to the interaction of three factors (Nakagawa and Yasui, 2009, p. 75):

1. Demographics. The ageing population is accumulating wealth in safe assets, including a large proportion in safe bank deposits and postal savings accounts – postal savings,
2. A consequence of the financial crisis of the 1990s, which steered households towards safer forms of investment,
3. The deflationary/disinflationary environment, which led to the liquidity trap that the Japanese economy has found itself in over recent decades, reducing asset returns.

Households are traditionally regarded as risk-averse investors; thus, they should be an important category of safe asset holders. They hold safe assets because they provide insurance against idiosyncratic shocks (Arslanalp and Eichengreen, 2023). The main category of safe assets for households is bank deposits.

What is more, the example of Japan shows that there are strong internal factors that shape the pattern of households' demand for safe assets at the country level. There is evidence that the demand for government debt is concentrated among the wealthiest households. The same conclusions can be drawn from Arrondel et al.'s (2014) empirical research on portfolio choices of European households. They indicated that safe financial assets, including deposits, life insurance contracts, and voluntary private pension plans, are held by almost every household, whether rich or poor. In particular, 93% of households in the euro area within the lowest wealth quintile hold safe financial assets, and this figure increases to 99% for the highest wealth quintile. Safe financial assets are held across all euro-area countries, but the share of risky assets (such as stocks, bonds and mutual funds) in a household's portfolio remains relatively low, with a noticeable uptick associated with the ascending distribution of net wealth (Arrondel et al., 2014).

In searching for factors that affect the wealth accumulation and portfolio choices of households, Arrondel et al. (2014) pointed to culture, history, the welfare state, the housing and credit markets, financial and institutions. The role of indirect investment in government bonds is also connected with factors such as population ageing and the establishment of funded pension pillars (ECB, 2021). Lastly, there are cross-country differentials as regards different categories of public debt. For example, in the United States, households traditionally have a key role as holders of municipal debt (ECB, 2021).

3.5 The Role of the Foreign Sector in the Ownership of Domestic Safe Assets – The Case of a Global Provider (USA)

Foreign ownership of US assets, including safe assets, has increased significantly in the course of transformations in the international monetary and financial system. Foreign demand for US official assets (including public debt instruments) increased from 1% of US GDP in 1946 to 34% in 2011. Similarly, foreign demand for financial sector assets that were deemed safe increased from 2% to 20% om the same period (Gourinchas, 2017, p. 9).

Assessing the demand for US Treasury securities, it can be asserted that, given the large size and depth of the US financial market, foreign investors' demand plays an important role. The structure of this demand is almost equally divided between official and private sector holdings at the beginning of 2023 (50.2% vs 49.8%; cf. Figure 3.17). However, looking back several decades, the dominant role of the official sector was evident. This tendency is visible in China, the single largest holder of foreign exchange reserves. According to estimates, it reduced its holdings of US Treasuries by $250 billion over the last two years, with the decline accelerating recently. It means that the level is now the lowest since 2010 (Slok, 2023, after: Arslanalp et al., 2023).

An analysis of the phenomenon from a historical perspective shows that foreign holdings of US Treasury securities have been changing over time,

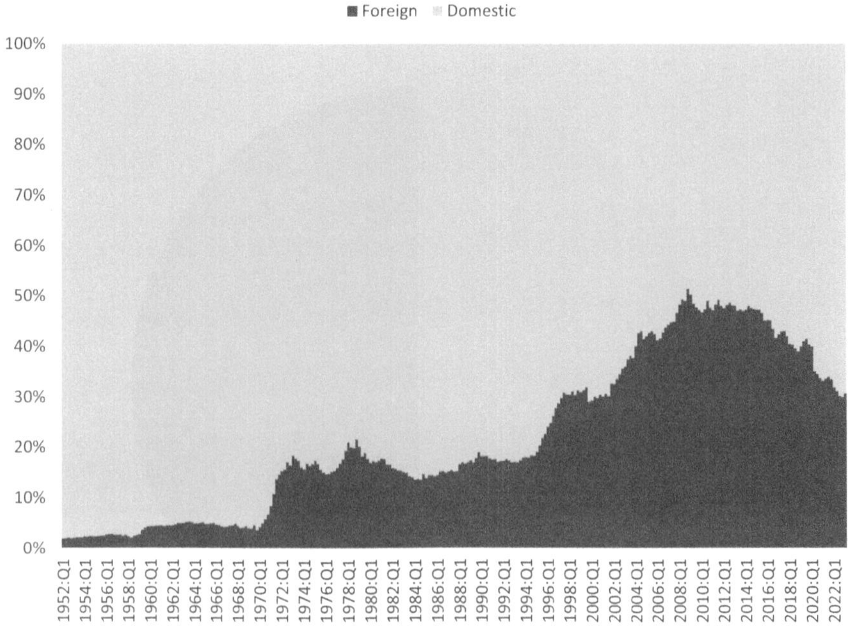

Figure 3.15 Foreign vs domestic holdings of US Treasury securities (share of total), 1952–2022.

Source: Authors' own compilation based on the Federal Reserve Board data.

largely responding to globalisation trends and economic sentiment. As Figure 3.15 shows, over seven decades, their share rose substantially, from a negligible 2% to a substantial 31% in 2023Q1. There are two noticeable periods of increasing shares, after which they stabilised at higher levels: the 1970s and the period starting in the mid-1990s and spanning the first two decades of the 21st century. It is symptomatic that these periods were marked by severe crises on a global scale, with implications of the IMS. The first period was marked by the collapse of the Bretton Woods system; the second period saw the Asian crisis and the GFC (in fact, in 2008Q4, the share of foreign holdings exceeded domestic holdings), clearly demonstrating a shift towards safety in times of stress (Figure 3.16).

Figure 3.17 shows foreign holdings of US Treasury securities, broken down by country of origin. Among the countries with the largest holdings of US Treasury securities, the dominance of Japan and China, that is the countries at the forefront of foreign exchange reserve accumulation, is noticeable. The inclusion of Luxembourg and Belgium in the top ten reflects the private sector demand, mainly from financial institutions. A large proportion of investment funds are registered in Luxembourg.[20] In addition, the importance of the country's banking system in the total balance sheet of EMU credit institutions should be highlighted.

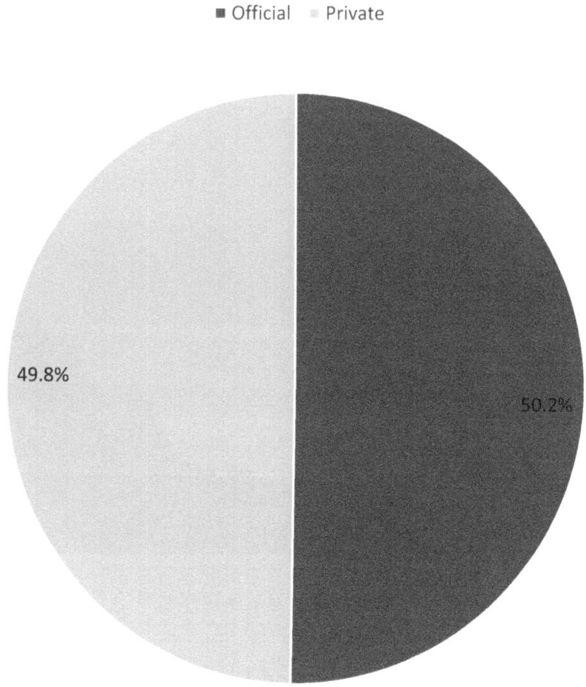

Figure 3.16 Official vs private foreign holdings of US Treasury securities in January 2023.

Source: Authors' own compilation based on Treasury Department International Capital System data. Data as of March 2023.

The group of countries shown in Figure 3.17 also includes countries classified as tax havens and offshore financial centres, that is Luxembourg, the Cayman Islands, Switzerland and Taiwan. Taiwan's large foreign assets may also reflect the anxiety about political isolation. The position of the United Kingdom and Ireland stems from the strong ties of their financial systems with the US system.

Table 3.4 presents the structure of foreign official holdings of US financial instruments, broken down by type. As can be seen, the share of US Treasury securities is dominant.

The relatively low share of corporate debt securities appears to be primarily attributed to the quality of these assets rather than the size of the market. McCauley (2019, p. 6) noted that in 2017, only a tenth of the corporate bonds in the Bloomberg index were rated AAA or AA. Central banks do not demand BBB-rated bonds, which are the ratings that dominate the US corporate segment. The small share of corporate bonds in the foreign official sector's portfolios, therefore, confirms that in addition to market size, liquidity is also key to its foreign asset portfolio management strategy.

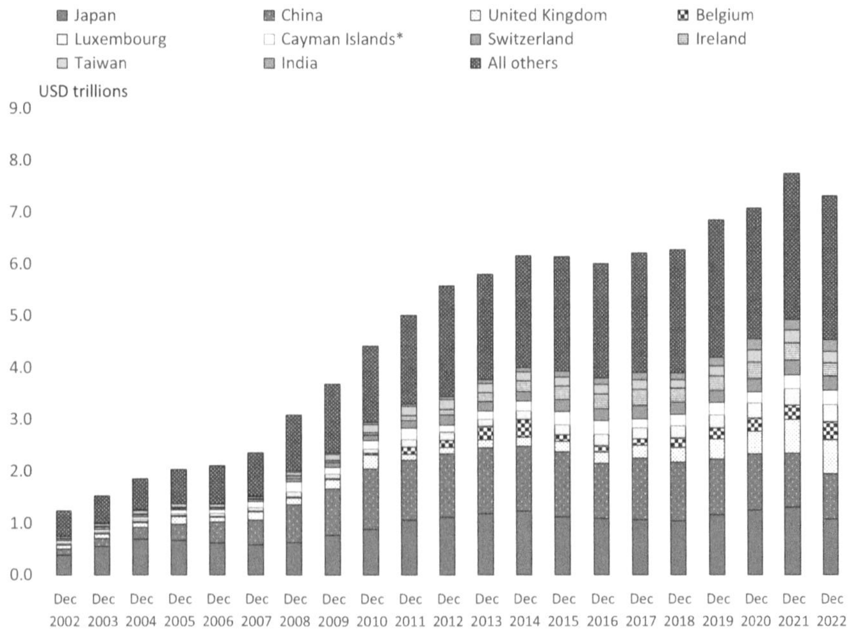

Figure 3.17 Major foreign holders of US Treasury securities

Source: Authors' own compilation based on US Department of the Treasury data.

Holdings at the end of the period.

* For 2002–2011, data presented for the Caribbean Banking Centres.

Prior to 2012, data for the United Kingdom included the Channel Islands and the Isle of Man.

Table 3.4 Holdings of US instruments by foreign official sector, as of June 2017 (%)

Financial Instrument	*Share in the US (%)*	*Share in Fixed Income in the US (%)*
Treasury securities	66	78
Debt securities issued by government agencies	7	8
Debt securities issued by companies	3	4
Bank deposits	8	10
Equity	16	0

Source: McCauley (2019, p. 5).

On the other hand, the larger share of another asset class in the foreign official sector's portfolio, that is debt issued by government agencies, is explained by its greater liquidity. However, the GFC experience demonstrated how the credit difficulties of the issuers of such assets, which increase their credit risk, may determine the demand from the foreign official sector. Despite the support of the federal government (the Paulson plan), central banks (Russia's central bank is a prime example) sold off debt issued by US government agencies that operated in the real estate sector, signalling that for these central banks, they had lost their security value. McCauley (2019, pp. 6–9) offers two explanations for this phenomenon:

1 Concerns about unfavourable domestic public opinion. Central banks were well aware of the scale of the global crisis generated in the property segment,
2 The lack of political agreement on the terms of government support for real estate sector finances in the United States undermined the perception of the large-scale support.

Paradoxically, therefore, despite the support of the federal government between 2008 and 2009, the holding ratio of government-guaranteed debt securities to foreign official sector treasuries fell from 52% in 2007 to 26% in 2009 and 23% in 2010 (McCauley, 2019, p. 7).

The foreign official sector maintains bank deposits in the US banking system in the form of unsecured (outright; about one-third of the total) or secured (reverse repo; about two-thirds of the total) deposits, which tend to be short term (McCauley, 2019, p. 10).

Analysing the impact of foreign demand on global supplier safe assets, the exchange rate comes to the fore. Empirical research by Jiang et al. (2018) confirmed that demand shocks for USD-denominated safe assets are significantly responsible for USD exchange rate volatility. The increase in convenience yields on global provider treasuries due to increased demand is simultaneously reflected in exchange rate appreciation. Jiang et al. attribute more than a 30% appreciation of the USD between 2008 and 2009 to the increased convenience yield of US Treasury debt securities, highlighting the pivotal role played by dominant safe assets and their issuers in the IMS.

Many empirical studies have confirmed the significant impact of foreign official sector demand on long-term interest rates for US Treasury securities. For example, Csonto et al. (2017) showed that a reduction in demand for Treasury securities of USD 100 billion would increase yields by 1.5 and 1.8 basis points for bonds with two- and three-year maturities, respectively. In turn, Sierra (2010) showed that the impact of foreign official sector demand gradually weakens for securities with longer maturities of more than six years. In addition, empirical studies on the impact of foreign demand on the yield of US Treasury securities show that:

1 It can only be temporary (BIS, 2004),
2 Globally, there is a global portfolio effect, which means that the price effect analysed also spills over to other markets (for treasury securities, but also for private issues), in particular to the yields on instruments in the United Kingdom, Japan and the euro-area countries (Gerlach-Kristen et al., 2012).

The previous view of the level of income earned by foreign investors, which includes the average convenience yield, has been challenged by Tabova and Warnock (2021). They found that investment portfolios comprised of US Treasury securities (the dominant part of safe assets) may have slightly higher risks and yields than is commonly believed. Foreign investors, particularly those in the private sector, who invest in US Treasury securities, achieve higher returns than US investors who place capital in the domestic market. The previous literature highlighted that yields on portfolios composed of US Treasury securities are low due to convenience yields (Krishnamurthy and Vissing-Jørgensen, 2007, 2012; Krishnamurthy and Lustig, 2019) and inelastic demand. Research on the returns of these portfolios of non-US investors has shown that they achieve higher returns, as indicated by higher Sharpe ratios than the portfolios of US investors. The above remarks and conclusions provide an important argument in the discussion on convenience yields and safe assets, challenging the prevailing perception of low yields on portfolios of US Treasury securities held by foreign investors.

Notes

1 Golec and Perotti (2017, p. 16) identify three key contractual conditions that strengthen debt security: collateralisation, maturity (time priority) and seniority.
2 The GIIPS countries – Greece, Ireland, Italy, Portugal and Spain.
3 Cf. *Unconventional Monetary Policy*, www.rba.gov (retrieved 14 October 2023).
4 Apart from Japanese government bonds, the BoJ also purchased other kinds of assets, including bills received from banks and Treasury Discount Bills (T-Bills).
5 Under CME, apart from previously used assets, commercial papers, corporate bonds, exchange traded funds and Japanese Real Estate Investment Trusts were also involved.
6 The QE policy was not completely abandoned between the two crisis episodes. This is clearly evident in the case of the ECB, which launched its asset purchase program (APP) in 2014. The stock of Eurosystem APP bonds stood at over EUR 2,500 bn in December 2018, that is the last month of net purchases before resumption in November 2019. Interestingly, before launching the APP, the ECB implemented negative deposit rates, which may discourage investors from selling their assets to the central bank. The BoJ also pursued QE in this period (in the negative interest rate environment). This combination made it introduce the policy of yield curve control to counteract the downward pressure on long-term interest rates that resulted from asset purchases).
7 Several measures of adequacy have been developed. The traditional rule of thumb relates to the number of months that imports can be sustained should all financial inflows in reserve currencies dry up. It is commonly argued that reserves should cover at least three months of imports. Another popular traditional metric (the "Greenspan-Guidotti rule") states that reserves should cover 100% of short-term external debt to insure against rollover risk in the event of a sudden stop in foreign financing. The IMF has recently developed its own risk-weighted reserve adequacy metric.
8 The shares do not add up to 100% due to the Other category (cf. Figure 3.6), which comprises entities such as BIS or the IMF.
9 Why the IMF is among the top holders of gold may raise questions? In fact, it does not require gold to establish confidence. The IMF's gold holdings are the relic of

past rules of the IMS, especially the rule of using gold to back the USD within the Bretton Woods system. When the IMF was founded in 1944, it was envisaged that member countries would make 25% of their initial payments into the fund in gold. As the IMF increased the quotas in subsequent decades, additional payments in gold were made. Member states also used gold to pay interest on loans obtained from IMF. After the collapse of the Bretton Woods system, the IMF's ability to purchase gold or make loans with gold came to an end. However, the fund still can sell gold. Operations of massive gold sales (13 million ounces) took place between 2009 and 2010 to strengthen the Fund's currency holding and boost lending to low-income countries.

10 World Gold Council, data as of July 2023.

11 In his speech, delivered at a press conference in Paris, he said; "No currency can compare, either by a direct or indirect relationship, real or imagined, with gold." Following his speech, between 1965 and 1966, $1.500 million in gold were added to the reserves of France. Although the motives for the dollar-to-gold conversions are widely debated in the literature, it is suggested that the main driver was a fear of the dollar's devaluation.

12 https://www.gold.org/what-we-do/official-institutions/central-bank-gold-agreements/european-central-bank-and-gold (retrieved 26 November 2023).

13 CDS spreads can be used as a country risk indicator because they show the extent to which a premium is demanded for insurance against a country's default risk.

14 Sometimes five broad classes of SWFs are used: (1) stabilisation funds, (2) savings and future generations funds, (3) pensions reserve and other future liabilities funds, (4) reserve investment funds and (5) strategic development sovereign wealth funds (strategic development priority).

15 Bills and bonds issued by the public and private sectors may constitute approximately 80% of a pension fund portfolio in the Czech Republic, whereas in Austria, they may represent less than 1% (OECD, 2021).

16 https://www.sifma.org/resources/research/us-treasury-securities-statistics/ (retrieved 4 August 2023).

17 ECB's estimates for 2020.

18 Japan: Japanese government bonds by type of holders 2022 | Statista (retrieved 21 November 2023).

19 Safe assets are defined broadly, including both credit instruments and non-credit instruments.

20 Refinitiv EIKON data.

References

Afonso, A., Gomes, P., & Rother, P. (2011). Short and long-run determinants of sovereign debt credit ratings. *International Journal of Finance & Economics*, *16*(1). doi:10.1002/ijfe.416

Aizenman, J., & Glick, R. (2009). Sterilization, monetary policy, and global financial integration. *Review of International Economics*, *17*(4), 777–801. doi:10.1111/j.1467-9396.2009.00848.x

Aizenman, J., & Inoue, K. (2012). Central banks and gold puzzles. *NBER Working Paper*, no 17894.

Aizenman, J., Jinjarak, Y., Nguyen, H. T., & Park, D. (2019). Fiscal space and government-spending and tax-rate cyclicality patterns: A cross-country comparison, 1960–2016. *Journal of Macroeconomics*, *60*, 229–252. doi:10.1016/j.jmacro.2019.02.006

Aizenman, J., & Lee, J. (2006). Financial versus monetary mercantilism: Long-run view of large international reserve hoarding? *IMF Working Paper*, no 06/280.
Aizenman, J., & Sun, Y. (2009). The financial crisis and sizable international reserves depletion: From fear of floating to the fear of losing international reserves? *NBER Working Paper*, no 15308.
Al-Hassan, A., Papaioannou, M., Skancke, M., & Chih Sung, C. (2013). Sovereign wealth funds: Aspects of governance structures and investment management. *International Monetary Fund*, *2013*(231).
Allen, W. (2013). *International liquidity and the financial crisis*. Cambridge: Cambridge University Press.
Arrondel, L., Bartiloro, L., Fessler, P., Lindner, P., Mathä, T. Y., Rampazzi, C., ... Vermeulen, P. (2014). How do households allocate their assets? Stylized facts from the Eurosystem household finance and Consumption Survey. *SSRN Electronic Journal*. doi:10.2139/ssrn.2796992
Arslan, Y., & Cantu, C. (2019). The size of foreign exchange reserves. *BIS Papers*, no 104.
Arslanalp, S., & Eichengreen, B. (2023), Living with high public debt. *Paper presented to Jackson Hole Symposium*, August 2023.
Arslanalp, S., Eichengreen, B. J., & Chima, S.-B. (2023). Gold as international reserves: A Barbarous Relic no more? *IMF Working Paper*, WP/23/14.
Bagliano, F. C., Fugazza, C., & Nicodano, G. (2009). *Pension funds, life-cycle asset allocation and performance evaluation, economics*. Available at: https://www.oecd.org/finance/private-pensions/43779973.pdf (Accessed: 15 June 2023).
Baur, D. G., & McDermott, T. K. J. (2009). Is gold a safe haven? International evidence. *Social Science Research Network*. https://doi.org/10.2139/ssrn.1516838
Bertaut, C., Tabova, A., & Wrong, V. (2015). The replacement of safe assets: Evidence from the U.S. bond portfolio. *FRB International Finance Discussion Paper*, no 1123.
BIS. (2004). International banking and financial market developments. Quarterly Review, March 2004.
Bissoondoyal-Bheenick, E. (2005). An analysis of the determinants of sovereign ratings. *Global Finance Journal*, *15*(3). doi:10.1016/j.gfj.2004.03.004
Bogołębska, J. (2020). *Stabilność międzynarodowego system walutowego. Problemy i kierunki reformy*. Łódź: Wydawnictwo Uniwersytetu Łódzkiego.
Bouis Romain. (2019). Banks' holdings of government securities and credit to the private sector in emerging market and developing economies. *Working Paper*, no 2019/224.
Brunnermeier, M., & Huang, L. (2018). A global safe asset for and from emerging markets. *NBER Working Paper*, no 25373.
Centre for Public Impact. (2019). *The Government Pension Fund Global (GPFG) in Norway*. Available at: https://www.centreforpublicimpact.org/
Csonto, B., & Tovar Mora, C. E. (2017). Uphill capital flows and the International Monetary System. *IMF Working Papers*, *2017*(174), doi:10.5089/9781484311424.001
Dąbrowski, M. (2009). Czy akumulacja rezerw walutowych przez kraje Azji Wschodniej jest przejawem internwencjonizmu państwowego? *Ekonomista*, nr 2.
Das, U. S., Mazarei, A., & van der Hoorn, H. (2010). Economics of sovereign wealth funds. *International Monetary Fund*. doi:10.5089/9781589069275.071

Drezner, D. W. (2015). Targeted sanctions in a world of Global Finance. *International Interactions*, *41*(4), 755–764. doi:10.1080/03050629.2015.1041297
ECB. (2008). Technical specifications for the temporary expansion of the collateral framework. [online; retrieved 20 September 2023].
ECB. (June 2009). Monetary and financial developments. *Monthly Bulletin*. Available at: https://www.ecb.europa.eu/pub/pdf/other/mb200906_focus01.en.pdf
ECB. (2019). Trends in central banks' foreign currency reserves and the case of the ECB. *Economic Bulletin*, Issue 7.
ECB. (2021). The role of households in financing government debt in the euro area. *ECB Economic Bulletin, Issue 3/2021*.
ECB. (2023a). *The international role of the euro*. Frankfurt am Main: European Central Bank.
ECB. (2023b). *Euro area insurance corporation statistics - Statistical release, May 2023*.
Erdem, O., & Varli, Y. (2014). Understanding the sovereign credit ratings of emerging markets. *Emerging Markets Review*, *20*. doi:10.1016/j.ememar.2014.05.004
ESRB. (2018). *Sovereign bond-backed securities: A feasibility study*. ESRB, Frankfurt am Main.
Fahri, E., Gourinchas, P., & Rey, H. (2011). Reforming the international monetary system. *NBER Working Paper*, no 22295. National Bureau of Economic Research, Cambridge.
Fang, X., Hardy, B., & Lewis, K. (2023). Who holds sovereign debt and why it matters. *NBER Working Paper Series*, no 30087.
Ferranti, M. (July 2023). Hedging sanctions risk: Cryptocurrency in central bank reserves, PhD thesis, Chapter 2 of Department of Economics, Harvard University, May 3; after: Frankel, J. (2023). Dollar Rivals. *NBER Working Paper*, no 31476.
Gerlach-Kristen, P., McCauley, R., & Ueda, K. (October 1, 2012). Currency intervention and the global portfolio balance effect: Japanese lessons. *BIS Working Paper*, no. 389. Available at SSRN: https://ssrn.com/abstract=2155645
Ghosh, A. (2016). What drives gold demand in central banks' foreign exchange portfolio. *Finance Research Letters*, No. 17.
Golec, P., & Perotti, E. (2017). Safe assets: A review. *Working Paper Series*, no 2035. European Central Bank.
Gourinchas, P. (2017). The fundamental structure of the international monetary system. In M. Bordo, & J. Taylor (Eds.), *Rules for international monetary stability. Past, present, and future*. Stanford, CA: Hoover Institution Press, pp. 169–203.
Gourinchas, P., & Jeanne, O. (2012). Global safe assets. *BIS Working Papers*, no 399.
Government Pension Fund Global Annual Report. (2022). Available at: https://www.nbim.no/
IMF. (2012). *Global Financial Stability Report*. Washington, DC. Available at: https://www.imf.org/external/pubs/ft/gfsr/2012/01/
IFSWF. (2016). Available at: https://www.ifswf.org/
Jiang, Z., Krishnamurthy, A., & Lustig, H. (May 2018). Foreign safe asset demand for US treasurys and the dollar. *AEA Papers and Proceedings*, *108*, 537–541.
Kacperczyk, M., & Maggio, M. (2017). The unintended consequences of the zero lower bound policy. *Journal of Financial Economics*, *123*(1). doi:10.1016/j.jfineco.2016.09.006

Kowalewski, P., & Shirai, S. (2023). A quarter of a century of the BoJ's efforts to overcome liquidity trap. *Bank i Kredyt*, *54*(4), 335–364.

Krishnamurthy, A., & Lustig, H. (2019). Mind the gap in sovereign debt markets: The U.S. treasury basis and the dollar risk factor. *Jackson Hole Economic Symposium*. Available at: http://www.kansascityfed.org/documents/6963/Krishnamurthy_JH2019.pdf

Krishnamurthy, A., & Vissing-Jørgensen, A. (2007). The demand for Treasury debt. *NBER Working Paper*, no 12881.

Krishnamurthy, A., & Vissing-Jørgensen, A. (2012). The aggregate demand for treasury debt. *Journal of Political Economy*, *120*(2), 233–267.

McCauley, R. (2019). Safe assets: Made, not just born. *BIS Working Papers*, no 769.

McDowell, D. (2020). Financial sanctions and political risk in the International Currency System. *Review of International Political Economy*, *28*(3), 635–661. doi:10.1080/09692290.2020.1736126

Megginson, W. L., Malik, A. I., & Zhou, X. Y. (2023). Sovereign wealth funds in the postpandemic era. *Journal of International Business Policy*, *6*, 253–275.

Mitchener, K. J., & Trebesch, C. (2021). Sovereign debt in the 21st century: Looking backward, looking forward. *SSRN Electronic Journal*. doi:10.2139/ssrn.3812076

Nakagawa, S., & Yasui, Y. (2009). A note on Japanese household debt: International comparison and implications for financial stability, in: Household debt: Implications for monetary policy and financial stability. *BIS Papers*, no 46.

OECD. (2019). *China Economic Snapshot*. www.oecd.org/eco/surveys/economic-survey-china.htm

OECD. (2021). Pension Funds in Figures June 2021. Available at: https://www.oecd.org/daf/fin/private-pensions/Pension-Funds-in-Figures-2021.pdf

Pilbeam, K. (1998). *International finance*. Basingstoke: City University, Palgrave Macmillan Business.

PWC Report. (2015). Available at: https://www.pwc.com/gx/en/sovereign-wealth-investment-funds/publications/assets/pwc-the-taxonomy-of-sovereign-investment-funds.pdf

Rathi, S., & Sahay, A. (2022). Central bank gold reserves and sovereign credit risk. *Finance Research Letters*, *45*. doi:10.1016/j.frl.2021.102127

Rzońca, A. (2014). *Kryzys banków centralnych. Skutki stopy procentowej bliskiej zera*. Warszawa: Wydawnictwo C.H. Beck.

Sierra, J. (2010). International capital flows and bond risk premia. *Bank of Canada Working Paper*, no 14.

Slok, T. (2023). *China: Holdings of treasuries have declined $250bn over the past two years, note*. Apollo Global Management.

SWFI. (2023). Available at: https://www.swfinstitute.org/fund-rankings/sovereign-wealth-fund

Tabova, A., & Warnock, F. (2021). Foreign investors and US treasuries. *NBER Working Paper*, no 29313. doi:10.3386/w29313

Taylor, A. M. (2012). The great leveraging. *NBER Working Paper*, no 18290.

The Wealth of Nations: Investment Strategies of Sovereign Wealth Funds. Available at: https://www.toptal.com/finance/market-research-analysts/sovereign-wealth-funds

Unconventional Monetary Policy, Reserve Bank of Australia. Available at: http://www.rba.gov

van den End, J. W. (2019). Effects of QE on sovereign bond spreads through the safe asset channel. *De Nederlandsche Bank Working Paper*, no 647. Available at SSRN: https://ssrn.com/abstract=3436805 or doi:10.2139/ssrn.3436805

Wiśniewski, P. (2017). *The recent investment activity of global sovereign wealth funds*. Wydawnictwo Uniwersytetu Łódzkiego. Available at: https://repozytorium.uni.lodz.pl/xmlui/handle/11089/20536

4 Safe Asset Shortages and the Implications for Financial Stability. In Search of New Sources of Supply

4.1 Financial Stability and Its Link with the Safe Assets Market

There is no single, widely accepted and used definition of financial stability. Schinasi (2004) defines it in terms of the sector's ability to facilitate and improve economic processes, manage risks and absorb shocks. He also argues that it should be considered a continuum, bearing in mind that it is changeable over time and consistent with multiple combinations of the constituent elements of finance (Schinasi, 2004). From the point of view of the market of safe assets, an appropriate definition seems to be the one given by Crockett (1997). He defines financial stability as an absence of instability, the latter being best illustrated as a situation in which economic performance is potentially impaired by fluctuations in the price of financial assets or by an inability of financial institutions to meet their contractual obligations.

In the context of a safe asset market, it is important to acknowledge that the risk of financial instability depends largely on the type of asset. In the case of non-credit safe assets, such as bank deposits, the risk is currently minimised by deposit insurance systems. They prevent the system from a 'bank run' type of crisis; however, the main risk is associated with transforming the run into a systemic banking crisis that involves massive total deposit outflows. Bank runs were the main driver of instability in the banking system in the past, although there have been some recent runs, unusually large and fast, facilitated by the digital channel. Apart from the 2023 case of Silicon Valley Bank, banks have experienced rapid online runs before. The 2007 deposit run on the UK bank Northern Rock took place mostly via the Internet; in effect, the bank lost almost 60% of its retail deposits in 2007, including 20% over just five days. Another example is the UK Internet banking branch of the Icelandic bank Landsbanki. In 2008, during the Icelandic banking crisis, it also suffered a rapid run (IMF, 2023b).

A market of credit-based safe assets is inherently connected with the risk of financial instability. In its extreme, it may take the form of a financial crisis or sovereign debt crisis. In both extremes, it means that the NQA attribute is gone for the market of safe assets (Gorton, 2016, p. 30). The high global demand for safe debt instruments puts unsustainable pressure on the financial system and may threaten its stability. A financial crisis follows

DOI: 10.4324/9781003376538-5

rapid growth in 'private safe assets'. It occurs when holders of short-term debt have doubts about the privately-produced collateral that backs their debt. Meanwhile, a sovereign debt crisis follows a rapid growth in public debt to unsustainable levels. A government may be tempted to reduce high public debt to a sustainable level, for example, through unanticipated inflation. However, relying on surprise inflation to bring down public debts may have adverse financial stability implications (Arslanap and Eichengreen, 2023). A good example is Silicon Valley Bank, which was caught by surprise inflation and the associated interest rate increases. It suffered large losses on its Treasury bond portfolio.

Factors that influence the safe asset market and may contribute to a potential increase in the financial system's fragility include:

- The interest rate level. In a low interest rate environment, private market participants can produce 'safe assets' to exploit arbitrage opportunities, such as small differences in the rates of return on different contracts that are treated as if they were equally safe for some purposes. However, a prolonged low interest rate environment creates uncertainty about future interest rate levels and shocks and the likelihood of a sharp correction in bond yields and associated default risk (Mitchener and Trebesch, 2021, p. 8). On the other hand, a higher interest rate environment creates greater challenges for reliable debt-service payments. In public finances, they may create possible negative feedback loops on investor sentiment (Boone et al., 2022, p. 23). What is more, inflation that accompanies higher interest rates can impose losses on central banks that have engaged in QE and acquired large government bond portfolios.
- Regulation and legislation in the banking system. Insufficient regulation may stimulate the proliferation of shadow banking.

From a financial stability perspective, the composition of government debt is of high importance. The structure of government debt holdings is relevant for the strength of the 'sovereign-bank nexus', the probability and effectiveness of sovereign debt restructuring, income inequality and the size of fiscal multipliers (ECB, 2021). When evaluating the government debt structure on overall financial stability, it is essential to consider the role of domestic and foreign holdings. Additionally, it is crucial to disaggregate the domestic holdings across different categories of savings providers. Feedback loops that originate from domestic holdings and potential cross-border spillovers from foreign government debt holdings are important parameters for financial stability (ECB, 2021).

The interconnectedness of debt and banking sector problems is illustrated by the 'sovereign-bank nexus' (also referred to as the 'diabolic loop' and 'doom loop'), of which the Silicon Valley Bank is a good illustration, up to a point. This phenomenon stems from the fact that the problems of sovereign debt sustainability and financial sector sustainability reinforce each other due to the mutual exposures of the two sectors. If sovereign debt loses value due to the deteriorating creditworthiness of the public sector, the financial sector balance sheets worsen as a consequence of its high exposure to domestic public debt. Weak bank balance sheets, in turn, lead governments to bail them out, increasing government spending and further deteriorating their fiscal position.

The negative feedback loop between banks and sovereigns was particularly strong during the euro-area sovereign debt crisis. This experience demonstrates that the mechanism under analysis can be characterised as a combination of direct and indirect links between the two sectors and the national economy (Véron, 2017, p. 8). Figure 4.1 presents the most important feedback loop channels.

The loop can be triggered either by the deterioration of the performance of the banking sector (e.g. in Ireland and Spain) or the public finance sector (e.g. in Greece). If the first direction of transmission is considered, the course of events may be as follows. The problems of the banking sector, whose stability is perceived as a global public good, may leave the government no choice but to provide assistance (e.g. in the form of direct recapitalisation), which adversely affects the general government deficit and debt statistics. In effect, the country's creditworthiness worsens, which results in downgrades of government bond ratings and an increase in their yields.

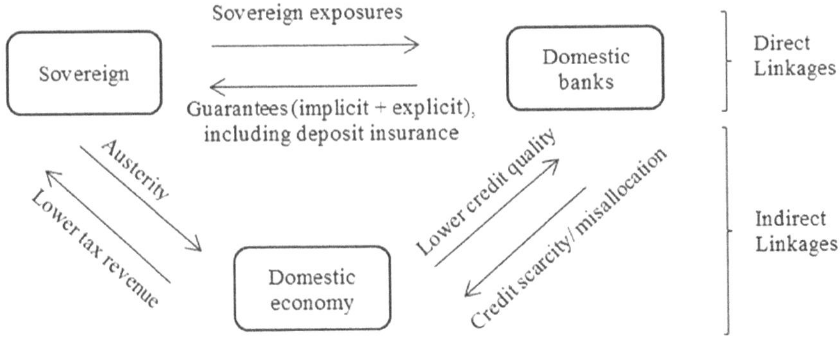

Figure 4.1 Selected contagion channels between banks and sovereigns

Source: Véron (2017, p. 8).

In an extreme scenario, the government may even lose access to market-based financing and be forced to apply to international creditors for assistance. Simultaneously, decreasing government bond prices worsen the balance sheets of banks that hold them in their portfolios. More specifically, banks may find it difficult to pledge these bonds as collateral in operations on the interbank market and with the central bank. The situation of banks is further complicated by the fact that the government's capability to grant additional support is severely curtailed (Stawasz-Grabowska, 2020).

Analysing indirect links, the austerity policy, including tax increases and public expenditure cuts, exerts a negative impact on the income of firms and households. Furthermore, the fall in government bond prices incurs losses for households that use these bonds, and it can also result in an increase in corporate bond yields (as implied by the sovereign ceiling policy[1]). The worsened condition of the real sector contributes to an increase in the share of non-performing loans in total bank loans, reducing their profitability and threatening the stability of the banking sector.

At the same time, there is ample evidence that banking crises are associated with economic slowdowns. When banks are forced to limit lending, entities that rely on bank financing sources will curtail consumption and investment, which will translate into lower tax revenues, compounding the already dire situation of the public finance sector (Dell'Ariccia et al., 2018, pp. 31–32). Therefore, the risk of feedback loops between the government and banks during the crisis is the main argument against large domestic holdings of government debt. This is the main argument in favour of increased funding diversification for governments, reducing the dependence on domestic banks. However, it is argued (e.g. ECB, 2021) that domestic debt holdings represent a more stable investor base. They can also make sovereign default less likely because they increase the incentives for debt repayment as the cost of a potential non-repayment is borne by residents.

In the global economy, with free international movements of capital, the risk of financial instability is strengthened by the asymmetrical position of countries in providing safe assets. The co-existence of economies that are unable to create regional/global safe assets with their providers makes the former prone to sudden outflows of capital (especially in short-term debt funding), while the latter leads to capital inflows. The first group of countries largely comprises emerging economies, while the second one mostly includes advanced economies. A sudden flight into safe-haven currencies, which occurs in periods of heightened uncertainty, can cause large disruptions and sharp currency movements, ultimately leading to financial instability and a crisis (Brunnermeier and Huang, 2018).

One of the signals of enhanced instability is visible in the level of convenience yield. Del Negro et al. (2017) point to the fact that the convenience yield on safe assets has risen by as much as 100 basis points since the turn of the century, which may illustrate a riskier economic, financial and political environment globally.

4.2 Imbalances in the Demand and Supply of Safe Assets

4.2.1 Causes of the Demand–Supply Mismatch of Safe Assets

Despite the lack of unanimity in the academic discussion, concerns have been expressed that the global economy is facing a macroeconomic shortage of safe assets (e.g. Caballero, 2006; IMF, 2012; Caballero et al., 2017; Temprano Arroyo, 2022).

As early as 2001, a study by the Bank for International Settlements (2001) warned that the supply of collateral in the form of instruments with low credit and liquidity risk could not keep up with the surge in collateralised transactions in financial markets. On the other hand, Caballero (2006, 2017) noted that, in 2006, the global economy was characterised by a scarcity of financial assets, which, in his view, was explained by a global excess of savings, low real interest rates, and low inflation. A few years later, the IMF warned: 'The shrinking set of assets perceived as safe, now limited to mostly high-quality sovereign debt, coupled with growing demand, can have negative implications for global financial stability' (IMF, 2012, p. 81).

It is believed that the shortage of safe assets emerged as a consequence of the GFC. However, some believe that its origins go much deeper – even to the Asian crisis of the second half of the 1990s (Blanchard et al., 2016), and that safe asset scarcity, though undoubtedly dynamised as a consequence of the GFC, exemplifies the 'secular stagnation hypothesis'. The IMF also stated that the intensive foreign exchange reserve accumulation policy pursued since the 1990s, combined with the weak level of development of emerging market financial markets, has contributed to the creation of imbalances in the supply and demand for safe assets (IMF, 2012, p. 82). This aspect is accentuated by the 'global imbalances hypothesis' formulated by Caballero (2010). It states that in response to excessive demand for Treasury debt instruments, the private sector began to make up the missing supply, leading to the creation of toxic assets.

Gorton (2016, p. 30) observed that the demand for safe assets has always been an intrinsic feature of the economy and that their scarcity limits transactions and the ability to smooth consumption.

Proponents of the hypothesis of safe asset scarcity in the global economy see the cause of the phenomenon in overlapping processes (ECB, 2021):

1 A decrease in their supply due to:

- A declining pool of sovereign assets of the highest quality (i.e. peripheral EMU countries),
- The cyclical nature of private sector supply,
- The limited capacity of reserve currency issuing countries to create public debt (e.g. the 'Laffer curve' for safe assets, a modern variant of the so-called Triffin dilemma/paradox).

2 An increase in demand – due to:

- Foreign exchange reserve accumulation policies,
- Surplus savings in the global economy,
- Regulatory reforms in the banking and insurance sectors, aimed at increasing the stability of the sectors,
- Asset purchase programmes implemented by central banks since the GFC,
- Demographic factors,
- Global risk aversion.

Thus, the prevailing view is that the shortage of safe assets has taken the form of a permanent, long-term phenomenon whose buildup has been driven by the mixture of factors mentioned above.

The 'global saving glut hypothesis', introduced by Bernanke (2005), is a theoretical concept that explains the factors that contribute to the accumulation of global imbalances, including the US current account deficit. He argued that global savings, combined with underdeveloped financial markets in the countries that accumulate them – mainly China and other emerging markets in Asia – along with favourable oil prices for oil-exporting nations and demographic trends, such as population ageing in Japan, resulted in the exportation of savings to the US financial market. This exerted downward pressure on real interest rates in the US financial market. The USD functions as the global reserve currency. Together with a deep financial market and an attractive expected rate of productivity growth, it provides an incentive to invest global capital in US dollar assets. However, it should be mentioned that in its original version, Bernanke's hypothesis focused on the overall shortage of assets, without 'isolating' the safe-asset component from it.

The role of recirculating capital generated by global imbalances in creating a credit boom was also mentioned by Caballero et al. (2008). They pointed out that countries differ in their ability to create safe financial assets for the value-preserving function. In particular, pledgeable income is limited due to a factor related to some countries' level of development. As they do not have a sufficient pool of local safe assets for portfolio value preservation purposes, they report a demand for foreign assets, thus leading to a current account deficit of a reserve currency issuing country and a decline in the global interest rate.

Blanchard et al. (2016), reflecting on the sources of the shortage of safe assets, mentioned the role of mismatches in savings and investment, which leads to an increasing decline in real interest rates. However, they view this phenomenon mainly through the prism of a poor match for the financial assets provided by real private sector investment and the financial assets sought by those with surplus savings to preserve their value.

The persistent occurrence of a supply and demand mismatch aligns well with the asymmetric role of emerging markets and developed countries in the global economy. The divergence in 'financial depth' between the two groups of countries – despite a gradual narrowing – is still significant. At the end of 2009, emerging market countries accounted for 40% of global GDP, while their contribution to financial depth was less than 20% of that of developed countries (IMF, 2012, p. 112). Furthermore, Prasad (2011) pointed out the stark contrast between the two groups of countries in terms of their contribution to global GDP growth and global debt. These factors have resulted in global net capital flows taking the form of flows from developing to developed countries (uphill capital flows), making China a major global net lender.

Given the asymmetric participation of both groups of countries in the global economy, Caballero and Farhi (2014) assert that the consequences, in the form of demand-supply mismatch, will exhibit a cyclical character. They point out that as a result of the faster economic growth of safe asset consumers compared to their producers, as well as the ageing population in rich countries, the shortage of safe assets will become a 'dormant' phenomenon during booms and intensify during downturns. The cyclical nature may be compounded by the fact that the shortage of safe assets increases global risk aversion after a downturn or financial crisis. Given the nature of safe assets and their characteristics, such as issuers and the links between demand and supply in the market, one can conclude that a key challenge for the stability of the international financial system is ensuring an adequate supply of global public safe assets.

4.2.2 *Consequences of the Demand-Supply Mismatch for Financial Stability*

A shrinking supply of safe assets with an increasing demand can have negative consequences for global financial stability. Gourinchas and Jeanne (2012, p. 2) argued that '[...] macroeconomic shortages of safe assets can create financial instability. Crises, when they occur, further exacerbate the shortage that gave rise to it'. Krishnamurthy and Vissing-Jørgensen (2012) showed empirically that financial crises are more likely to materialise when the stock of US Treasury securities is low and private sector-created debt is high.

Analyses of the relationship between demand-supply mismatch and financial instability, which can lead to financial crises, attempt to isolate the transmission channels of the disturbances and the factors that trigger them. The IMF (2012, pp. 81–83, 112–114) recognises the danger that an increase in the price of safety due to safe asset scarcity may force investors to lower their expectations regarding safety. Forced to compete for access to such assets, investors may move towards higher-risk assets. As a consequence, especially in an environment of an extended period of low interest rates and increased uncertainty in financial markets, changes in risk assessment in terms of investors' perception of the safety of different assets may lead to:

1 Price volatility, including short-term price spikes and the danger of asset bubbles accumulating. Rapid changes in investors' perceptions of asset safety and insufficient differentiation in the risk categorisation of the assets concerned, both in terms of creditworthiness and liquidity, can lead to a 'cliff effect'. This is when the market deteriorates, and a downgrade of assets can result in an automatic reclassification of assets to a lower category and a sudden drop in their price. Such an unintended 'cliff effect' – a lack of sufficient differentiation between the required assets for regulatory purposes – can trigger a sudden drop in prices when certain assets that were previously considered safe lose this status and can no longer meet regulatory criteria. Moreover, the burden of price distortions in the mispriced safety asset segment is borne unevenly among different categories of investors. For example, prudential requirements may lead to greater stress in the market for safe assets with shorter maturities. Therefore, investors who allocate capital in assets with shorter maturities, including banks, in particular, will suffer greater consequences.
2 Herding behaviour.
3 A run-on government debt. Short-term debt, in particular, is vulnerable to a run, threatening a systemic financial crisis (Gorton, 2016, p. 1).

Blanchard et al. (2016) distinguished two channels for the spread of the effects of safe asset scarcity: macroeconomic and microeconomic. In the context of the macroeconomic channel, the scarcity of safe assets and the resulting downward pressure on real interest rates creates a persistent form of the Keynesian liquidity trap named by Caballero and Farhi (2014) a 'safety trap'.[2]

Caballero and Farhi (2014) demonstrated that when there is a sudden increase in demand for safe assets, accompanied by a sharp decrease in supply, the usual mechanisms for equilibration and policy effectiveness weaken (or do not work at all). The standard equilibrating mechanism for the safe asset market involves the central bank reducing real interest rates and using accommodative monetary policy, such as a reduction in nominal interest rates. However, when this shortfall brings the economy close to a dangerous level of near-zero nominal interest rates, this mechanism and the effectiveness of conventional central bank tools are weakened or do not work at all. The only way out of the 'safety trap' is for the market participants to reduce consumption or investment, but the resulting deflationary pressure reduces aggregate demand. The adjustment channel in a 'safety trap' situation, therefore, becomes a deep recession, reducing demand for safe assets through the wealth effect. In the model proposed by Caballero et al. (2017), safe assets are thus held by risk-averse agents unwilling to invest in risky assets; a shortage of safe assets arises when monetary policy is constrained by a zero lower bound.

By lowering their yields relative to other instruments (safety spreads), the scarcity of safe assets creates tensions in the financial system, simultaneously reducing the effectiveness of conventional monetary policy.

The operation of the macroeconomic channel can generate:

- The risk of speculative asset bubbles,
- The misallocation of capital,
- The problem of the credibility of the international monetary and financial system, which arises from the potential insolvency of a sovereign debt-issuing country (the Triffin II paradox).

Because safe assets in the form of debt securities provide a benchmark for risky instruments' expected return, any disturbance in the segment of these assets may have important consequences from the perspective of capital allocation in the economy. A decline in interest rates on government securities as a consequence of a shortage of supply may induce financial intermediaries to underprice all risks.

The efficient functioning of markets may also be adversely affected by accepting lower-quality collateral (if prime collateral becomes too expensive). Such distortions in financial markets can reduce the ability of financial institutions (including investment banks and hedge funds) to secure funding (IMF, 2012, p. 113).

A decrease in the supply of safe assets can also generate financial instability through the emergence of the risk of asset bubbles (Gourinchas and Jeanne, 2012). The importance of this risk was also highlighted by the IMF (2012), which noted that it can be a consequence of increased volatility in financial markets due to uncertainty.

In turn, the microeconomic channel creates an incentive for financial system participants to increase the issuance of safe assets. In fact, as the GFC experience shows, it is very difficult for the private sector to create truly systemic safe assets in sufficient quantity. This is particularly true of the financial sector, whose natural behaviour is to leverage.

Consistent with Caballero's 'safety trap' model, the scarcity of safe assets is also considered a reason for low capital investment and low growth rates in the global economy over the past decade (Financial Times, 2020). The shortage of safe assets became apparent during the GFC. Following a decline in supply from private and public sources in the peripheral EMU countries (as a result of the sovereign debt crisis), the gap was filled by rising US government debt. Under fiscal stimulus between 2007 and 2013, consolidated US government debt (in nominal terms) rose from 57.8% of GDP to 96.9%. This increase was faster than the growth of US dollar foreign exchange reserves, which was largely a consequence of the strong US dollar exchange rate. Thus, as McCauley (2019, p. 2) pointed out, from the point of view of reserve-accumulating countries, there can be no shortage of US Treasury debt to meet their demand during that period.

Table 4.1 Global supply of safe assets as % of global GDP

Safe Assets Category	*GFC*		*COVID-19 Economic Crisis*	
	2007	*2011*	*2019*	*2021*
US government debt	9.2	15.8	232	31.3
American ABS	20.2	–	12.8	13.5
Government debt of EU core countries	4.3	5.0	4.8	6.8
Government debt of EU peripheral countries	2.9	–	3.7	4.5
Government debt of the UK and Japan	14.9	16.9	15.9	18.8
Total gross safe assets	51.5	37.7	60.4	74.9
Central banks' asset purchase operations	2.7	4.3	12.8	19.1
Total safe assets, excluding central bank holdings	48.9	33.5	47.5	55.8

Source: Financial Times (2020).

In the analysis of the consequences of the economic crisis triggered by the COVID-19 pandemic, opinions have been voiced that, paradoxically, the crisis may have alleviated the shortage of safe assets (Financial Times, 2020). This may be due to the increase in the scale of public debt as a consequence of the fiscal expansion being implemented. Additionally, it was noted that in the pandemic economic crisis, unlike in the GFC, the financial system was more insulated from the resulting shocks, so there were no negative consequences of their transmission to the system (Financial Times, 2020).

Table 4.1 presents changes in the supply of various safe asset classes after the GFC and the COVID-19 pandemic crisis, in particular, the scale of the fiscal expansion of the main global provider of these assets, complemented by the fiscal expansion of regional providers. It also shows the increasing role of central banks as investors in the Treasury securities segment.

However, it has also been argued that there may be pressure on the demand for safe assets to rise as a consequence of geo-economic fragmentation (GEF).[3] Aiyar et al. (2023) pointed to the fact that GEF is likely to lead to heightened uncertainty during the fragmentation. Uncertainty can increase households' precautionary savings and their demand for risk-free assets. At the country level, greater uncertainty, together with disrupted international cooperation (which weakens the capacity of the GFSN to support crisis countries and complicates the resolution of a prospective sovereign debt crisis), may prompt a shift towards self-insurance by accumulating higher foreign exchange reserves. Therefore, Aiyar et al. (2023, p. 19) warned: 'At a global level, a synchronised deleveraging by many countries or an increased competition for scarce safe assets can be self-defeating'.

4.3 The Evolution of Public Debt Levels of Safe Asset Supplier Countries

Public debts have soared to unprecedented levels after two 21st-century crisis episodes (the GFC and COVID-19). At the end of 2020, gross US government debt was 134% of GDP, the highest in US history, and well above its previous record – 121% just after World War II in 1946 (Reis, 2022). In 2020, the global average public debt as a ratio to GDP[4] approached 100%, and it is expected to remain above pre-pandemic levels for about half of the world (IMF, 2023a).

What is more, in the last three decades, the increase in public debt has been accompanied by a decrease in debt servicing. In 2021, debt ratios for the median OECD country were historically high, and the ratio of interest payments to GDP was historically low, as global interest rates were falling faster than debt accumulation (Boone et al., 2022).

These high levels of public debt are more of a problem for emerging markets than for most major advanced economies, as the latter are subject to structural sources of demand, making them much more manageable (Arslanalp and Eichengreen, 2023). However, problems with the sustainability of debt across reserve currency issuing countries, illustrated best by Triffin Dilemma II and 'the Laffer curve', may cause their safe assets to be re-valuated as unsafe. Thus, this group of countries must take care to avoid actions that could bring about such a scenario (Arslanalp and Eichengreen, 2023).

When assessing the sustainability of increased public debts, it is crucial to look through the creditors' base to ascertain which investor group absorbs the rising debt levels most. To this end, Fang et al. (2023) constructed a data set of sovereign debt holdings by foreign and domestic banks, non-bank private investors (non-financial corporations, pensions and insurance companies, households and other financial institutions largely represented by investment funds) and official investors for 95 countries over 20 years. They demonstrated that private non-bank investors, mostly investment funds, absorb disproportionately more sovereign debt supply than other investors. Thus, when the supply of government debt increases, it is mostly investment funds that play a significantly larger role than other categories of investors in absorbing this expansion. Furthermore, creditor groups are particularly responsive to changes in yields, resulting in a higher elasticity of demand compared to other groups. Counterfactual analysis of emerging market sovereigns shows that a 10% increase in debt leads to a 6.7% increase in costs but an out-sized 9% increase if non-bank investors are absent. This observation highlights the dependence of emerging market governments on the sentiments of non-bank investors.

The analysis of advanced countries shows that debt ratios remained flat in the run-up to the GFC; they then rose sharply between 2008 and 2014. As part of their management of the global financial crisis, developed countries embarked on fiscal expansion (essentially to recapitalise banks, take over the debts of distressed financial institutions and introduce programmes to stimulate demand recovery). It was reflected in an increase in their public debt-to-GDP ratios, thus raising concerns about its level, given the ageing populations and low levels of economic growth in these countries (Cecchetti et al., 2010). This period was followed by modest fiscal consolidation until the COVID-19 crisis, when debt ratios soared again. However, as indicated by Arslanalp and Eichengreen (2023, p. 4), the share of advanced countries that experienced sharp increases in the COVID-19 crisis is lower than during the GFC crisis, when more than 70% of advanced countries experienced debt spikes.

Mitchener and Trebesch's (2021, pp. 6–7) analysis of the evolution of public debt in developed countries points out that the problem of excess levels concerns two aspects that determine the extent of possible fiscal expansion (fiscal space):

1 Its sustainability, which is understood as the distance between its current level and the attainable limit,
2 'Debt overhang', which results from a negative correlation between debt levels and growth, ultimately leading to a low investment rate.

Despite the lack of unanimity regarding the threshold value at which the negative impact of excessive debt on growth is triggered, empirical justification can be found for a level above 90% of GDP (Reinhart and Rogoff, 2010). Empirical estimation of the limits of the debt sustainability level yields mixed results; however, an interpretation can be found that it is in the range of 150%–250% of GDP (Mendoza and Ostry, 2008). Studies also show that when public debt exceeds a certain (country-specific) upper threshold, interest rates can rise sharply, leading to debt unsustainability. This alludes to the concept of a self-fulfilling crisis (Mitchener and Trebesch, 2021, p. 8).

Figure 4.2 shows the ratio of general government (g.g.) debt to GDP in major advanced economies, including the reserve currency issuers and the Group of Seven (G7) members between 2001 and 2022. It shows that the ratio is the highest in Japan (over 250%), and it has increased compared to other countries since 2001. This indicates that Japan's fiscal potential may (soon) be exhausted, meaning that further debt growth may be considered unsustainable by investors. Considering the countries from the euro area, Germany is the only one with a ratio below 100%; it actually hovers around the threshold of 60%, deemed as sustainable in line with the Maastricht Treaty convergence criteria. In contrast, following fiscal stimulus during the COVID-19 pandemic, g.g. debt to GDP exceeded 140% in Italy and 110% in France in 2022. Meanwhile, US debt has more than doubled since the beginning of the 21st century, when it accounted for around 50% of GDP; it is deemed unlikely that the ratio will fall in the foreseeable future (Arslanalp and Eichengreen, 2023, p. 3). The largest scope for increasing debt is found in Switzerland, where it stands at around 40% of GDP.

Figure 4.3 shows China's g.g. debt-to-GDP ratio (2001 and 2022 levels) against the reserve currency issuers. Its debt-to-GDP ratio was the lowest in 2001 and one of the lowest in 2022. Hence, Chinese public debt appears low and sustainable (OECD, 2019). What follows is the conclusion that China can play the role of a global safe asset issuer in the future, as there is both the potential (fiscal capacity) and the economic rationale to increase debt

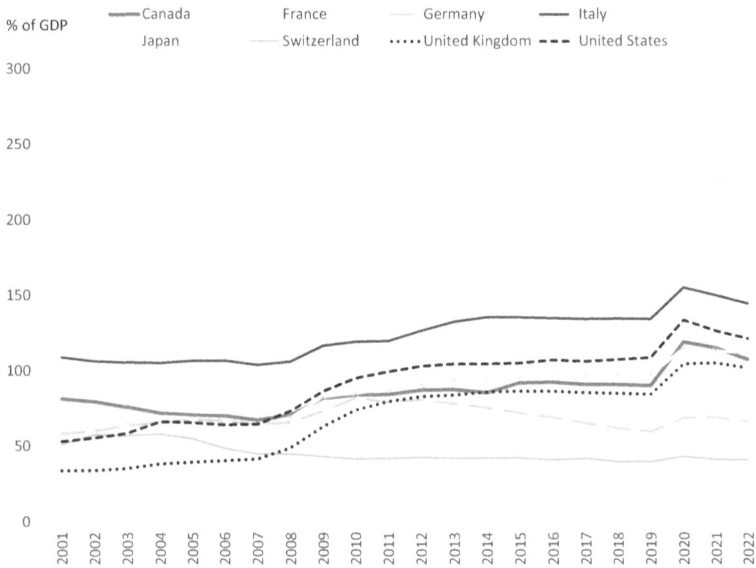

Figure 4.2 General government debt of major advanced economies, 2001–2022 (% of GDP)

Source: Own compilation based on World Economic Outlook IMF data.

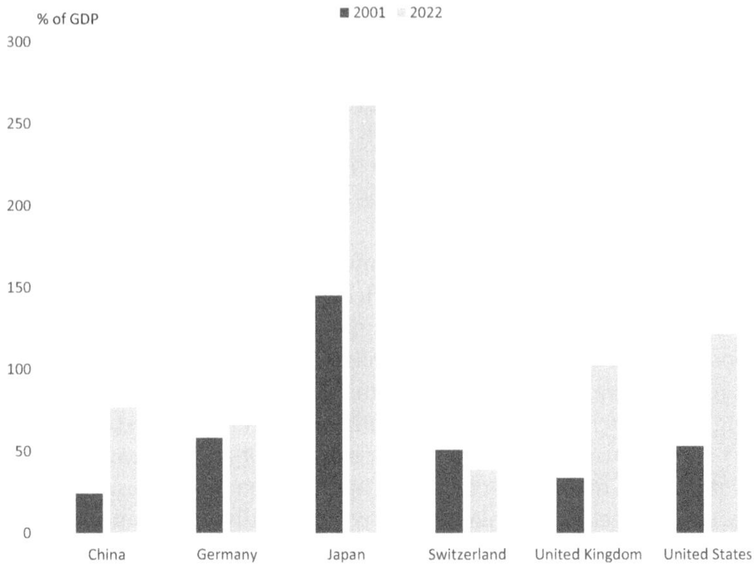

Figure 4.3 China's public debt compared to reserve currency issuers in 2001 and 2022 (% of GDP)

Source: Own compilation based on World Economic Outlook IMF data.

through the issuance of government debt instruments. At the same time, it should be noted that over the analysed period, Chinese debt grew at the fastest rate – it increased more than three times.

In light of the 'safe assets Laffer curve', a significant increase in debt in reserve currency issuing countries may indicate limited potential for economies traditionally seen as providers of safe assets to increase their supply. At the same time, the data clearly show that debt levels in China remain relatively low.

Increases in debt ratios have led to calls for debt reductions (IMF, 2023a). It is argued that in order to achieve a lasting reduction in debt ratios, fiscal consolidation is essential. However, it must be adequately timed (e.g. during economic expansions) and appropriately designed (e.g. more expenditure-than revenue-based in advanced countries). Furthermore, the positive effects of fiscal consolidation should be accompanied by growth-enhancing structural reforms and strong institutional frameworks. At the same time, since fiscal consolidation tends to slow GDP growth, consolidations, on average, have negligible effects on debt ratios (IMF, 2023a).

Taking into consideration the aforementioned conditions, it is broadly accepted that high levels of public debt are not going to be reduced in the foreseeable future. Arslanalp and Eichengreen (2023) are sceptical about the possibilities of debt reduction for the following reasons:

a There is limited scope for large, sustained primary surpluses. Primary budget surpluses achieved through a combination of tax increases and spending cuts will be difficult to sustain at a level and duration needed to significantly reduce debt ratios. To make it work, political solidarity at the national level and strong economic growth are essential. In the discussion on why debt consolidation in the US is harder today than a few decades ago, they point to the fact that the 1990s in the US were characterised by faster economic growth and less economic polarisation (Arslanalp and Eichengreen, 2023, p. 17).
b Real interest rates have trended downward to very low levels, and it is hard to foresee them falling lower. In effect, favourable interest rate–growth rate differentials to reduce debt ratios in an accounting sense would be impossible to achieve in the face of slower, not faster, anticipated growth.
c The inflation trajectory does not translate into reducing public debt.[5] Although an anticipated increase in inflation may reduce debt ratios in the short run by raising the denominator of the debt-to-GDP ratio, in the long run, it is likely to raise interest rates and shorten maturities. At both horizons, these effects are unlikely to be economically important.
d Any measures of financial repression (e.g. statutory ceilings on interest rates) are less feasible today than in the past, mainly due to investors' behaviour, as they are capable of lobbying against them and the high level of financial liberalisation.

Boone et al. (2022) pointed to the role of the following structural trends that can put significant upward pressure on public finances in the long run:

1. Ageing populations. This is associated with rising public expenditures on pensions, health and long-term care. What is more, this factor also has an indirect impact on public finances via its effect on GDP. Ageing populations will lead to a slowdown in the effective labour force, reducing GDP per capita growth.
2. Climate change and the transition to a low-carbon economy. This raises expenditure on investment in clean energy infrastructure, R&D support, and subsidies. Apart from this direct influence, climate change is likely to affect public finances indirectly through reduced short-term growth.

Other structural trends that may bring challenges to fiscal policy include the following:

1. Continued productivity slowdowns. They can undermine tax revenues, thus threatening debt sustainability along and improved living standards.
2. A continued rise in within-country income and wealth inequalities. They can add pressure on government social programmes and undermine growth and political stability.
3. Accelerated digitalisation. This can require new investments in technology and human capital, the reorganisation of businesses and governments, and a redesign of welfare systems. On the other hand, however, it can improve productivity.

4.4 Mechanisms of Safe Asset Creation and the Stability of the International Monetary System

The contemporary literature emphasises the importance of safe assets for the stability of the international monetary system. Gourinchas (2017) writes explicitly that the fundamental function of the IMS is to allocate scarce safe assets across countries. On the demand side, emerging market countries do not need their holdings of foreign exchange reserves assets to grow with their nominal GDP growth. On the supply side, the US government does not need to have a monopoly in producing safe assets denominated in the US dollar (McCauley, 2019, p. 1). As a consequence, a natural space for supplier diversification arises, both from the new category of countries and from the new currency of denomination. Thus, the emergence of a multi-polar system of safe asset creation can be linked to the move away from a mono-currency system based on the supremacy of the USD to a system based on different currencies acting as international currencies.

The link between the supply of global safe assets and the currency composition of reserves was empirically confirmed by Caballero (2006) and

Caballero et al. (2017). Such a direction for the evolution of the IMS would be a natural response to contemporary trends in the system, where the status of an international currency becomes largely based on the willingness and ability of the issuer to pursue accommodative monetary and fiscal policies to become a net global supplier of safe assets. Relating the determinants of safe asset creation to the assumptions of chartalism, it is important to recognise that foreign confidence in the nominal safety of an international currency is more important than confidence in the stability of its real value: 'the international currency issuer must be the world's provider par excellence of safe assets whose nominal payment needs to be guaranteed and contain no default risk' (Vermeiren, 2019, p. 55).

Another argument in favour of diversifying the IMS was expressed by Eichengreen et al. (2018). They pointed out that due to changes in market technology, the digitalisation of currency trading has reduced transaction costs, contributing to the ease of making transactions, the declining importance of scale and network effects, and the diversification of the IMS while probably embracing emerging market currencies. In the view of Aiyar et al. (2023), the tendency to diversify away from traditional reserve assets – accelerated by digitalisation – should be perceived as the outcome of the fragmentation of policy-driven geo-economics. Faced with GEF, with less international risk sharing and higher macroeconomic volatility, countries are looking to mitigate fragmentation risk.

Considering that an increase in global providers of public safe assets would address the shortage of safe assets, the question arises about the consequences of such a multipolar system of their creation. Views and arguments prevail in favour of the pro-stability (from the point of view of the IMS and the provision of an adequate supply of international liquidity) consequences of increasing the sources of creation and increasing competition among issuers. However, Gourinchas and Jeanne (2012, p. 39) see an element of risk in such an action. They argue that as a result of arbitrage among safe assets, volatility in financial markets may increase rather than decrease. This is a key argument for the involvement of the IMF, in coordination with national monetary authorities, in the management of safe asset creation by global providers.

In the context of the evolution of the IMS, including currency substitution and the internationalisation and de-internationalisation of currencies, given the role of the official sector in purchasing US dollar-denominated treasury securities, a more diversified system may help to mitigate the shortage of safe assets. A good measure of the degree to which diversification in the IMS is underway is to analyse the evolution of the process in relation to the portfolio of central bank reserves.

In addition to the diversification of instruments that comprise investment portfolios (debt versus equity), currency diversification is taking place in the policy of foreign reserves. Its slow pace is due to the way the IMS functions, including its inertia, which is reflected in a lag in currency portfolio changes in relation to economic and political events and the powers of reserve currency issuers.

The 'big four' play an important role in the global structure of foreign exchange reserves, with their respective shares: USD 58.4%, EUR 20.5%, JPY 5.5% and GBP 4.9%.[6] In the role of reserve currency, the supremacy of the USD is still apparent, even though its share in global reserves has been gradually declining in recent decades. Indeed, while the USD's share of global reserves was 75% in the late 1970s, at the beginning of the 21st century, it was around 70%, and two decades later, it had fallen to less than 60% (Bogołębska, 2020, pp. 60–62). Despite the dominance of the USD in the reserve currency function, the contemporary IMS is widely considered to be a bipolar system, with the EUR being the second international currency that plays an important role in the reserve function. The fluctuations in the share of the USD and EUR in the reserve currency function, presented in Figure 4.4, largely reflect passive diversification; that is it results from fluctuations in the USD/EUR exchange rate.

A policy of intentional diversification of the currency structure of reserves (active diversification) can be observed in the decline in demand for the euro after 2011 as a consequence of the EMU debt crisis. This trend in demand for the EUR shifted after 2018, which can be explained by concerns about

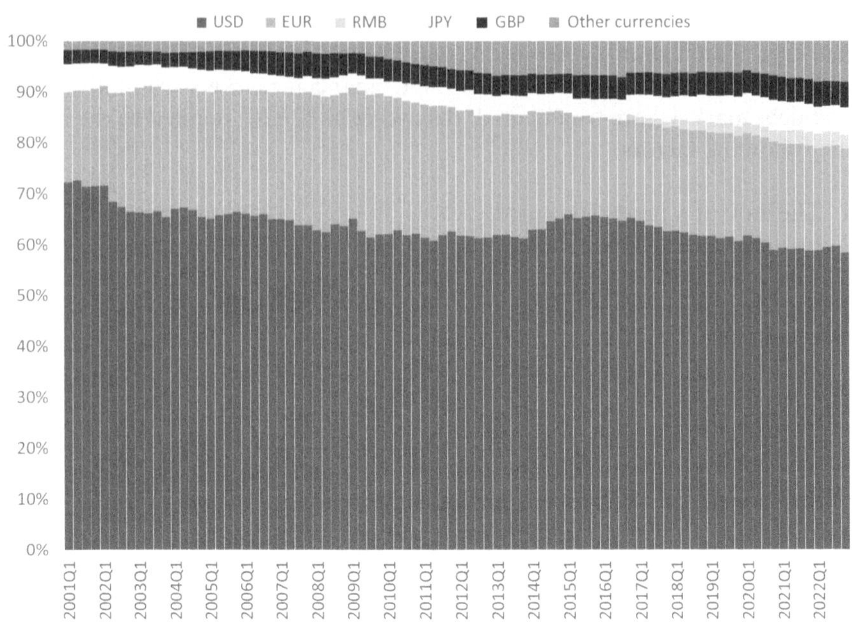

Figure 4.4 World currency composition of official foreign exchange reserves (shares of allocated reserves)

Source: IMF COFER (access: 10 June 2023).

international trade tensions and sanctions in which the United States was actively involved. An interesting example of an active policy of diversifying foreign exchange reserves is the strategy of the Central Bank of Russia, which has increased the share of EUR and RMB, while reducing the USD. With a share of up to 32.3%,[7] the EUR is the main reserve currency in its reserve portfolio, followed by the USD (16.4%) and RMB (13.1%) (Bank of Russia, 2022, p. 6).

This potential increase in the use of the euro in the reserve currency function, and (in line with the hypothesis of network externalities, although it is disputed in the contemporary literature) also in other functions of an international currency, could become an important catalyst for the perception of instruments issued in this currency as global safe assets.

A factor that supports the potential of the euro to increase its use in international currency functions is the strong position of the EMU as a global exporter. Gopinath and Stein (2018) hypothesised that the invoicing and payment function of the currency should translate into the use of the currency to issue safe assets. Ilzetzki et al. (2020) pointed out that a quarter of global exports originate from euro-area countries (by comparison, the corresponding figure for the United States is 9%), indicating a weaker – relative to potential – use of the currency in international currency functions.

However, there are factors, both economic and non-economic, that have limited the euro's role in international functions and that may weaken the perspectives for its future internationalisation. The integration of financial markets, which should ensure diversification of capital raising sources and investments, is still not finished. In fact, financial markets (capital markets and debt markets) are fragmented. Ilzetzki et al. (2020) pointed to the role of the following factors:

1 The lack of a financial centre,
2 Its limited geopolitical reach,
3 The dominance of the United States and China in technology research,
4 The comparatively scarce supply of (safe) euro-denominated assets,
5 The ECB's lack of policy clarity, that is its policy of expanding its arsenal of credit facilities to European banks and sovereigns since the times of the GFC.

In particular, they analysed the function of an anchor currency. The choice of the euro as a stabilising nominal anchor by many economies in the region (with EMU countries, the CFA franc pegged to the euro, and a number of Eastern European countries with crawling pegs to the euro) makes it 'only' a regional currency compared to the global reach of the USD. The perspective of a freely floating renminbi and the de-anchoring of Asia from the USD, as a consequence, may enhance the position of the Chinese currency, further weakening the role of the EUR.

Another phenomenon in the composition of foreign exchange reserves has appeared, namely the increasing role of non-traditional reserve currencies (which are defined as currencies other than the 'big four'). The share of nontraditional reserve currencies rose from negligible levels at the turn of the century to 11% of total official reserves in 2022 (Figure 4.4). The Chinese RMB accounts for about one-quarter of this increase, while non-SDR currencies (the Australian Dollar, Canadian Dollar, Swiss Franc, Korean Won, Swedish Krona, Singapore dollar, Norwegian Krone, Danish Krone, New Zealand dollar and Hong Kong dollar) make up the remaining three-quarters. The above trend may alleviate the problem of a shortage of safe assets in the future.

Arslanalp et al. (2022) pointed to three factors that contribute to the growing role of nontraditional reserve currencies:

1 Growing market liquidity,
2 The active management of foreign exchange reserves as an effect of high levels of accumulated reserves,
3 The pursuit of yield strategies in central bank management policies amid yields on bonds issued by the governments of the 'big four' falling toward zero ('secular stagnation').

Changes in the currency composition of foreign exchange reserves can be attributed to the GEF phenomenon, in addition to the growing role of EME countries. The prospective transformation of trade, finance, and global value chains will surely influence transactional demand, invoicing and the international usage of currencies. As Aiyar et al. (2023, p. 20) put it, an accelerated transition towards cross-border trade in national currencies, as well as a redirection of global value chains towards geopolitically aligned countries, may reduce the demand for the USD as an international currency. For example, Kazakhstan and the Kyrgyz Republic hold Russian rubles in their portfolio of foreign exchange reserves due to their close relationship with Russia (Arslanalp et al., 2022).

Another factor that potentially diminishes the role of USD and EUR as international currencies and influences the reserve management policy of countries that do not have friendly relations with the US and EU is the policy of sanctions and freezing foreign exchange reserves. Examples of freezing foreign exchange reserves include Afghanistan, Iran, Libya, North Korea, Syria and Venezuela. However, the freezing of USD 300 billion of the Russian Central Bank's (RCB) foreign reserves as a consequence of Russia's invasion of Ukraine is believed to have stimulated diversification policies worldwide (Muhleisen, 2022). Indeed, the number of countries facing sanctions from the United States and its allies (the EU, Japan and the United Kingdom) rose from 10% in the early 90s. to 30% of all countries (Sharma, 2023). Western powers embarking on sanctions against such a big player as Russia was a wake-up call for many other countries, and BRICS in particular, that the weaponisation of the dollar can be used against any economy.

When analysing trends in changes in the global currency composition of reserves in conjunction with the development of reserve demand, Aizenman et al. (2019) showed that the phenomena taking place are comprehensive and complex:

1 Emerging markets with a high share of trade with the 'big four' countries and debt issued in their currencies maintain high levels of foreign exchange reserves. However, for these countries, maintaining a higher level of accumulated reserves relative to GDP encourages them to diversify their currency structure from the 'big four' currencies. Given the key role of these countries in the accumulation of foreign exchange reserves in recent decades, this conclusion is a good proxy for the prospects of IMS diversification.
2 Developed countries show a different propensity to diversify than emerging markets: the higher the level of reserves, the greater the concentration of their structure on the currencies of the 'big four'.
3 The presence of SWFs in a country significantly affects the composition of reserves portfolio: developed countries with SWFs with high asset values tend to diversify and move away from the 'big four' currencies. However, the presence of these entities in emerging markets does not affect the share of the 'big four' currencies in reserves.
4 Commodity-exporting countries tend to diversify their reserve portfolio away from the 'big four' currencies when their terms of trade improve. Given the significance of this group of countries in reserve accumulation processes, a similar conclusion to the first case can be drawn.
5 An analysis of diversification processes during the GFC period shows that the increasing scarcity of safe assets is prompting countries to increase the role of the 'big four' currencies in their portfolio composition. In better economic conditions, the concentration on the 'big four' currencies decreases. This conclusion provides empirical confirmation of the flight-to-safety attribute of safe assets.

4.5 Alternative Sources of Safe Asset Supply

The assumption that only US fiscal deficit can provide USD-denominated global safe assets is based on a narrow understanding of the creation of this asset class. This perspective overlooks the potential for increasing the asset base with public involvement, such as mortgages, export credits and development loans. Both the US central government and other governments with recognised credibility can provide such support (government backing) and thus enable the creation of safe assets without increasing fiscal deficits (Bordo and McCauley, 2017). An example of this would be the 2008 US government recapitalisation of both government-sponsored enterprises (GSEs) and major national banks.

Government support for the liabilities of entities in such sectors may indicate that the government does not need to have a monopoly on creating safe assets. Nevertheless, it must be able to control the supply of assets of these institutions, thereby transforming them into a safe asset category (McCauley, 2019, p. 4). However, empirical experience has shown that, in this case, government action does not translate into increased demand for such asset classes.

The search for ways to increase the supply of safe assets alternatively suggests the potential use of financial engineering, exemplified by a risk-pooling system among quasi-safe public entities. This approach allows the share of safe debt to be increased within existing public assets (Caballero et al., 2017, p. 39). The issuance of bonds based on the willingness and ability of a group of countries to jointly honour payment obligations can provide a valuable channel for the creation of public safe assets. By sharing creditworthiness, such assets could reduce the likelihood of sharp increases in borrowing costs as a result of country-specific events. However, such assets would only be perceived as safe to the extent that the framework within which they were issued ensured the fiscal sustainability of all the countries. Moreover, while such assets would increase the amount of safe assets available to investors (in terms of credit risk and market liquidity), sovereigns whose creditworthiness was higher than the pooled credit quality underlying the new bond would face higher borrowing costs (IMF, 2012, p. 116).

Brunnermeier and Huang (2018) pointed out that a pooling solution linked to the ring-fencing of tranches for the common debt market may be particularly appropriate for the creation of regional safe assets, especially for emerging market countries. They demonstrated that the current strategy of unilateral insurance through the accumulation of foreign exchange reserves (the buffer approach), which in fact leads to flight-to-safety destabilising capital flows (uphill) for the IMS, should be replaced by a regional strategy that allows for the redirection of these flows (the rechannelling approach). There should be a redirection of demand for developed countries' public debt towards their own (regional) public debt instruments, thus creating a self-stabilising mechanism for capital flows. At the same time, they acknowledge that a solution based on separating two tranches from the debt pool, the 'senior bond' and the 'junior bond', may be an optimal solution given the heterogeneity of countries that characterise this group of economies, as it exploits diversification benefits. Separating the two tranches could prove particularly important in a negative shock environment. This would allow the 'senior bond' tranche to complement the pool of regional, and perhaps prospectively global, safe assets. Indeed, any losses resulting from a partial insolvency would first be absorbed by the 'junior bond'. Only when this tranche covers the losses would the 'senior bonds' begin to absorb the losses. This means that bonds from this tranche would find it much harder to lose their safe asset status. This concept, inspired by the search for a common debt mechanism within the EMU environment (cf. Section 4.6.2), is called Global Sovereign Bonds (GloSBies).

An example of regional integration mechanisms aimed at producing public safe assets is the experience of Asian countries with a common bond market. Established in 2005, the Asian Bond Fund 2 (ABF 2) is a pooling of bonds issued in 11 countries. However, it is not based on tranching; thus, there is no senior bond concept to act as regional safe assets.[8] Its main goal is to improve liquidity in the major government bond markets.

Despite the empirically well-established awareness of the limited substitutability of private versus public assets in the role of safe assets, the importance of enhancing the ability of the private sector to supplement the supply of these assets is also highlighted.

In the IMF's (2012) view, private markets can create safe assets by combining existing instruments that have inherently higher risk and hedging strategies. To ensure that such products perform the functions of safe assets, some new measures and solutions are needed:

1 A surveillance system,
2 Better issuers incentives (e.g. giving the issuer compensation for creating longer-term assets),
3 Relevant regulations,
4 Improved communication with the markets, ensuring that the instruments are understood and that the information available about them allows them to be priced and risk-managed.

Detailing the set of recommendations above, the IMF sees room to incentivise the creation of private safe assets, for example, through appropriate structures and regulations for covered bonds or by establishing sound rules for securitisation practices (IMF, 2012).

McCauley (2019, p. 5) asserted that, in addition to US entities, issuers of US dollar safe assets are non-US entities (e.g. banks, domestic and supranational public institutions). When analysing the composition of the foreign official sector's holdings of US dollar-issued assets outside the United States, he showed that in 2017, 48% were non-US bonds and 52% were non-US deposits. At the same time, each of these positions accounted for 8% of global fixed-income instruments. Thus, while fixed-income instruments issued by US entities accounted for 84% of assets held by the official foreign sector, instruments issued in US dollars by non-US entities accounted for 16%. The off-shore US dollar bank deposit market may, therefore, represent a promising source of safe assets for the official sector.

Similarly, the USD-denominated bond market issued by reputable non-US entities (i.e. governments and government agencies) can substitute for US government bonds in the asset portfolio of the foreign official sector. The role of US dollar bonds issued by supranational institutions (e.g. the European Investment Bank, World Bank, Kreditanstalt für Wiederaufbau, Oesterreichische Kontrollbank Aktiengesellschaft) should also be highlighted.

McCauley (2019, p. 12) pointed out that the age of instruments issued by such institutions held by the foreign official sector fluctuates around 50%. In particular, he draws attention to the large share (over 70%) of this sector in the primary market purchase of bonds issued by the ESM.

Unilateral action resulting from the transformations that take place in the global economy may also become an important channel to increase the supply of public safe assets. Given the increasing role of emerging markets countries in global GDP, and the gradual increase in the 'financial depth' of these countries, with their small share in global debt, they represent a significant and promising area for the creation of safe assets.

An increase in the ability of emerging market countries to provide public safe assets depends on the design of their fiscal policies and the development of their domestic financial infrastructure, including regulation, clearing and payment systems, and transparency of issuance procedures. These measures are necessary to support the development of local and national markets for public debt instruments. In the long term, the implementation of the above measures can facilitate the use of these assets in the role of safe assets, both in the national, regional and global space (IMF, 2012, p. 116).

For emerging markets countries, the benchmarking function of government debt instruments is crucial for the development of local financial markets. The existence of a liquid government bond market of various maturities is seen as a prerequisite for the development of other financial market segments, including derivatives and corporate bond markets (IMF, 2012, p. 103).

4.6 The EMU

4.6.1 Fiscal Frameworks within the EMU and Its Evolution

For the EMU countries, joining the euro area meant giving up autonomous monetary and exchange rate policies, although their competences to conduct fiscal policy remained at the national level. However, this also meant that no central fiscal authority capable of imposing taxes, making financial transfers among countries, absorbing asymmetric shocks, or rescuing financial institutions or strategic enterprises with the use of public funds was established. Hence, countries were fully responsible for the sustainability of their debt, which, due to the prohibition of monetary financing, they issued in currency beyond their direct control (De Grauwe and Ji, 2018).

Maintaining fiscal prudence was based on two pillars: a dedicated legal framework and the disciplinary role of financial markets. Within the former, the following played a crucial role:

1 Fiscal Maastricht criteria. These criteria established limits for general government deficit and debt as a ratio to the country's GDP (no more than 3% and 60%, respectively).

2 The stability and growth pact (SGP). It envisages sanctions for non-compliance with fiscal discipline rules.
3 The prohibition of monetary financing (Article 123 of the Treaty on the Functioning of the European Union (TFUE)).
4 The prohibition of privileged access of public authorities to financial institutions (Article 124 of the TFUE).
5 The no-bail-out clause (Article 125 of the TFUE).

Regarding the disciplinary role of financial markets, it was assumed that countries would care about the best possible macroeconomic fundamentals, as they translate into more favourable financing conditions.

The GFC demonstrated that both of these pillars did not meet the expectations placed on them. For example, the SGP proved to be toothless as early as 2003, when the two largest Member States, France and Germany, circumvented the Commission's recommendations to reduce structural deficits. This non-compliance resulted in the imposition of sanctions (Collignon, 2004). This event set a very bad precedent for other EMU countries, signalling that they could also act against the spirit of the Pact.

In the pre-crisis years, which coincided with the Great Moderation, market discipline appeared dormant. Empirical studies that investigated the role of macroeconomic fundamentals and non-fundamental factors in determining sovereign bond spreads for euro-area countries before and after the outbreak of the GFC corroborate this observation. They also showed that the impact of the two categories changed over time. In the pre-crisis period, investors paid scant attention to differences in variables reflecting the economic situation, such as fiscal standing and international competitiveness, considering bonds issued by euro-area countries as close substitutes. Instead, variables that approximated the global aversion to risk (for example, VIX) proved to be significant (Oliveira et al., 2012; De Grauwe and Ji, 2013; Giordano et al., 2013).

However, during the crisis period, the role of macroeconomic fundamentals increased significantly. Following the revelation of Greece's fiscal problems, investors divested sovereign bonds of the peripheral euro-area countries in response to problems identified in other countries form this group, reflecting the 'wake-up-call contagion' (Beirne and Fratzscher, 2013). At the same time, somewhat in opposition to the spirit of the SGP, European banking regulations allowed for the application of a risk weight of zero to debt issued by all EU countries. This approach created the false impression that public sector bonds of all EU member states are equally safe (van Riet, 2017).

Before the crisis, capital flowed from the core euro-area countries to the peripheral countries. As long as the latter economies prospered and saw asset prices increase, market participants paid little attention to their macroeconomic imbalances, which were mainly external and fiscal. This was evident in increasing current account deficits across all peripheral countries and general government debt-to-GDP ratios well above the threshold of 60% in Greece, Italy, and Portugal. Sovereign bonds issued by euro-area countries were treated as similar, that is of high safety and liquidity and an NQA attribute. This similarity translated into the compression of spreads with regard to German bunds soon after the inception of the euro area (Figure 4.5). However, some economists suggest that, rather than being dormant, investors implicitly assumed that – due to possible spillover effects – in the unlikely event of one country defaulting, the other countries and/or institutions (the ECB, in particular) would have no choice but to intervene and organise a bailout (Eijffinger et al., 2015).

With the onset of the GFC, there was a change in the perception of sovereign-specific default risk. Sovereign assets of the most vulnerable countries abruptly lost their safe status and began to be perceived as risky. van Riet (2017) called this phenomenon a regime switch, from NQA mode to information sensitivity or even hyper-sensitivity. As the first tensions emerged, the German bund proved to be the 'truly safe' cornerstone of the euro-area financial system and a safe haven, while investors started to shed GIIPS assets. This process accelerated around 2009 and 2010, when the misreporting of fiscal statistics by Greece came to light. The

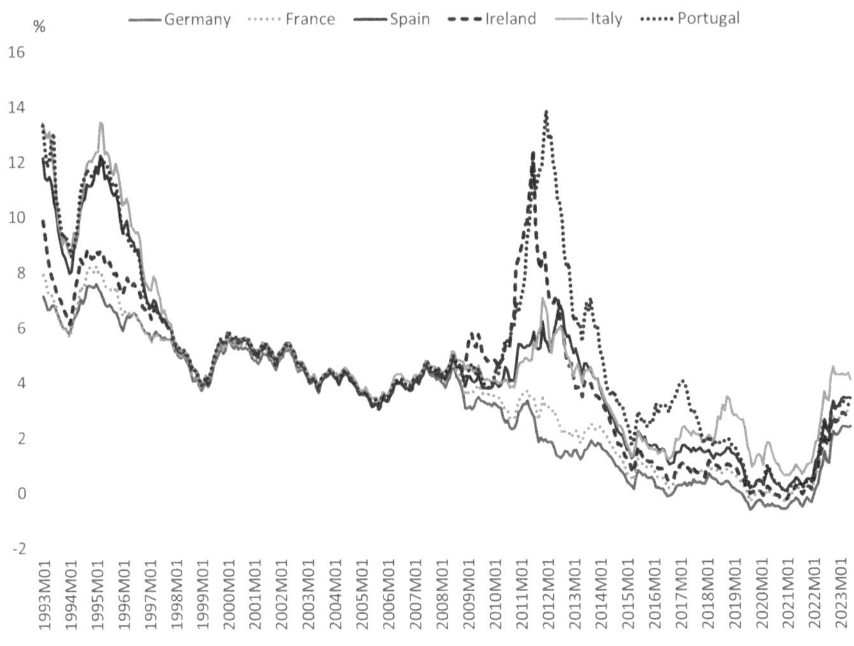

Figure 4.5 Long-term sovereign bond yields of some euro-area countries

Source: Authors' own compilation based on Eurostat data.

Note: Due to data gaps, the time series for Greece is not presented.

compression of spreads was quickly reversed, and GIIPS countries faced market pressure and rising risk premia.

The euro area soon found itself in a situation of mounting tensions, which had been unimaginable before the GFC. All of the GIIPS countries experienced massive private-capital outflows ('sudden stops'; Merler and Pisani-Ferry, 2012) and negative feedback loops between banks and sovereigns (Véron, 2017). The mood was not improved by the rating agencies' decisions to downgrade the sovereign debt of the most distressed countries through a series of fast and sharp cuts (Figure 4.6). According to some studies, the Big Three played an active role in aggravating the crisis in the EMU (De Santis, 2012).

After Greece, Ireland and Portugal were the next to lose access to market financing at manageable interest rates, and they had to apply for a bailout. Nonetheless, the successive anti-crisis measures were assessed as insufficient.[9] At the height of the sovereign debt crisis, euro-area financial markets saw deep fragmentation along national lines, and the EMU project itself started to be questioned. This triggered a general repatriation of funds aimed at matching domestic assets and liabilities in case the redenomination risk materialised (van Riet, 2017). The turning point came on 26th July 2012, when the ECB announced the OMT programme, which assumed unlimited interventions in

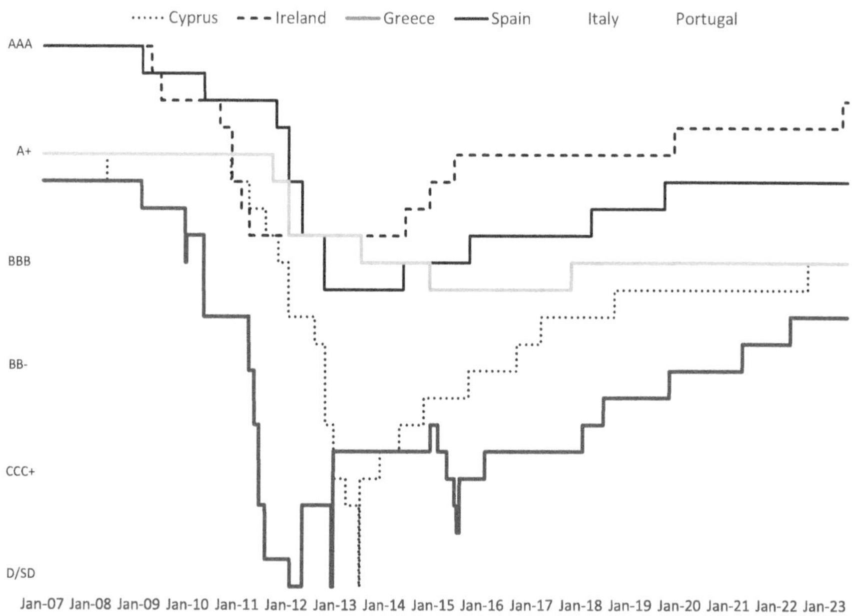

Figure 4.6 Credit ratings of the selected euro-area economies (according to S&P)

Source: Authors' own compilation based on Trading Economics data.

the secondary sovereign bond markets. With this measure, the ECB became the lender of last resort for euro-area sovereigns.

Since the outbreak of the crisis, various stabilisation measures have been taken in the euro area. Some were launched at the national level, while others were aimed at improving the economic situation of the euro area/EU as a whole. Among the former, the following should be highlighted:

1 Risk-sharing mechanisms – the temporary European Financial Stability Facility and the permanent European Stability Mechanism (ESM) (operating since 2012). Their purpose is to provide financial support for EMU countries experiencing serious financial difficulties,
2 Fiscal strengthening measures, including the Six-Pack, Two-Pack and Fiscal Pact,
3 The Macroeconomic Imbalance Procedure,
4 ECB measures, including liquidity-providing operations and the above-mentioned OMT programme,
5 The banking union. Its current shape is based on two pillars – the Single Supervisory Mechanism (SSM) (since 2014) and the Single Resolution Mechanism (SRM) (fully operational since 2016).

In the post-crisis years, a reduction in euro-area sovereign bond yields and compression of spreads compared to Germany have been observed, although the spreads have not returned to pre-crisis levels. Nonetheless, as noted by van Riet (2021), this phenomenon does not reflect fiscal sustainability achieved by ambitious structural reforms, as would be desirable, but the ECB's exceptional monetary accommodation during that period. This accommodation includes ultra-low interest rates, targeted longer-term refinancing operations, and the asset purchase programme. With these measures in place, market participants were able to renew their search for yield while paying less attention to credit quality.

More than a decade after the outbreak of the GFC, the euro area remains vulnerable to destabilising capital flows and is divided along national lines of creditworthiness, as evidenced at the beginning of the COVID-19-induced crisis. During this time, the spreads of the hardest-hit countries rose substantially. The ECB's announcement on 12 March 2020 that it was not there 'to close spreads' (ECB, 2020a) only added insult to injury, further widening the spreads.[10] A few days later, on 18 March 2020, the ECB withdrew its initial, somewhat reserved attitude, when it announced a new asset purchase programme – the Pandemic Emergency Purchase Programme (PEPP), and it relaxed its collateral standards (ECB, 2020b). These measures had calming effects on the markets, as they managed to reduce the spreads.[11]

The insufficient supply of euro-denominated safe assets (i.e. bonds of the highest credit ratings issued in euros by EMU countries) is one of the most severe consequences of the GFC. As can be seen from Table 4.2, before the crisis, the euro-area countries enjoyed the highest ratings. There were eight

Table 4.2 Credit ratings in euro-area economies

Country	*2007*	*2015*	*2023Q2*
Austria	AAA	AA+	AA+
Belgium	AA+	AA	AA
Cyprus[(a)]	A	BB–	BBB
Estonia[(c)]	A	AA–	AA–
Finland	AAA	AA+	AA+
France	AAA	AA	AA
Germany	AAA	AAA	AAA
Greece	A	CCC+	BB+
Ireland	AAA	A+	AA
Italy	A+	BBB–	BBB
Latvia[(d)]	BBB+	A–	A+
Lithuania[(e)]	A	A–	A+
Luxembourg	AAA	AAA	AAA
Malta[(a)]	A	BBB+	A–
Netherlands	AAA	AAA	AAA
Portugal	AA–	BB+	BBB+
Slovakia[(b)]	A	A+	A+
Slovenia	AA	A–	AA–
Spain	AAA	BBB+	A

Source: Authors' own compilation based on Trading Economics data.

Note: The table presents end-of-period ratings according to the S&P scale.
Euro members since: (a) 2008, (b) 2009, (c) 2011, (d) 2014, (e) 2015.
Data for Croatia are not presented due to its short membership in the euro area (since 2023).

triple-A-rated governments, while the lowest grade of single A was granted to only two then-EMU countries. The crisis reduced the number of countries with prime investment grades to three (Germany, Luxembourg and the Netherlands). As of 2023Q2, almost half of the euro-area countries are rated as single A or lower. The same three countries maintain the highest rating of AAA.

The substantial deterioration in the quality of debt issued by euro-area countries after the GFC is presented in Figure 4.7. In the pre-crisis period, AAA-rated securities constituted more than 50% of total sovereign debt securities issued by the EMU sovereigns. However, a sharp decline in the share of this category took place in 2012 and has not risen much since then. In 2009, the first downgrade to BBB grade occurred (Greece). The lower medium grade (triple-BBB) became the dominant category from 2012 to 2016. However, the last five years analysed show an improvement in credit quality, with increasing shares of A and AA categories, despite the deteriorating fiscal positions of EMU countries due to the COVID-19 shock.

The downgrades of many euro sovereigns during the GFC had a substantial and negative impact on the global pool of safe assets. As shown by Temprano Arroyo (2022), most of the fall in the world's safe assets since 2009 has been led by the decline in euro-denominated assets.

Finally, the insufficient availability of euro-based assets of the highest quality is evident in relative terms when compared with the supply of such assets

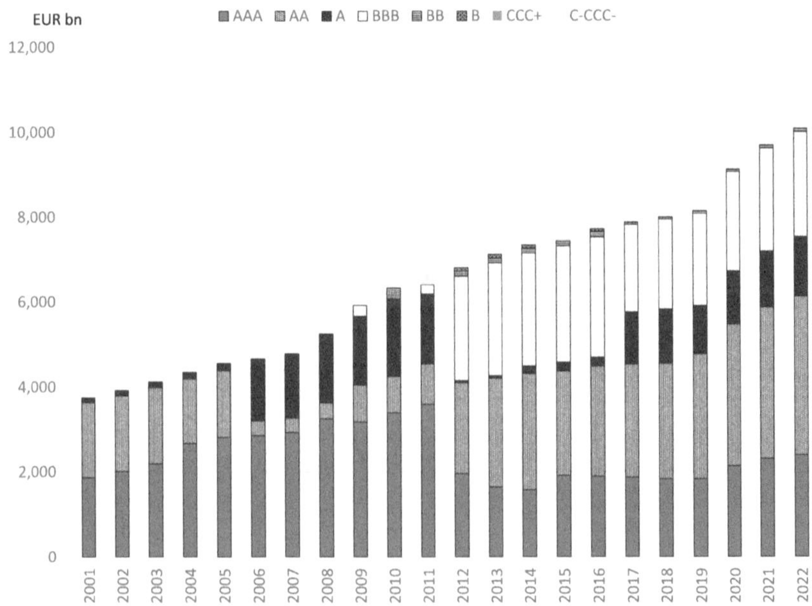

Figure 4.7 The stock of euro-area sovereign debt securities broken down by credit rating

Source: Authors' own compilation based on Eurostat and Trading Economics data. Inspired by Papadia and Temprano Arroyo (2022).

Note: The figure uses end-of-year ratings supplied by S&P.

Euro-area changing composition.

by the United States. For example, Gossé and Mourjane (2021) estimated that in 2019, EU countries had only 37% of sovereign bonds rated at least AA relative to GDP, while the United States had 89%. Temprano Arroyo (2022) argued that this is well below the economic and financial wealth of the EMU, given that the EU is not much smaller than the United States. Similarly, Ilzetzki et al. (2020) explored the reasons for the euro's underperformance. In the context of the undersupply of euro-denominated safe assets, they refer to the different financial system models adopted by the two economies: a bank-based model in the euro area and a market-based model in the United States. Using central banks' demand for safe assets as an example, official reserves are mainly held in securities, not in the form of bank deposits. Furthermore, compared to the United States, the euro-area capital market is both fragmented and characterised by insufficient depth and liquidity.

4.6.2 A Common Safe Asset for the Euro Area. An Overview of Proposals

There is a broad consensus that a common safe asset would benefit the euro area in a number of ways. Bini Smaghi and Marcussen (2019) stated that this asset is not 'a nice to have' but 'a need to have'. There are numerous potential intertwined benefits that stem from the introduction of a common safe asset. They are characterised by high credit quality, resilience to idiosyncratic and widespread sovereign shocks, compliance with regulatory and market standards, as well as eligibility as collateral for Eurosystem credit operations (Alogoskoufis et al., 2020), and include the following:

1. A euro-area safe asset should reduce the interdependence between sovereigns and domestic banking sectors. By diversifying away from national sovereign bonds, the banking sector automatically reduces its home bias and becomes less dependent on the position of the sovereign. Moreover, it gets the high-quality collateral needed to secure wholesale funding and central bank liquidity (Bini Smaghi and Marcussen, 2019). It might also be useful to the sovereign in solving banking crises.
2. A common safe asset should foster financial stability in the euro area by eliminating or reducing the problem of destabilising capital flights from vulnerable countries' assets towards safe havens (e.g. German bunds) in times of distress.
3. It should also support the effective transmission of monetary policy across all euro-area countries by facilitating its 'singleness'. The ECB's conduct of monetary policy during the GFC was largely impaired by financial fragmentation in the EMU along the national lines of creditworthiness and the resulting divergent sovereign bond yields. A common debt instrument should ensure the smooth transmission of the bank's monetary policy through the sovereign bond markets to the borrowing costs of households and businesses, and ultimately to aggregate demand (Šreiberytė and Spurga, 2021).
4. A liquid market for a euro safe asset should foster financial development and integration in the EMU, accelerating progress towards banking and capital market unions.
5. A euro-area safe asset should benefit European citizens as it would finance common projects aimed at addressing the challenges of green and digital transitions.
6. A common safe asset should also bring benefits in the international field. They include the expected higher attractiveness of the euro as a reserve currency, strengthening its international role, curtailing the global shortage of safe assets, and enhancing the credibility of the euro area in the eyes of international investors, all of which should support efforts to enhance Europe's self-sufficiency and independence.

The fact that such an asset has not yet been introduced reflects the lack of political consensus on the rules of joint bond issuance. More broadly, it demonstrates the old dispute between the (ordoliberal) German and French visions of European integration. The former emphasises the role of responsibility/accountability and bringing moral hazard concerns to the fore, while the latter recognises the need for flexibility in the crisis management policy (Cabral, 2021).

Furthermore, the experience of the GFC crisis heightened divisions along economic and cultural lines into debtors and creditors, the periphery and the core, the North and the South, or, more figuratively, 'sinners' and 'saints'. The first group, represented by the GIIPS countries, are notorious for their willingness to free ride on the fiscal discipline of other Member States. The second group, composed of countries such as Germany, Austria, Finland and the Netherlands, are often referred to as the frugal states, 'obsessed with punishment'. As described by Verdun (2010), this shows that the EMU is not a politically embedded entity; it lacks a sense of community and partnership. Against this backdrop, one should understand the number of proposals for the creation of a euro-area safe asset after the GFC. These proposals have evolved from the most far-reaching ones, that is those that envisaged a fiscal/political union, to those considering the introduction of a 'synthetic' instrument and excluding any amendments to the Treaty. Below, the most frequently discussed proposals will be presented (Šreiberytė and Spurga, 2021). In particular, they differ in terms of the guaranteed structure of common debt, the risk of moral hazard and the options to address it, and the need to introduce changes to the Treaty.

1 Eurobond 1

A 'genuine' Eurobond would be issued under several and joint guarantees. Each participating Member State (MS) would be liable for the totality of the incurred debt. The proportions of the liability of each MS would be specified. At the same time, if another country fails to meet its obligations, an investor gets legal recourse to all the participating MS. Hence, the proposal does not automatically entail fiscal transfers. They occur only when an MS does not meet its financial obligations or if it receives a higher share of the Eurobond funds than implied by its repayment share. In its basic design, the option assumes the complete substitution of national debt issuance with joint issuance (introduced either in a more or a less-gradual approach). Given the shared liability, the Eurobond 1 would be a true safe asset for the euro area, expected to lower borrowing costs and volatility of interest rates for all members.

The nature of the 'genuine' Eurobond, therefore, makes it the most vulnerable to the risk of moral hazard. To address this risk, the fiscal sovereignty of individual MSs may need to be curtailed, either by transferring decisions to issue the bonds to a European authority or enforcing strict fiscal rules.

The issuance of Eurobonds with several and joint guarantees would go against Article 125 of the TFUE, which stipulates that an MS cannot assume the liabilities of another MS. Therefore, this option of debt mutualisation would require an amendment to the Treaty.

2 Red and blue bonds

The Eurobond 1 proposal involves a complete substitution of national issuance. A modification of this proposal, known as the blue-red approach

(Delpla and Weizsäcker, 2011), suggests that national issuance would be replaced only partially. While this approach would not create as large and liquid a market of euro-area safe assets as full substitution, it would be more beneficial in terms of containing moral hazard. More specifically, the approach envisions the issuance of two types of bonds – blue and red. The former would finance each MS's debt up to 60% of GDP (the threshold established within the Maastricht convergence criteria). These bonds would be underpinned by joint and several guarantees, and they would be enhanced by the seniority clause. By contrast, MSs would remain fully responsible for red bonds, that is any debt issued beyond the 60% threshold. This means that the red bonds would not be guaranteed by other MSs and would not be eligible for a bailout from any EU rescue mechanism. In fact, the no-bail-out clause would apply to red bonds. As a result, the cost of the red bonds should be higher, which should encourage fiscal prudence, in accordance with the spirit of the Treaty, which recognises debt level below 60% of GDP as sustainable.

Given the joint and several liability attached to the blue bonds, implementing this proposal would require an amendment to the Treaty. Nevertheless, fiscal transfers seem unlikely due to the limited volume of blue bonds and their priority over the national debt.

A potential weakness of the proposal arises from the threshold itself and its credibility. Especially in times of crisis, once the blue bond allocation has been exhausted, even countries with stable macroeconomic conditions may encounter problems with debt financing at short notice. This, in turn, could trigger political pressure to raise the threshold. Succumbing to such pressure would set a very dangerous precedent, undermining the disciplining effect emphasised in the blue and red bonds concept (Gilbert et al., 2013 after Šreiberytė and Spurga, 2021).

3 Eurobond 2

The second Eurobond proposal envisions the issuance of a common debt instrument under several but not joint guarantees. Each MS would be liable only for the interest payments and principal redemption based on its share of the bond. The amount of funding secured would correspond to the same weights as those applied in the guaranteed structure. Hence, from an investor's perspective, such a bond would be similar to a diversified portfolio of national sovereign bonds. Consequently, the credit rating of the instrument would be close to a weighted average (based on their relative shares) of the ratings assigned to the participating MS.

Eurobond 2 would still carry a risk of moral hazard, although it is lower than Eurobond 1. Additionally, it is argued that this instrument would not attain the true safe asset status as countries with the highest credit standing would not be liable for the debt of other issuers. Importantly, as there is no joint liability, no amendments to the Treaty would be necessary, making this option easily deployable.

4 Sovereign Bond-Backed Securities

The concept of Sovereign Bond-Backed Securities (SBBS) was proposed by Brunnermeier et al. (2016) and later developed by the European Systemic Risk Board (ESRB, 2018). The proposal aims to overcome debt mutualisation and all the related concerns. In other words, it aims to create safe assets for the euro area without risk sharing (*Banque de France*, 2021, p. 5). The issuer of these assets, that is a private or a public financial institution (such as the European Investment Bank), would buy a diversified portfolio of euro-denominated sovereign bonds (the weights would be defined, e.g. by the shares in the capital of the ECB) and would later use them as collateral to issue their own securities. The project provides for two tranches – a senior one (the senior SBBS tranche) and a junior one (the junior SBBS tranche). The first tranches would be protected against losses of up to 30% on the underlying bond portfolio, which would allow it to perform the function of a safe asset for the euro area. The other would be much riskier. As the proponents of the project argue, the introduction of SBBS would help delink banks from their sovereigns and curtail destabilising capital flows among the euro area. More specifically, capital would flow from more to less risky asset classes, that is from junior SBBS to senior SBBS, thus replacing flows from countries with worse macroeconomic foundations to safe havens. On the other hand, critics claim that the complexity of the SBBS would work to the disadvantage of its safe status in times of high stress, which are characterised not only by flights to safety but also flights to simplicity (De Grauwe and Ji, 2018).

Under the proposal, no Treaty changes would be required as it entails no joint liability nor fiscal transfers. Moreover, the risk of moral hazard is contained as each MB remains fully responsible for managing its debt and addressing its own credit spreads.

The discussion on Eurobonds was revived by the COVID-19 pandemic shock, hence the name 'coronabonds'. In a letter to European Council president

Table 4.3 Main characteristics of joint debt proposals

Proposal	*Guarantee Structure*	*Treaty Changes Required*	*Fiscal Transfers*	*Moral Hazard*
Eurobond 1	Several and joint	Yes	Possible	High
Red and blue bonds	Several and joint up to the threshold (blue bonds)	Yes	Unlikely	Contained
Eurobond 2	Several but not joined (capped)	No	Unlikely	Contained
SBBS	N/A	No	No	Contained

Source: Authors' own elaboration

Note: N/A – not applicable.

Charles Michel from March 2020, leaders from nine euro-area countries appealed for 'a common debt instrument issued by a European institution to raise funds on the market on the same basis and to the benefits of all Member States'. The signatories stressed the symmetric nature of the shock, which adversely affected all common currency block countries, and called for a united response. 'This common debt instrument should have sufficient size and long maturity to be fully efficient and avoid roll-over risks now as in the future', they wrote. Funds obtained that way would be used to invest in the healthcare system and temporary policies aimed at protecting European economies.

Regarding the above-presented proposals for joint debt issuance in the EMU, coronabonds would feature jointly and severally guaranteed euro-area debt instruments with partial substitution. The idea, however, was rejected by Germany, the Netherlands, and other northern members as fundamentally contradictory to their vision of the common currency area (Financial Times, 2020).

Recognising that there is no political appetite for the creation of a common debt instrument for the euro area, Papadia and Temprano Arroyo (2022) proposed another option to increase the supply of safe assets in the EMU, namely the expansion of national safe assets. The proposal focuses on implementing fiscal consolidation and ambitious growth-oriented reforms by sub-triple-A euro-area sovereigns, which should translate into them being upgraded to triple-A.[12]

As of 2023 q2, there were seven AA-rated euro-area countries, four of which were triple-A before the outbreak of the GFC (Table 4.2). Of these seven countries, Austria and Finland are rated AA+ (group 1), Belgium, France, and Ireland are rated AA (group 2), while Estonia and Slovenia are AA- (group 3). Papadia and Temprano Arroyo (2022) estimated the impact of the upgrades of each group to triple-A on the supply of safe assets in the euro area. They showed that by 2026 (the last year of net issuance under NextGenerationEU), the total supply would increase by EUR 0.6 trillion, EUR 4.1 trillion and EUR 5.0 trillion with each consecutive group upgrade relative to the baseline scenario (the number triple A-rated governments does not increase).[13] For 2032, these estimates are as follows: EUR 0.7 trillion, EUR 5.1 trillion, and EUR 6.2 trillion, respectively.

The increase in safe asset supply due to the rating upgrades of all double A-rated euro-area countries is estimated to be five and seven times as large as the maximum issuance of bonds under SURE[14] and NGEU[15] facilities combined. Furthermore, the proposal performs favourably in comparison to the well-known proposals of creating a common debt instrument for the euro area, envisaging a volume of safe assets issued in the range of EUR 0.7 trillion – EUR 7.3 trillion (Papadia and Temprano Arroyo, 2022).

4.6.3 The Role of Supranational Debt in Safe Assets Creation. The Case of EU

In addition to government bonds from the highest rated EMU countries, the 'European pool' of safe assets embrace bonds issued by European supranational providers[16]:

- The European Investment Bank,
- The European Financial Stability Facility,
- The European Stability Mechanism,
- European Union.

The four aforementioned supranational issuers differ as regards their scope of operation, institutional bases, guarantee schemes.

Historically, the first European safe asset was created by the EIB, while the second came from the EU. It issued several Community bonds on private markets since the 1970s, which were guaranteed by the Member States and distributed to countries where required. The first European Community bond was issued in 1976 and used for Italy and Ireland (Janse, 2023).

The debt created by supranational issuers aimed at responding to various challenges that appeared in course of integration process, and globally, increasing over time.

The European Commission had issued bonds in the past to fund:

1 Macro-Financial Assistance (MFA) – a financial aid programme extended to countries outside of the EU, experiencing a balance of payments crisis,
2 European Financial Stabilisation Mechanism (EFSM) – an emergency funding programme for any EU member experiencing or threatened by severe financial difficulties,
3 Balance of payments (BoP) assistance – facility for non-euro-area EU countries experiencing or threatened by difficulties regarding their balance of payments,
4 European Atomic Energy Community – financing eligible projects on behalf of Euratom.

Nevertheless, before 2020, the EU's presence in the capital markets was limited. Between 2009 and 2019 the Commission issued only EUR 77.8 bn (European Commission, 2023). This has changed with the onset of the COVID-19 pandemic. To face challenges it posed, including the economic impact, anti-crisis measures have been taken at the EU level (i.e. with the participation of non-euro-area Members States) that seem to represent the most significant step towards debt mutualisation in the history of the European integration.[17]

More specifically, in response to the COVID-19 shock, the EU countries empowered the European Commission to borrow in the international capital markets to finance two facilities – the temporary SURE and NGEU, worth up to EUR 100 bn and EUR 806.9 bn, respectively. Due to its unprecedented size, the EU is expected to become the largest supranational issuer in the world and also one of the largest European issuing entities (Krautzberger, 2020).

As for the two facilities themselves, SURE was established to mitigate the socio-economic impact of the COVID-19 pandemic shock. It was intended to cover public expenditure related to maintaining employment, whatever its form (employees and self-employed). SURE has provided EUR 98.4 bn to crisis-affected EU countries in the form of back-to-back loans. Altogether, 19 countries received aid, with Italy (EUR 27.4 bn), Spain (EUR 21.3 bn) and Poland (EUR 11.2 bn) being the largest beneficiaries. The financing of the SURE facility was based on the issuance of social bonds by the European Commission.[18] The Commission carried out 9 issuances, consisting of bonds of 5 to 30-year maturities. SURE was deactivated on 31 December 2022.[19]

NGEU is a temporary economic recovery instrument worth EUR 806.9 bn (EUR 750 bn at 2018 prices). It aims to make Europe greener, more digital, and more resilient to crises after the COVID-19 pandemic. A key element of the NGEU is the Recovery and Resilience Facility (RRF), with a budget of up to EUR 723.8 to be allocated to EU countries in the form of grants (EUR 338 bn) and loans (EUR 385.8 bn). To receive support under RRF, the EU countries have submitted national recovery and resilience plans, indicating the reforms and investments (with clear milestones and targets) they will carry out by the end of 2026. The RRF is performance based, meaning that the funds are disbursed according to country's implementation of the agreed milestones.

To finance the NGEU, the European Commission – on behalf of the EU – raises debt on capital markets, on more favourable terms than most Member States could obtain. The Commission then redistributes these amounts. As a result of the first transaction, which took place on 15 June 2021, the Commission raised EUR 20 bn through a 10-year bond issuance. This was the largest ever institutional bond issuance in Europe and the amount raised was the largest the EU had ever raised in a single transaction. The Commission borrowing under NGEU will cease in 2026. The loans provided under the RRF facility will have to be fully repaid by 2058.[20]

Regarding the Commission's debt issuance in the context of the creation of euro-area safe assets, the EU enjoys the highest credit rating of AAA from almost all major rating agencies. S&P is the only rating agency which rates it at AA. The EU draws from several layers of debt-service protection, which makes its debt low in default risk. The Commission's borrowings are direct and unconditional obligations of the EU. Article 323 of the TFEU binds the EU to service this debt. The beneficiaries of EU loans have always serviced their debts. Furthermore, if a loan beneficiary fails to honour its obligations, the EU budget is the ultimate guarantor for all EU debt (European Commission, 2023). Finally, for SURE and NGEU-related debt issuances additional guarantees were established.

The SURE and NGEU bonds enjoyed substantial interest by investors. This was particularly reflected by large primary market demand (vastly oversubscribed issues) and low spreads with regard to German bunds compared to previously issued EU supranational bonds. When strengthening the international role of the euro is concerned, EU issuances have been demanded by international investors, which may be an indicative of latent demand for euro-denominated safe assets. As evidenced by (Temprano and Arroyo, 2022), around 44% of the SURE bonds and around 49% of the NGEU bonds, which were issued by April 2022, were demanded by investors outside the euro area (with even higher shares (60%–70%) in the shorter end of the maturity structure).

At the same time, there are serious obstacles preventing the SURE and NGEU-related bonds from achieving the status of genuine euro-area safe assets. The most evident one lies in the one-off and time-limited nature of the EU's response to the COVID-19 crisis. Furthermore, they also miss the euro-area dimension. Additionally, without particular hedging instruments, such as futures for German bonds, they are priced using the euro-denominated interest rate swap curve as a benchmark and lastly, bonds of supranational issuers are not included in the global sovereign bond indices limiting the index funds interest in such investments (Janse, 2023).

4.7 The Role of EMEs in Producing Safe Assets

4.7.1 The Rising Role of EMEs in the Global Economy

Emerging markets have been playing an increasingly important role in the global economy. Strong economic growth in developing Asian countries, mainly China and India, has significant global and regional implications. In 2022, the top three largest world economies, measured by share in global GDP (based on purchasing power parity – PPP), were China (18.4%), the United States (15.5%) and India (7.3%). Prior to 2016, the United States was number one, but China took the lead after a prolonged period of strong economic growth (cf. Figure 4.8).

Apart from their rising share in global GDP, the economic expansion of EMEs is visible in their growing share in the supply of primary commodities, as well as their growing share in manufacturing. China now accounts for one-third of the global manufacturing value added (Aiyar et al., 2023). These countries also have a bigger share of the global population compared to advanced economies. Major emerging markets have also become an increasing source of outward foreign direct investments, which is an evident shift from their receiving-country status a few decades ago (Aiyar et al., 2023).

Since the GFC, large inflows of foreign capital into bonds[21] denominated in local currencies in EMEs have occurred. This was an important change compared to the 1990s, when investors in those countries were attracted to foreign exchange-denominated debt (Agur et al., 2018). By reducing currency (and maturity) mismatches, the increased role of local currency-denominated debt made EMEs less vulnerable to capital outflows and currency crises. Although emerging markets' sovereign bonds are generally categorised as risky assets, the growth in size and increased interest raise the question of whether they may become potential safe assets in the (foreseeable) future.

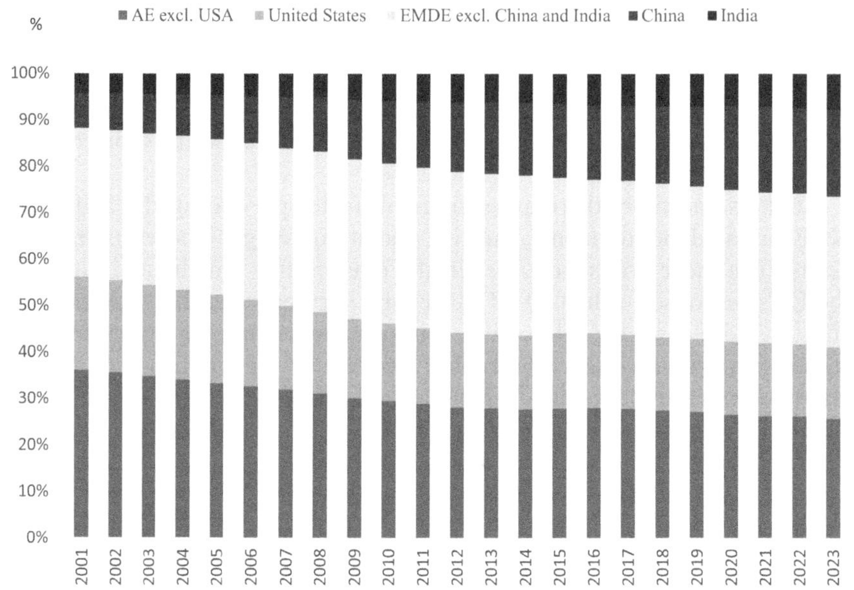

Figure 4.8 GDP based on PPP, global share (%)

Source: IMF, World Economic Outlook database and IMF calculations.

Note: AE – advanced economies, EMDE – emerging market and developing economies

The growth of EMEs' sovereign bond markets has mostly been driven by local currency debt.[22] The governments of EMEs have deepened the local currency bond markets, substantially improving their credit ratings, with local currency debt now constituting the majority of outstanding bonds (Arslan et al., 2020). Market capitalisation is concentrated in Asia and Latin America, with Asia accounting for over 30% of the share of the EM local currency bond market. China has the largest government bond market of the emerging economies, followed by Brazil and India (Agur et al., 2018). Additionally, China is the second-largest global bond market (cf. Figure 4.10).

The increase in foreign ownership of EME bonds is a sign of increasing integration with global financial markets, a trend that gained momentum, particularly after the GFC. In some countries, like Brazil, Indonesia, and Malaysia, foreign investors own more than 30% of the outstanding debt stock. Factors that contribute to increased foreign participation in the market include stronger institutions and policies, lower inflation, and currency risk (Ottonello and Perez, 2019; Engel and Park, 2022). Apart from greater macroeconomic and financial stability, an important driver has been better access to these markets. Although the openness of EME capital accounts varies, improvements have taken place. The development of bond markets is primarily driven by improvements in the investability of EME debt. Investability can be defined in terms of the following dimensions: market access, market taxation, market efficiency and regulation, market infrastructure and investor base, market size and instruments. Improvements in these dimensions have attracted investors, both to the domestic and foreign bond markets of EMEs (Agur et al., 2018). The attractiveness of EME bond markets has also grown due to include EME debt in various key benchmark indices. Initiatives to stimulate the development of bond markets, namely the ABMI[23] and ABF, provide an argument in favour of providing regional public safe assets in the Asian region.

Experience from COVID-19 shows that local currency government bonds in EMEs are not perceived as safe assets, as during this period of high global uncertainty, there were record portfolio outflows, as well as currency depreciation. Meanwhile, EME local currency bond spreads spiked (BIS, 2020). Even if they are deemed to be safe assets in times of stability, they easily lose this status in turbulent times when investors show their preferences for treasuries of advanced countries.

In the medium term, the quantity of safe assets may increase via public debt issuance in China, India, and other EMEs. In the short term, China may provide global safe assets in substantial quantities, but this is still not certain. To reduce the problem of safe assets shortage, emerging markets that hold safe assets issued by a limited number of high-income countries could eventually provide them while their economies grow (Caballero et al., 2017). However, in the long term, some threats may appear which could hamper the potential role of EME as providers of global safe assets.

First, GEF could hinder cross-border capital flows, reducing the options for external financing and impeding economic development. The introduction of new barriers to capital mobility would fragment capital markets, reducing financing choices and leading to less investment (Aiyar et al., 2023). Financial globalisation would be substituted by financial regionalisation, at best. Second, there are concerns about the risk of EMEs falling into the 'middle-income trap' (MIT).[24] This risk is mostly evident in China, as its economic growth has recently decelerated.

4.7.2 *China*

4.7.2.1 *The Dynamics and Determinants of China's Bond Market Development*

The bond market has been a rapidly growing segment of China's financial market. As of 2023Q2, the size of Chinese local currency bond market reached approximately 107.4% of the country's GDP (Asia Bond Monitor, November 2023). This growth is expressed in the scale of issuance, trading volumes and the diversification of issuer and investor categories. The bond market has become the main channel for direct financing for enterprises in China, although traditionally, it was the banking system and bank credit that played a crucial role in private sector financing. The specific monetary policy environment of the central bank, which shapes the term structure of banking lending and deposit rates, was also a factor that inhibited the development of the bond market and thus affected the dynamics of returns in the Chinese bond market (Fan et al., 2023). The main driver of bond market development has been the deregulation of interest rates. They were carried out sequentially in recent years and contributed to a decline in the influence of monetary policy on market pricing mechanisms.

Other important drivers of bond market development include the following:

1 Organisational and regulatory measures. These measures aim to develop the primary and secondary markets and improve liquidity. Notable initiatives include:

- The establishment of the Shanghai Stock Exchange in 1990, allowing government bonds to be listed and traded, analogous to shares.
- The creation of the interbank bond market in 1997, which functions as an OTC market and currently constitutes the main segment of trading in these instruments (over 90% of transactions).

2 The progressive internationalisation of the renminbi (RMB). This includes:

- Promoting the use of the RBM primarily in trade invoicing and currency settlement, which is consistent with Gopinath and Stein's (2018) empirical research on the determinants of safe asset status.
- The use of the RMB as a reserve currency. A manifestation of this was the inclusion of the RMB in the SDR basket (2016), which signalled to foreign investors that the Chinese currency was being treated as 'freely usable' and that the financial system was becoming more market-oriented. As a result, foreign central banks' holding of foreign exchange reserves in the RMB increased more than threefold between 2016 and 2022, accounting for 2.7% of global official foreign exchange reserves as of 2022Q4 (cf. Figure 4.4). The internationalisation of the RMB demonstrates that it has the potential to become a new global reserve currency, thereby increasing foreign demand for Chinese financial assets in the future and diversifying the portfolio of global safe assets.
- Creating a global network of renminbi currency swaps and official clearing banks.

The internationalisation of the RMB has been strengthened by growing exports and imports of the economy, the Belt and Road Initiative,[25] and the development of a central bank digital currency (e-CNY).[26]

3 Opening up the bond market to foreign investors. This is an integral part of a broader strategy of liberalising capital flows, and it is being implemented gradually, sequentially and asymmetrically (Schipke et al., 2023). Key initiatives and regulatory actions include:

- Providing foreign investors with access to the domestic bond market, free of quotas and limits; currently, most foreign institutional investors have unrestricted access to the bond market.

- Allowing non-Chinese issuers (corporations, sovereigns) to issue RMB-denominated bonds in the Chinese onshore market under the 'Panda bonds' programme since 2005.
- Ensuring currency convertibility.
- The creation of the Bond Connect Program in 2017. It is a reciprocal bond market access platform that enables reciprocal bond trading through a connection between China and Hong Kong. It allows foreign investors to participate in the bond market without having to maintain onshore accounts.

Despite systematic liberalisation measures, the share of foreign entities that hold Chinese bonds should still be considered modest; the share of foreign-owned debt is one of the lowest in the emerging markets group. Cerutti and Obstfeld's (2018) cross-country comparative analysis showed that in 2018, only 1.6% of issued bonds in China were held by foreign entities. The small share is apparent when juxtaposed with other countries; for example, in Korea, foreigners hold 5% of Korean bonds (Schipke et al., 2023). Furthermore, this share is even less than the share of foreign entities in the capitalisation of the Chinese stock market, which stood at 2.4% in 2018 (Cerutti and Obstfeld, 2018). By way of comparison, the corresponding figures for India are 3.2% (bond market) and 16.2% (equity market).[27] This observation led them to conclude that there is substantial room to improve foreign investments in the Chinese bond markets in both size and structure.[28] Significantly, the foreign sector's holdings are dominated by government bonds, followed by policy bank bonds, that is securities with the potential to be safe assets on the international financial market.

A step that accelerated the sector's integration into the global financial market and could lead to an increase in foreign participation in the Chinese bond market was the inclusion of these bonds in global indices:

1. In 2017, Chinese government bonds were included by Citigroup in some bond indices,
2. In April 2019, government bonds and task banks were included in the Bloomberg Barclays Global Aggregate Bond Index.

The inclusion of Chinese bonds in global indices is undoubtedly indicative of the growing perception of Chinese bonds as part of international financial markets.

4.7.2.2 *Segments of the Chinese Bond Market – The Role of Public Sector Issuance*

There are different classifications of the segments of the Chinese bond market, which translates into heterogeneous assessments of their scale and importance. Amstad and He (2019) distinguished three broad categories of bonds:

- Government bonds,
- Financial bonds,
- Corporate bonds.

The government bonds segment includes treasury bonds, municipal bonds, policy bank bonds and others (e.g. central bank bonds). Financial bonds include securities issued by the private financial sector and corporate bonds by the private non-financial sector.

According to Hu et al.'s (2018) classification, there are four categories of bonds:

- Government bonds,
- Central bank bonds,
- Non-financial sector credit bonds (corporate credit bonds),
- Financial bonds.

Government bonds include treasury bonds and local government bonds.

Meanwhile, Schipke et al. (2023) distinguished two categories of bonds:

- Government and quasi-government bonds. Like Amstad and He's (2019) classification, they include government bonds, local government bonds and policy banks,
- Credit bonds. They include financial bonds, corporate bonds, commercial papers and other securities.

The basis of this classification is, therefore, the emphasis on distinguishing issuers not by sector but by ownership (public or private issuers). Consequently, it may be surprising to include bonds issued by state policy banks as government bonds. However, due to the peculiarities of China's economic and financial system, such a classification of government bonds may be justified when assessing their prospects of fulfilling the safe asset function. As policy banks are entities backed by the central government (ownership, government guarantees), these bonds are considered an almost risk-free instrument. Furthermore, due to the depth and size of the market, they have the status of a liquid instrument, almost as attractive to investors as government bonds.

Analysis of the issuers of safest assets, a classification that broadly captures government bonds, shows how extensive the scale of Chinese debt creation aspiring to the safe asset category can be. When considering the potential for safe asset creation, it is essential to note that, in broadly defined government bonds issued by public sector entities, the safest assets currently account for around 70% of local currency bonds outstanding (Asia Bond Monitor, November, 2023).

A noteworthy development is the dynamically developing[29] local government bond market since 2015. The increase in the scale of issuance is related to the implementation of the state's financial policy, specifically, the need to refinance the debt issued for fiscal stimulation in the wake of the GFC (through the use of LGFVs[30]). Despite the dynamic growth of this segment of the bond market, inhibiting factors are identified, which include low liquidity, the lack of customary use of credit as an external source of financing, a narrow investor base and fragmented regulatory structures (Lam and Wang, 2018; Schipke et al., 2023).

Government bonds, despite their different maturities, are characterised by low market liquidity and are concentrated at the short end of the yield curve. As 70% of these bonds are held by banks (often right up to maturity), the functioning of the secondary market is very limited. Consequently, the information function that these currencies traditionally perform in the financial market is limited (Asia Bond Monitor, November, 2023; Schipke et al., 2023). These bonds are a key instrument for the implementation of monetary policy by the Chinese central bank today. As of 2019, government bonds constituted approximately 18% of the total bond market. Compared to the corresponding share for US government bonds (46%), it illustrates the still relatively low importance of this bond segment in China (Amstad and He, 2019).

The size of the policy bank bond market is similar to government bonds, although the market is more liquid. Furthermore, due to the larger scale of trading, it is more responsive to changes in fundamental factors.

Figure 4.9 shows that the main Chinese bond issuers are the central government, policy banks, and local governments, which jointly account for more than 55% of the total outstanding bonds. There is also a high share of corporate bonds/companies. It should also be noted that state-owned enterprises (SOEs) are an important issuer of debt instruments, confirming the thesis of the noticeable dominance of the public sector in Chinese bond issuance (Table 4.4).

The rapid growth of China's total (government, corporate and household) debt-to-GDP ratio (from 164% of GDP in 2007 to 290% in 2020),[31] which is one of the highest in emerging markets, may raise concerns about its manageability. However, rising overall debt is not perceived as a destabilising factor for the following reasons:

1 China is a net lender globally. Its investment position is positive, reflecting the low degree of foreign ownership of Chinese domestic assets. Its sustainability is further ensured by the current account surpluses it achieves; net foreign liabilities account for 40% of GDP, in stark contrast to the US (around 160% of GDP) and Japan (115%). The structure of foreign liabilities, with stocks and bonds accounting for only one-fifth of the total, reflects the potential for further market integration with the international financial market (Cerutti and Obstfeld, 2018).
2 China's high savings rate, reaching 50% of GDP, makes the economy less reliant on foreign capital to transform savings into investment. Moreover, the high savings rate means that deeper integration with the international bond market can contribute to a more productive allocation of global savings, with benefits for both borrowers and lenders (Cerutti and Obstfeld, 2018).

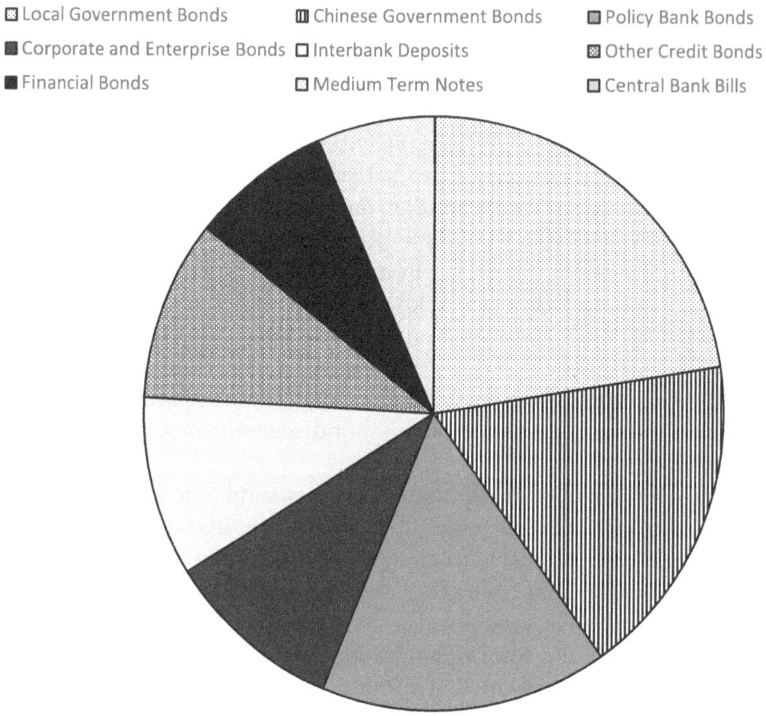

Figure 4.9 Chinese onshore bond market structure (% of total bonds outstanding)

Source: Authors' own compilation based on Wind data (after: Invesco, 2021).

Note: This classification used by Wind is different than those presented by Amstad and He (2019) and Schipke et al. (2023).

Table 4.4 Segments of the Chinese government bond market

Type of Government Bond	*Sector and Key Issuers*	*Maturity Period*	*Regulatory Authority*	*Trading Venue*
Treasury Bonds	Ministry of Finance (public sector)	3 months–50 years	Ministry of Finance	Interbank or stock market
Policy Bank Bonds	China Development Bank, Agricultural Development Bank of China, Export-Import Bank of China (quasi-public sector)	1 year–10 years	Central Bank (PBC), Banking and Insurance Regulatory Commission (CBIRC)	Interbank or stock market
Local Government Bonds	Local and municipal authorities (municipal sector)	1 year–20 years	Ministry of Finance	Interbank or stock market

Source: Own compilation based on Furey et al. (2018).

3 China has a financial buffer in the form of the world's largest foreign exchange reserves, exceeding USD 3 trillion.
4 The overwhelming majority of its debt is held by domestic creditors. While foreign indebtedness has risen over the past few years, it accounts for only 5% of overall debt. This eliminates the risk of a 'sudden stop' by foreign investors (Boone et al., 2022).
5 There is a minimal risk of large-scale capital flight by Chinese domestic investors due to capital account restrictions. China's high household savings are invested in the domestic capital market and/or held in domestic bank accounts (Boone et al., 2022).
6 Much of the debt resides within the public sector, with SOEs constituting 60% of overall corporate debt and reaching 100% of GDP. In addition, central government and local government debt together account for almost 70% of GDP. The lenders to SOEs – highly indebted local governments and quasi-fiscal LGFV – are banks that are directly or indirectly controlled by the government. This implies that controlled defaults and the gradual recognition of non-performing loans are the norm (Boone et al., 2022).
7 The central government, apart from having the ability to regulate the banking system and control banking lending, has sufficient fiscal space to prevent a systemic credit crisis. What is more, Chinese sovereign debt trades like 'hard duration' (government bond yields fall during the financial crisis), which enables the government to borrow more at a lower cost.

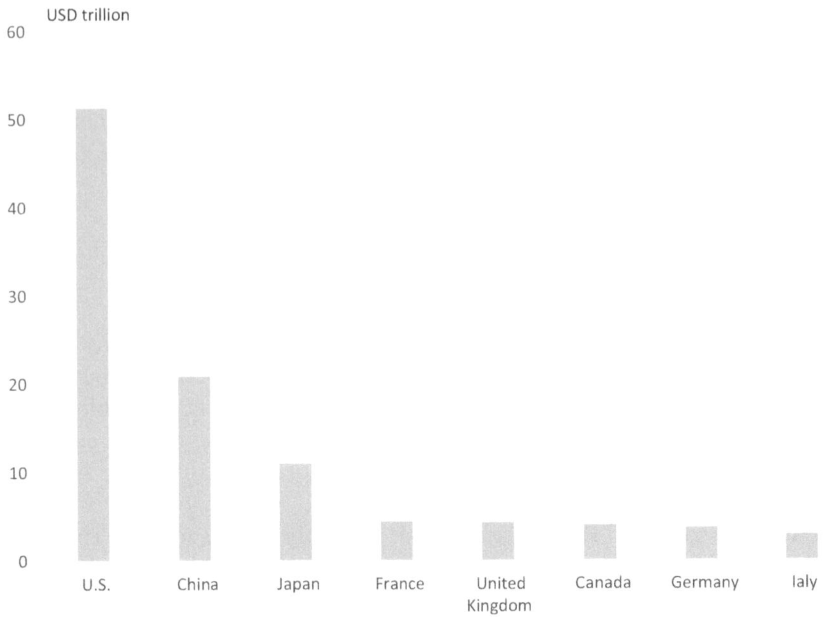

Figure 4.10 The largest bond markets in the world

Source: Authors' own compilation based on World Economic Forum data.

The government can also instruct the central bank to provide liquidity to the banking system or even engage in direct lending to corporates (Boone et al., 2022).

The Chinese bond market demonstrates strong growth rates; for example, in 2016, total bond issuance grew by 29% year-on-year. The scale of its growth is illustrated by its position as the second-largest market in the world as of 2022. The capitalisation of the bond market relative to GDP increased from 35% in 2008 to over 90% in 2017, in contrast to the relatively constant level of just over 200% in the US (Amstad and He, 2019). Simultaneously, China's bond market capitalisation rose from 1% of global GDP in the early 2000s to 9% by the end of 2017 (Cerutti and Obstfeld, 2018).

When analysing the potential for increased interest in Chinese government bonds, including from foreign investors, the following factors should be considered:

1 The high rating of Chinese government debt (A+ according to Fitch rating agency), which ranks it at the highest levels in the emerging markets group and even in a similar range to developed countries (e.g. Ireland according to Fitch rating agency),[32] creates demand from foreign investors for government bonds.
2 Other incentives include attractively shaped yields compared to other investments in a similar asset class (Furey et al., 2018). In addition, there are favourable yield prospects as a consequence of expected higher economic growth rates than in developed countries and low and stable inflation.
3 The co-existence of two trading platforms (the interbank market and the exchange market) limits liquidity and pricing mechanisms in the government bond segment. This consequently leads to market segmentation, higher information acquisition costs, and regulatory arbitrage (Amstad and He, 2019; Schipke et al., 2023).

However, the demand for government bonds may also involve the following risks:

1 Political risk. Political risk arises from institutional and regulatory instability, a lack of central bank independence and monetary policy transparency. An important source of this risk may be the possible use of instruments to control capital outflows (e.g. to stabilise foreign exchange reserves and the exchange rate), which, for foreign investors, poses concerns about profit repatriation.
2 Exchange rate risk. Exchange rate risk is mainly related to concerns about RMB devaluation/depreciation (Furey et al., 2018).
3 Financial instability risk. As the sensitivity of China's bond market to the global financial cycle will increase as it becomes more integrated with the international financial market, there is a risk of financial instability

and reduced monetary policy independence (Cerutti and Obstfeld, 2018). Therefore, it is crucial to support the creation of safe assets through measures that eliminate sources of political risk and increase the degree of market-based exchange rate formation.

There have been structural changes in China's balance of payments in recent years, transitioning from a structural balance of payments surplus to a deficit in the first quarter of 2018 and, subsequently, a small current surplus after the GFC. Therefore, the country will be more dependent on foreign capital inflows in the form of foreign direct investment or portfolio investment. In this context, opening the market to foreign capital can be an important factor in stabilising the country's payment position. Creating demand from foreign investors for a liquid, deep and open debt market could be an important factor in transforming China's economic development model.

4.7.3 India

India is classified as the third largest economy after the United States and China, having experienced strong economic growth since embarking on major structural reforms and economic liberalisation in 1991. The Indian economy was impacted by external and domestic shocks, some of which were directly related to the financial sector or the effects of spillovers through international trade and global supply chains. The Indian financial sector plays a crucial role in the country's economy and had provided an important foundation for sustained economic growth in recent years. India has introduced many reforms aimed at financial deepening, including the development of the private banking sector, the introduction of flexible inflation targeting, and the Insolvency and Bankruptcy Code (IBC), all of which occurred in 2016. Generally, India's long-term growth outlook is positive, supported by strong population growth and a young labour force. Nonetheless, there is a strong desire for further financial development and increasing financial sector efficiency to unlock India's full economic potential (Schipke et al., 2023).

India's financial system has changed as a consequence of the above-mentioned economic growth factors, which reflect the increased reliance on market-based financing and the emergence of digital money and financing. Financial intermediaries, mostly public sector banks (60% of total bank assets), dominate the financial system. In 2015, after the reforms, non-banking financial companies grew rapidly, resulting in 30% credit growth in 2018, mainly for micro, small and medium Indian companies. The most important aspect of the Indian financial system is market-based financing, which has grown rapidly over the past ten years. At the end of 2023, the total outstanding debt amounted to more than 80% of GDP (IMF, 2023c).

The Indian debt market is regarded as one of the largest in Asia, providing a solid alternative to traditional investments. The government debt market is the largest and oldest component of the Indian debt market, and it is perceived as a core segment of the Indian financial system. The bond market emerged as very attractive to international investors by including the country's sovereign bonds in global bond indices such as the FTSE and JPMorgan Chase & Co.

An important stimulus for the development of a government bond market can be the inclusion of government debt in J.P. Morgan's global bond index. It should lower the cost of borrowing and help fund infrastructure, thereby stimulating new investments. This step may translate into it being included in other indexes, such as the Bloomberg Global Aggregate Index.

In India, the government bonds market accounts for 68% of the fixed-income market, while in 2021, corporate bonds accounted for 20%. Foreign ownership of Indian sovereign bonds accounts for just 1.9% of the federal government's outstanding debt, creating room for the development of the debt market. From legal and regulatory perspectives, India has implemented two frameworks: the Foreign Portfolio Investor (FPI) and External Commercial Borrowing schemes. Under the FPI, portfolio debt investment quotas by non-residents are specified, and a list of designated government securities is created, outlining what can be purchased by foreign investors without any limit or macroprudential control. These investment restrictions are eased progressively, with investment limits increased for both corporate and government debt securities (Schipke et al., 2023).

A special kind of instrument in the financial system is the Sovereign Gold Bond, issued by the Reserve Bank of India on behalf of the Government of India. These instruments combine the attributes of gold with the safety of government bonds, thus potentially fulfilling the functions of safe assets. Sovereign Gold Bonds offer a good investment vehicle for individuals seeking safe assets while also acting as substitutes for holding physical gold.

However, as the global economy ends its rate hike cycle in 2023 and bond yields are increasing significantly, emerging market debt is becoming an attractive investment option for international investors. Increased foreign investment in the Indian public sector can potentially provide funding for the country's economic growth. A larger issuer and investor base can increase competition among financial intermediaries, expand the availability of long-term debt, and lower interest rates.

The capitalisation of the Indian equity market has also grown rapidly, becoming the fifth largest in the world after the United States, China, Japan and Hong Kong as of 2022. Additionally, India has developed an efficient digital payments infrastructure that enhances financial inclusion. The financial sector plays a key role in allocating resources and influences the economy. India's economic fluctuations can be magnified by the banking sector (credit), asset prices (stock exchange) and the real economy (output).

In summary, India is still a relatively lower-middle-income country with favourable growth prospects, positive demographic trends, and development needs. However, its economic outlook is shaped by foreign capital inflows, which strengthen domestic investments (Schipke et al., 2023).

4.8 Evolution of the Forms of Money and the Supply of Safe Assets

The emergence of digital currency, based on blockchain technology, together with the growing global cryptocurrency market, represents a breakthrough in the development of the financial market in the 21st century. In essence, digital currency is a form of money that is available only in digital or electronic form; it does not have physical attributes or a physical equivalent. Similar to physical currency, digital currency has utility, meaning that it can be used to purchase goods and pay for services. Generally, digital currencies are used for investment, operational and transactional purposes in international financial markets. Both central bank-issued money and privately issued digital money have the potential to significantly improve payment efficiency domestically and across borders (Kosse & Mattei, 2023). Unlike fiat currency (physical money), which has a centralised system of production and distribution by a central bank, the most popular cryptocurrencies have decentralised digital currency systems like bitcoin has.

Blockchain technology[33] is a decentralised distributed record of data grouped into interconnected blocks. Transactions within the system are transmitted simultaneously to all participants in the system, essentially creating a ledger that contains a list of transactions made in a given cryptocurrency and serving as a transaction system in one (Ciupa, 2018).

One of the main features of a cryptocurrency is that it acts as a virtual currency. Access is not geographically restricted, and it is not subject to the supervision of national and international financial institutions. The dispersion, transparency, spectacular growth in the value of cryptocurrencies, and the lack of centralisation of trading have attracted great interest from financial market participants, particularly those in the capital market. The involvement of investors and financial market institutions, as well as the potential application of blockchain technology in international payment systems, is particularly important. The market for cryptocurrencies, mainly bitcoin, may offer an interesting alternative to fiat money and traditional banking as they are more resilient to devaluation and political factors that arise in individual economies that issue international currency (Nakamoto, 2008).

The rapidly growing market for private digital currencies has forced central banks to accelerate the reform of their monetary systems, addressing a key challenge of today's economy – its increasing digitalisation. Concerns that the market for private digital currencies will crowd out public issuers from providing assets that fulfil the functions of money have resulted in what can be described as a rivalry between central banks in a technological race to maintain (or gain) their position in the IMS. The increasing adoption of digital money could offer additional opportunities for reserve diversification, such as its increased use in cross-border payments (Aiyar et al., 2023).

However, there are risks associated with the development of new forms of electronic currency in the real economy. Firstly, the financial laws, directives and regulations that impact digital currencies are complex and unstable, and the situation in Europe is very different compared to the United States. Secondly, there are new sources of risk to users, including the currency exchange acting negligently, unexpected exchange rate fluctuations, manipulation, mining pool fees, being denied access after losing the password, and payment errors because of the irreversibility of transactions. Thirdly, new threats may arise for the regulatory authorities and financial integrity, such as tax evasion, attempts to evade regulation within the financial sector, and efforts to avoid the seizure of assets and confiscation (Tasca, 2015).

There are different types of digital currencies, and this term is used to describe different types of currencies that exist in electronic form, that is cryptocurrencies, virtual currencies and Central Bank Digital Currencies (CBDCs; Figure 4.11).

Cryptocurrency is sometimes called a 'crypto-asset', and it is a digital representation of value that is a digital, encrypted and decentralised medium of exchange. While it is not issued by a central bank or public authority nor attached to a fiat currency, it can be used as a means of exchange and can be transferred, stored, or traded electronically (EBA, 2014, p. 5). Cryptocurrencies are obtained through a process called 'mining', which is defined as solving cryptographic equations with the use of computers. The most popular type of cryptocurrency is Bitcoin, which is the most widely recognised and used cryptocurrency, surpassing Ethereum and Tether in popularity.

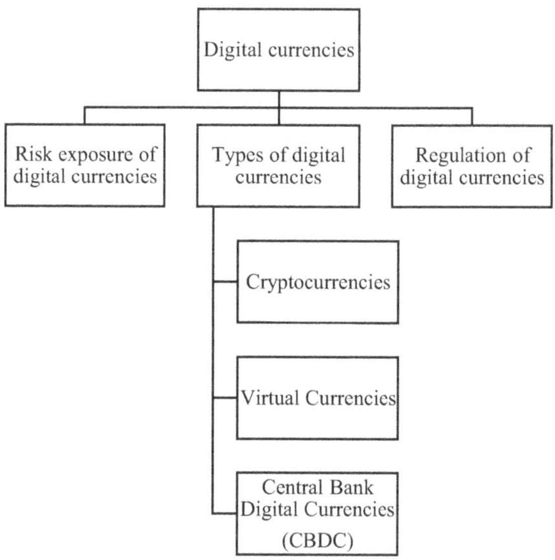

Figure 4.11 Types of digital currencies and the main issues surrounding classification
Source: Own elaboration based on Alsalmi et al. (2023).

Virtual currencies are unregulated digital currencies issued by private developers or a founding organisation. They are denominated in their own unit of account, distinct from fiat currency (i.e. not tied to legal tender). They can be stored, accessed or transacted electronically for different purposes, as agreed upon by the transacting parties. Virtual currencies have different levels of convertibility to real-world goods and services (IMF, 2016).[34]

CBDCs are defined by the IMF as 'a new form of money, issued digitally by the central bank and intended to serve as legal tender' (IMF, 2018, p. 7). Typically, they are digital currencies issued by the central bank. However, in contrast to a fiat currency, which can exist in both physical and digital forms, CBDCs exist only in digital form. Currently, all G20 member countries are exploring the use of CBDC, with 16 projects already in development or at the pilot stage (Aiyar et al., 2023).

The move by central banks to introduce central bank digital currency should be viewed as both a search for an alternative to cash and strategy to preserve the position of central banks amidst the proliferation of private payment systems. Moreover, the CBDC project has the potential to influence the position of the currency-issuing country in the global economy and the IMS, thereby shaping conditions for the operation of existing safe assets. The impact of CBDC issuance on the ability of governments and financial institutions to secure funding through the creation of safe assets will depend on the flexibility to substitute these currencies (Muller, 2020, p. 4). At the same time, by offering a new asset class to different actors (e.g. households and non-financial and financial firms), it has the potential to change the structure of the assets they hold.

The issuance of a digital currency can have both positive and negative consequences for the country issuing the reserve currency. However, identifying the effects of introducing such new financial assets is characterised by considerable uncertainty, given the current reliance on hypothetical assumptions. Hypothetical assumptions, while useful, have limitations in predicting the real-world impact of new financial assets. Experimental cases like Ecuador and Uruguay offer crucial data to address this gap (Muller, 2020, p. 4).

There are three key benefits of issuing a 'digital fiat currency':

1 Potential transactional savings,
2 Increased accessibility of financial products (financial inclusion), thereby eliminating financial exclusion,
3 Improvement in the transmission of monetary policy impulses.

The introduction of CBDCs is expected to accelerate the digitisation of financial settlements, a necessity in view of the rise of cashless transactions and electronic payments. Improving the accessibility of the payment system and eliminating financial exclusion are particularly strong motivations for central banks in emerging markets, where the lack of access and competition in the operation of payment systems raises transaction costs. Finally, by directly influencing the interest rates on the funds of all CBDC holders, central banks could, in theory, increase the efficiency of the monetary policy transmission mechanism.

The central bank's digital currency will be a new form of money with two key characteristics of safe assets: no liquidity risk and no credit risk. As these are the characteristics of safe assets, it will enable the CBDC to compete with other safe and liquid assets. Considering CBDCs according to the model of alternative safe assets proposed by Golec and Perotti (2017, p. 42), they can be placed at the level of cash (Muller, 2020, pp. 4–7). The effect of CBDCs may result in crowding out private financial sector safe assets, essentially bank financial instruments, from the market due to the greater degree of safety offered by central bank instruments. The extent of the effect of CBDC on the demand for alternative safe assets depends on whether it would be a better substitute for financial instruments in the retail or wholesale sector. To reduce the crowding-out effect and the possibility of funding private financial sector activity, it is suggested that CBDCs could be designed to limit access to this type of currency. This may involve reducing the services connected to CBDC use or requiring safe collateral for the use of this form of money (Muller, 2020, p. 21).

The stimulation of competition between currencies following the increased role of such central bank-issued safe assets in cross-border use could radically redefine the concept and essence of money. This could weaken the international role of existing international currencies, fostering de-internationalisation (mainly of the USD) and currency substitution (digital 'dollarisation' in countries with instable currencies and weak fundamentals). From the IMS point of view, such an evolution of global liquidity allocation would be beneficial, reducing the central role of the USD in the system and pushing for its diversification. The ECB recognises the link between CBDCs and currency internationalisation, stating that an increase in the internationalisation of the euro is not the direct objective of the CBDC project. However, implementing its own digital currency could increase the use of the currency at the global level (ECB, 2021).

On the other hand, there is a risk that the ongoing geo-economic fragmentation may both limit and increase risks stemming from digitalisation of the global payment system. What is more, a fragmented global payment system could, in turn, reinforce GEF through its effects on trade and capital flows (Aiyar et al., 2023).

Notes

1 The experience of emerging countries and distressed advanced economies demonstrates that the sovereign rating downgrade is followed by cuts in the ratings of domestic debt instruments. This policy of credit rating agencies reflects the widespread belief that private debt is always riskier than sovereign one (Luitel et al., 2016, p. 288).

2 Unlike a liquidity trap, which concentrates on the general asset shortage, a safety trap focuses on the shortage of safe assets. This kind of trap, as Blanchard et al. (2016) argue, is unresponsive to forward guidance – type policies or to the emergence of financial bubbles.
3 The GEF should be seen as a reversal of global economic integration. This policy-driven process is likely to affect the global economy through different distinct but interconnected channels, such as trade, technology, labour, capital and the provision of global public goods. The GEF may hinder cross-border capital flows, reducing the options for external financing and impeding economic development (Aiyar et al., 2023).
4 Henceforth 'debt ratios'.
5 In theory, high inflation can influence debt ratios through at least two channels: (1) higher nominal GDP and (2) higher nominal interest rates. The second mechanism depends on whether inflation is anticipated or comes as a surprise. Unanticipated inflation jumps may affect debt ratios only through the channel of higher nominal GDP (IMF 2023a).
6 IMF data for Q4 2022.
7 Data as of June 2021; percentage of foreign exchange and gold asset.
8 The ABF 2 is not the only policy initiative taken over to encourage the development of local currency bond markets in the region. Another example is the Asia Bond Market Initiative (ABMI), launched in 2002 under the ASEAN+3 framework.
9 The case in point here is the Securities Markets Programme announced by the ECB in May 2010. Due to its temporary nature and limited scale of interventions, the programme managed to calm down the markets only in the short term.
10 For example, Delatte and Guillaume (2020) estimate that after this announcement widened the spreads of heavily indebted countries by 7.9 basis points.
11 According to Delatte and Guillaume (2020), the PEEP announcement on 18 March reduced the spreads in largely indebted countries by 53.4 basis points.
12 Papadia and Temprano Arroyo (2022) narrowly define the set of euro area safe assets as including only sovereign bonds with a AAA credit rating.
13 In Papadia and Temprano Arroyo's (2022) study, the group of AA-rated countries comprised Belgium and France. In May 2023, S&P upgraded the Irish rating from AA- to AA.
14 The European instrument for temporary Support to mitigate Unemployment Risks in an Emergency.
15 Next Generation EU.
16 They were mentioned in Chapter 2, section 2.2.2.
17 Therefore, although the concept of pan-European bonds have so far been analysed in the context of the EMU, this section renders the considerations to be moved to the Community level.
18 Social bonds are meant to convince investors that the funds raised will be used to serve a truly social objective.
19 https://economy-finance.ec.europa.eu/eu-financial-assistance/sure_en (Retrieved on 30 November 2023).
20 https://commission.europa.eu/strategy-and-policy/eu-budget/eu-borrower-investor-relations/nextgenerationeu_en (Retrieved on 30 November 2023).
21 Both public, and private.
22 The necessity to rely on foreign portfolio investors was also the effect of relatively small domestic institutional investor base (BIS, 2020).
23 Since the ABMI was established, the five original members of ASEAN – Indonesia, Malaysia, the Philippines, Singapore, Thailand, Vietnam, plus China and Korea (ASEAN+2), have achieved remarkable progress in developing their domestic

bond markets. The total size of these local currency bond markets climbed from USD 1.06 trillion to USD 22.3 trillion at the end of 2021.

24 The MIT concept is derived from the observation that some countries have failed to progress from middle-income to high-income brackets in recent decades. After initial rapid growth, which is driven by abundant and cheap labour and the import of foreign technologies through foreign direct investment, continued strong growth increasingly requires high and sustained total factor productivity growth (Dieppe et al., 2018).

25 It emerged as a regional integration project to improve infrastructure connectivity and boost trade and investment along the ancient Silk Road (connecting Asia, Europe and Africa). Since its launching in 2013, it has expanded into disaster prevention, environmental degradation and innovation.

26 In 2014, China became one of the first major countries to start exploring a CBDC. Since then, it has been a leader in the development of domestic and cross-border payment via digital currencies. China began piloting its e-CNY programme in 2019 and has begun large-scale testing. The pilot has about 260 million wallet users (more detailed information can be found at: www.atlanticcouncil.org).

27 Cf. Cerutti and Obstfeld (2018, p. 5).

28 More recent data show that improvement is taking place. In recent years, the share of foreign investors has increased to around 3% (HKEX, 2022). However, the share of foreign investments in government (only sovereign) bonds increased from around 2.7% in 2016, to around 8.5% in 2019. This shows that foreign investors mainly invest in Chinese sovereign bonds.

29 The market for these bonds developed virtually overnight. Prior to 2015, it was largely impossible for local authorities to borrow funds. The drivers for this sector of the bond market include the implementation of the debt-for-bond swap programme and regulatory changes. However, the pricing of Chinese local government bonds is still highly regulated (Liu 2020). The scale of growth of the local government bond market (which is now one of the largest in the world) is illustrated by the fact that in 2017 it exceeded the size of the government bond market.

30 Local Government Financing Vehicles (LGFVs) are public enterprises established by local authorities. They are equipped with capital, land or other public resources and can borrow funds from banks or issue bonds.

31 Most of the debt is corporate debt of non-financial enterprises, including state-owned enterprises. China's overall debt ratio is thus comparable to that of high-income advanced economies like the United States (296%) and the euro area (292%t). I far exceeds debt levels in other major emerging market economies such as India (181%), Brazil (189%), Russia (136.9%) and Indonesia (80%).

32 The ratings were obtained from Trading Economics, n.d.

33 Otherwise known as distributed register technology.

34 Sometimes virtual currencies are a form of digital currency.

References

Aiyar, S., Chen, J., Ebeke, C., Garcia-Saltos, R., Gudmundsson, T., Illyina, A., … Trevino, J. (January 2023). Geoeconomic fragmentation and the future of multilateralism. *IMF Staff Discussion Notes*.

Aizenman, J., Jinjarak, Y., Nguyen, H. T., & Park, D. (2019). Fiscal space and government-spending and tax-rate cyclicality patterns: A cross-country comparison, 1960–2016. *Journal of Macroeconomics*, *60*, 229–252. doi:10.1016/j.jmacro.2019.02.006

Agur, I., Chan, M., Goswami, M., & Sharma, S. (2018). On International integration of emerging sovereign, Bond Markets, *IMF Working Paper 2018*.

Alogoskoufis, S., Giuzio, M., Kostka, T., Levels, A., Vivar, L. M., & Wedow, M. (2020). *How could a common safe asset contribute to financial stability and financial integration in the Banking Union?* European Central Bank. Available at: https://www.ecb.europa.eu/pub/fie/article/html/ecb.fieart202003_02~2b34819f75.en.html (Accessed: 29 December 2023).

Alsalmi, N., Ullah, S., & Rafique, M. (2023). Accounting for digital currencies. *Research in International Business and Finance*, *64*, 101897. doi:10.1016/j.ribaf.2023.101897

Amstad, M., & He, Z. (February 2019). Chinese bond market and interbank market. *NBER Working Paper*, no 25549. Available at SSRN: https://ssrn.com/abstract=3336500

Arslan, Y., Drehmann, M., & Hofmann, B. (2020). Central bank bond purchases in emerging market economies, BIS Bulletins 20, Bank for International Settlements.

Arslanalp, S., & Eichengreen, B. (2023). Living with high public debt. *Paper presented to Jackson Hole Symposium*, August 2023.

Arslanalp, S., Eichengreen, B., & Simpson-Bell, C. (2022). The stealth erosion of dollar dominance and the rise of nontraditional reserve currencies. *Journal of International Economics*, *138*, 103656. doi:10.1016/j.jinteco.2022.103656

Asian Development Bank, Asia Bond Monitor. Available at: https://www.adb.org/publications/asia-bond-monitor-november-2023 (November 2023).

Bank for International Settlements. (2001). *Collateral in wholesale financial markets: recent trends, risk management and market dynamics*. Committee on the Global Financial, Basel.

Bank of Russia. (2022). *Annual Report 2021*. Available at: https://www.cbr.ru/Collection/Collection/File/43443/ar_2021_e.pdf

Beirne, J., & Fratzscher, M. (2013). The pricing of sovereign risk and contagion during the European sovereign debt crisis. *Journal of International Money and Finance*, *34*, 60–82. doi:10.1016/j.jimonfin.2012.11.004

Bernanke, B. (2005). *The global saving glut and the U.S. current account deficit, Speech 77*. Board of Governors of the Federal Reserve System (U.S.).

Bini Smaghi, L. & Marcussen, M. (2019). Domesticating the euro. *Intereconomics*, *54*(2), 78–84. doi:10.1007/s10272-019-0798-z

Blanchard, O., Rajan, R., Rogoff, K., & Summers, L. H. (Eds.) (2016). *Progress and confusion: The state of macroeconomic policy*. Cambridge: The MIT Press.

Bogołębska, J. (2020). *Stabilność międzynarodowego system walutowego. Problemy i kierunki reformy*. Łódź: Wydawnictwo Uniwersytetu Łódzkiego.

Boone, L., Feis, J., Jorda, O., Schularick, M., & Taylor, A. (2022). "Debt: The eye of the storm", Centre for Economic Policy Research. *Geneva Reports on the World Economy*, no 24.

Bordo, M., & McCauley, R. (December 2017). A global shortage of safe assets: A new Triffin dilemma? *Atlantic Economic Journal*, *45*(4), 443–451.

Brunnermeier, M., & Huang, L. (2018). A global safe asset for and from emerging market economies. *NBER Working Paper*. doi:10.3386/w25373

Brunnermeier, M., Langfield, S., Pagano, M., Reis, R., Van Nieuwerburgh, S., & Vayanos, D. (2016). ESBies: Safety in the tranches. *Working Paper Series*, no 21 / September 2016. doi:10.2139/ssrn.2840935

Caballero, R. J. (2006). On the Macroeconomics of Asset Shortages. *Social Science Research Network*. https://doi.org/10.2139/ssrn.947587

Caballero, R. J. (2010). *The "Other" imbalance and the financial crisis*. https://doi.org/10.3386/w15636

Caballero, R. J., Farhi, E., & Gourinchas, P.-O. (2008). Financial crash, commodity prices, and global imbalances. *Brookings papers on economic activity*, 1–55. Available at: http://www.jstor.org/stable/27720394

Caballero, R. J., Emmanuel, F., & Pierre-Olivier, G. (2017). The safe assets shortage conundrum. *Journal of Economic Perspectives*, *31*(3), 29–46.

Caballero, R. J., & Farhi, E. (2014). *The safety trap*. https://doi.org/10.3386/w19927

Caballero, R. J., Farhi, E., & Gourinchas, P.-O. (2017). The safe assets shortage conundrum. *Journal of Economic Perspectives*, *31*(3), 29–46. doi:10.1257/jep.31.3.29

Cabral, N. C. (2021). Borrowing in the European Union: From a pure national model to the antechamber of a European federal fiscal solution. *Journal of European Integration, 43*(8), 939–954. Available at: https://www.tandfonline.com/doi/full/10.1080/07036337.2021.1881499

Cecchetti, S. G., Mohanty, M., & Zampolli, F. (2010). The future of public debt: Prospects and implications. *Social Science Research Network*. https://doi.org/10.2139/ssrn.1599421

Cerutti, E., & Obstfeld, M. (December 2018). China's bond market and global financial markets. *IMF Working Paper*, no 18/253. Available at SSRN: https://ssrn.com/abstract=3314584

Ciupa, K. M. (2018). Technologia Blockchain i jej wpływ na rozwój infrastruktury rynku kapi-tałowego, [w:] T. Czerwińska, A. Z. Nowak (red.), Rynek kapitałowy – regulacje i fundamenty, Wydawnictwo Naukowe Wydziału Zarządzania Uniwersytetu Warszawskiego, Warszawa, s. 95–112. Available at: http://www.wz.uw.edu.pl/portaleFiles/6133-wydawnictwo-/Rynek_kapita%C5%82owy_-_regulacje_DRUK.pdf#page=95

Collignon, S. (2004). The end of the stability and growth pact? *International Economics and Economic Policy*, *1*(1), 15–19. doi:10.1007/s10368-004-0009-6

Crockett, A. (1997). The theory and practice of financial stability. *GEI Newsletter Issue*, no 6. Cambridge: Gonville and Caius College Cambridge, 11–12 July.

De Grauwe, P., & Ji, Y. (2013). Self-fulfilling crises in the Eurozone: An empirical test. *Journal of International Money and Finance*, *34*, 15–36. doi:10.1016/j.jimonfin.2012.11.003

De Grauwe, P., & Ji, Y. (2018). How safe is a safe asset? *CEPS Policy Insights 2018-08*, Centre for European Policy Studies.

De Santis, R. (2012). The euro area sovereign debt crisis: Safe haven, credit rating agencies and the spread of the fever from Greece, Ireland and Portugal. *Social Science Research Network*. https://doi.org/10.2139/ssrn.1991159

Del Negro, M., Giannone, D., Giannoni, M., & Tambalotti, A. (2017). Safety, liquidity, and the natural rate of interest. *Staff Reports*, no 812, Federal Reserve Bank of New York.

Delatte, A.-L., & Guillaume, A. (2020). Covid 19: A new challenge for the EMU? *CEPR Discussion Paper*, no 14848.

Dell'Ariccia, G., Rabanal, P., & Sandri, D. (2018). Unconventional monetary policies in the euro area, Japan, and the United Kingdom. *Journal of Economic Perspectives*, *32*(4), 147–172.

Delpla, J., & Weizsäcker, J. V. (2011). Eurobonds: The blue bond concept and its implications. *Bruegel Policy Contribution*, *6*. Available at: https://www.bruegel.org/policy-brief/eurobonds-blue-bond-concept-and-its-implications

Dieppe, A., Gilhooly, R., Han, J., Korhonen, I., & Lodge, D. (2018). The transition of China to sustainable growth – implications for the global economy and the Euro Area (January 26, 2018). *ECB Occasional Paper No. 206*. Available at SSRN: https://ssrn.com/abstract=3113109 or https://doi.org/10.2139/ssrn.3113109

EBA. (2014). *The European Banking authority*. Available at: https://www.centralbank.ie/consumer-hub/consumer-notices/eba-opinion-on-virtual-currencies

ECB. (2020a). Introductory statement press conference 12 March 2020. Available at: https://www.ecb.europa.eu/press/press_conference/monetary-policy-statement/2020/html/ecb.is200312~f857a21b6c.en.html#qa (Accessed: 12 March 2020).

ECB. (2020b). ECB announces €750 billion Pandemic Emergency Purchase Programme (PEPP). Available at: https://www.ecb.europa.eu/press/pr/date/2020/html/ecb.pr200318_1~3949d6f266.en.html (Accessed: 18 March 2020).

ECB. (2021). *The international role of the euro*. Available at: https://www.ecb.europa.eu/pub/pdf/ire/ecb.ire202106~a058f84c61.en.pdf

Eichengreen, B., Mehl, A., & Chitu, L. (2018). *How global currencies work. Past, present and future*. Princeton: Princeton University Press.

Eijffinger, S., Kobielarz, M. L., & Uras, B. (2015). Sovereign debt, Bail-Outs and contagion in a monetary union. *Social Science Research Network*. https://doi.org/10.2139/ssrn.2574210

Engel, C., & Park, J. (2022). Debauchery and original sin: The currency composition of sovereign debt. *Journal of the European Economic Association*, *20*(3), 1095–1144. https://doi.org/10.1093/jeea/jvac009

ESRB. (2018). *Sovereign bond-backed securities: a feasibility study*. Frankfurt am Main: ESRB.

European Commission. (2023). *EU investor presentation – Investing in EU-bonds & EU-Bills (2023)*. Available at: https://commission.europa.eu/strategy-and-policy/eu-budget/eu-borrower-investor-relations/investor-presentation_en

Fang, X., Hardy, B., & Lewis, K. (April 2023). Who holds sovereign debt and why it matters? *NBER Working Paper*, no 30087.

Financial Times. (2020). *The safe asset shortage after Covid-19*. Available at: https://www.ft.com/content/b98078c0-6acc-43e6-929b-13883c211288 (Accessed: 12 October 2021).

Furey, D., Zhang, B., & Binny, J. (2018). *Opening of China's bond market: What global investors need to know*. Available at: https://www.ssga.com (Accessed 17 December 2018).

Gilbert, N. D., Hessel, J., & Verkaart, S. (2013). Towards a stable monetary union: What role for Eurobonds? (SSRN Scholarly Paper ID 2269538). *Social Science Research Network*. doi:10.2139/ssrn.2269538

Giordano, R., Pericoli, M., & Tommasino, P. (2013). Pure or wake-up-call contagion? Another look at the EMU sovereign debt crisis. *International Finance*, *16*(2), 131–160. doi:10.1111/j.1468-2362.2013.12033.x

Golec, P., & Perotti, E. (2017). Safe assets: A review. *Working Paper Series*, no. 2035, European Central Bank.

Gopinath, G., & Stein, J. (2018). Trade invoicing, bank funding, and Central Bank Reserve Holdings. *AEA Papers and Proceedings*, *108*, 542–546. doi:10.1257/pandp.20181065

Gorton, G. (2016). The history and economics of safe assets. *NBER Working Paper*, no 22210.

Gossé, J., & Mourjane, A. (2021). A European safe asset: New perspectives. *Bulletin de la Banque de France*, *234/6*, March–April.

Gourinchas, P. (2017). The fundamental structure of the international monetary system. In M. Bordo & J. Taylor (Eds.), *Rules for international monetary stability. Past, present, and future*. Stanford, CA: Hoover Institution Press, pp. 196–203. Available at: https://static1.squarespace.com/static/5e6033a4ea02d801f37e15bb/t/5ee29d92e132c77e196e1730/1591909780220/rulesforinternationalmonetarystability-ch4.pdf

Gourinchas, P. O., & Jeanne, O. (2012). Global safe assets. *BIS Working Paper*, no 399. Available at SSRN: https://ssrn.com/abstract=2247974

HKEX. (2022). *Hong Kong Exchanges and Clearing Market Website*.

Ilzetzki, E., Reinhart, C., & Rogoff, K. (2020). Why is the euro punching below its weight? *NBER Working Paper*. doi:10.3386/w26760

IMF. (2012). *Global financial stability report*. Washington, DC. Available at: https://www.imf.org/external/pubs/ft/gfsr/2012/01/

IMF. (2016). *Monetary and capital markets, legal, and strategy and policy review departments virtual currencies and beyond: Initial considerations*. Available at: https://www.imf.org/external/pubs/ft/sdn/2016/sdn1603.pdf.

IMF. (2018). *Casting light on central bank digital currencies*. Available at: https://www.imf.org/en/Publications/Staff-Discussion-Notes/Issues/2018/11/13/Casting-Light-on-Central-Bank-Digital-Currencies-46233

IMF. (2023a). Coming down to earth: How to tackle soaring public debt; Chapter 3. In *World* ***economic*** *outlook*, pp. 69–89.

IMF. (October 2023b). *Global financial stability report*, Chapter 2: A new look at global banking vulnerabilities.

IMF. (2023c) World Economic Outlook, 2023 database.

Janse, K. (2023). Developing European safe assets, intereconomics. *Review of European Economic Policy*, *58*(6), 315–319.

Kosse, A., & Mattei, I. (2023). Making headway - Results of the 2022 BIS survey on central bank digital currencies and crypto, *BIS Papers, Bank for International Settlements*, number 136.

Krautzberger, M. (2020). *The implications of EU bond issuance*. Available at: https://www.ecb.europa.eu/paym/groups/pdf/bmcg/200923/20200923_Item_3a_The%20implications_of%20EU_bond_issuance_Blackrock.pdf

Krishnamurthy, A., & Vissing-Jørgensen, A. (2012). The aggregate demand for treasury debt. *Journal of Political Economy*, *120*(2), 233–267.

Lam, W. R., & Wang, J. (2018). China's local government bond market (September 2018). *IMF Working Paper No. 18/219*. Available at SSRN: https://ssrn.com/abstract=3267242

Luitel, P., Vanpée, R., & De Moor, L. (2016). Pernicious effects: How the credit rating agencies disadvantage emerging markets. *Research in International Business and Finance*, *38*, 286–298. https://doi.org/10.1016/j.ribaf.2016.04.009

Liu, K. (2020). Chinese local government debts: Institutional change, roles in economic growth and pricing. *International Journal of Economic Policy in Emerging Economies*, *15*(1). doi:10.1504/IJEPEE.2022.10043337

McCauley, R. (2019). Safe assets: Made, not just born. *BIS Working Papers*, no 769.

Mendoza, E. G., & Ostry, J. D. (2008). International evidence on fiscal solvency: Is fiscal policy "responsible"? *Journal of Monetary Economics*, *55*(6), 1081–1093. https://doi.org/10.1016/j.jmoneco.2008.06.003

Merler, S., & Pisani-Ferry, J. (2012). Sudden stops in the euro area. *Review of Economics and Institutions*, *3*(3). doi:10.5202/rei.v3i3.97

Mitchener, K. J., & Trebesch, C. (2021). Sovereign debt in the 21st century: Looking backward, looking forward. *SSRN Electronic Journal*. doi:10.2139/ssrn.3812076

Muhleisen, M. (2022). *The international role of the euro and the dollar*. Washington, DC: The Atlantic Council.

Muller, C. (2020). The demand for safe liquid assets and the implications of issuing a Central Bank Digital Currency for bank funding instruments, Norges Bank, Staff Moemo, No. 8/2020, Norges Bank, Oslo. Available at: http://hdl.handle.net/11250/2690368

Nakamoto, S. (2008). *Bitcoin: A peer-to-peer electronic cash system*. Available at: https://bitcoin.org/bitcoin.pdf

OECD. (2019). *China Economic Snapshot*. Available at: www.oecd.org/eco/surveys/economic-survey-china.htm.

Oliveira, L., Curto, J. D., & Nunes, J. P. V. (2012). The determinants of sovereign credit spread changes in the euro-zone. *Journal of International Financial Markets, Institutions and Money*, *22*(2), 278–304. doi:10.1016/j.intfin.2011.09.007

Ottonello, P., & Perez, D. J. (2019). The currency composition of sovereign debt. *American Economic Journal: Macroeconomics*, *11*(3), 174–208, doi:10.1257/mac.20180019

Papadia, F., & Temprano Arroyo, H. (2022). Don't look only to Brussels to increase the supply of safe assets in the European Union. *Policy Briefs*, Bruegel. Available at: https://www.bruegel.org/policy-brief/dont-look-only-brussels-increase-supply-safe-assets-european-union

Prasad, E. S. (2011). Role reversal in global finance. *NBER Working Papers*, no 17497. National Bureau of Economic Research, Inc.

Reis, R. (2022). Debt revenue and the sustainability of public debt. *Journal of Economic Perspectives, American Economic Association*, *36*(4), 103–124, Fall.

Reinhart, C., & Rogoff, K. (2010). Growth in a time of debt. *American Economic Review*, *100*(2), 573–578. doi:10.1257/aer.100.2.573

Sharma, R. (2023, April 23). What strong gold says about the weak dollar. *Financial Times*. Available at: https://www.ft.com/content/e9c78b99-8a29-47e2-b5bf-9f7542608cf6 (Accessed: 23 April 2023)

Schinasi, G. (2004). Defining financial stability. *IMF Working Paper*, no WP/04/187.

Schipke, A., Turunen, J., Choueiri, N., & Gulde-Wolf, A.-M. (Eds.) (2023). *India's financial system: Building the foundation for strong and sustainable growth*. Washington, DC: IMF.

Šreiberytė, E., & Spurga, S. A. (2021). *Joint debt arrangements in EMU: From NextGenEU to eurobonds*. (Issue 2021; Issue 2037 of Occasional Paper Series).

Stawasz-Grabowska, E. (2020). Negative feedback loop between banks and sovereigns in the euro area – experience of the crisis and post-crisis perspective.

Comparative Economic Research. Central and Eastern Europe, *23*(3), 41–61. doi:10.18778/1508-2008.23.19

Tasca, P. (2015). Digital currencies: Principles, trends, opportunities, and risks. *Social Science Research Network*. doi:10.2139/ssrn.2657598

Temprano Arroyo, H. (June 2022). The EU's response to the COVID-19 crisis: A game changer for the international role of the euro? *Discussion Paper*, no 164 (europa.eu).

van Riet, A. (2017). Addressing the safety trilemma: A safe sovereign asset for the eurozone. *Social Science Research Network*. doi:10.2139/ssrn.3723381

van Riet, A. (2021). *From Euro Crisis to Covid Pandemic: The Changing Universe of Safe Public Debt in Europe*. https://fbf.eui.eu/wp-content/uploads/2022/06/VAN_RIET_2021-10-01-Changing-universe-of-public-debt-in-Europe-DebtCon5-v2.pdf

van Riet, A. (2021). Safe and risky sovereigns in the Euro area capital market: Financial drivers of fiscal policies in Germany and Italy. *German Politics*, *30*(3), 2021.

Vermeiren, M. (2019). Meeting the world's demand for safe assets? Macroeconomic policy and the international status of the euro after the crisis. *European Journal of International Relations*, *25*, 30–60.

Véron, N. (2017). *Sovereign concentration charges: A new regime for banks sovereign exposures*. Brussels: European Parliament.

Verdun, A. (2010). Ten years EMU: An assessment of ten critical claims. *International Journal of Economics and Business Research*, *2*(1/2), 144–163, Inderscience Enterprises Ltd.

Conclusion

These concluding remarks bring together the main findings from the book. Drawing insights from the material presented in each chapter, the book establishes new guidelines within the safe asset dilemma. It also addresses the main questions and outlines future trends in the global economy. This book discusses many concepts that financial market participants and policymakers can use when formulating the investment strategy, building a portfolio or communicating public opinion. This unique book makes numerous contributions and has implications for investors and policymakers that have not been mentioned so far. First, it defines and describes safe asset instruments with their supply and demand characteristics. Second, it offers a unified framework that links the safe asset discussion with the post-crisis environment (the Global Financial Crisis (GFC) and COVID-19), monetary policy and the banking sector, portfolio theory, and digital currency issues. Third, it highlights the problem of safe asset shortages and their implications for financial stability and economic growth. It presents alternative sources of potential safe asset creation, such as European Union, common debt issuance within Economic and Monetary Union or the emerging economies of China and India.

Safe assets are financial instruments that are desired by investors as they provide full protection from credit, the market, inflation, currency and idiosyncratic risks; they are also highly liquid. They aim to supply the real economy with money through a network of international stock markets, financial intermediaries and other institutions. At the same time, safe assets perform numerous functions, such as hedging in financial transactions, storing value, being a key component of prudential regulation or a benchmark for other, riskier financial instruments. In addition, they have a number of attributes: moneyness, insensitivity to information or the convenience yield. The difference between safe assets and the safe-haven concept is mainly visible in the short-lived phenomenon of the latter, increasing its value during a market turmoil. Today, high price volatility and changing financial conditions, aided by the rapid circulation of information, create a natural place for the emergence of investments that can mitigate safety requirements.

Although many assets have some safety attributes, the dominant role in the provision of safe assets is played by public sector financial instruments,

DOI: 10.4324/9781003376538-6

including government bonds with the highest rating. Issuers of these assets must fulfil a number of economic (debt market size) and noneconomic (institutional quality) conditions, resulting in a narrow pool of issuers, mostly the United States. However, there are limits to the issuance of public debt. The historical experience of the global economy, illustrated by the Triffin paradox and by theoretical considerations of the Laffer curve, raises questions about the risk of main safe assets providers' loss of debt sustainability.

The contemporary structure of safe asset supply is shaped by the United States, as a key global provider. Currently, more than half of the global safe asset supply is made up of government bonds with the top credit ratings, securitised instruments, investment-grade corporate debt, and gold. The main question is whether the supply is likely to satisfy the global demand, given that the issuance of sovereign debt by advanced economies is a key source of safe assets in the global financial markets. Debt instruments issued by advanced economies have a special characteristic of safe assets, but they can be lost very rapidly if a country's market perception is questioned. As a consequence, deterioration in fiscal and monetary conditions has an important endogenous effect on safe assets supply. In periods of financial instability, the role of global safe asset providers should be supplemented by smaller regional providers. Private sector production of safe assets is closely linked to economic conditions and may collapse when the onset of a global crisis occurs.

Different economic sectors, such as commercial banks, central banks, individual and institutional investors, and non-financial corporations, contribute to the creation of safe assets, thanks to the broad range of functions they can perform. This makes safe assets an important portfolio component for different investor groups, especially banks. The high demand of central banks for safe assets, driven by policies to accumulate foreign exchange reserves, has become an important determinant of monetary and fiscal conditions in the issuing countries, thus affecting the stability of the IMS. Financial globalisation, which has resulted in cross-border transactions in financial instruments, is reflected in the scale of foreign holdings of safe assets, which are prominent in central banks. Thus, safe asset creation dilemmas are a global problem, not just a domestic one. Furthermore, the role of gold as a safe asset in central banks' portfolios is also important. The analysis of gold prices and central banks' policies towards gold allows us to make the assumption that after decades (the 1970s–1990s) of gold's diminishing role, it will play a significant role in their portfolios as a result of high market uncertainty in the global economy.

The safe assets shortage problem prompts the question about the possibility of increasing global supply. In view of the above concerns, further increases in public safe assets from the United States, as a key global supplier, should be complemented by regional suppliers. The euro area may have a special place here, provided that it can develop a system for creating common debt. The debt issuance processes currently taking place within the framework of crisis management in the EU are a good proxy for further, more systemic measures within the EMU. Moreover, the potential of emerging market countries, led by China and India, in providing safe assets cannot be overlooked. The depth of China's financial market and the booming bond markets point to the country's potential to provide safe assets in the future.

The emergence of new safe asset-issuing countries is linked with the internationalisation of their currencies and strong interdependence with the global economy. However, safe assets cannot be provided without increasing fiscal deficits, either by covering instruments with government guarantees or by using more sophisticated financial engineering treatments (pooling, tranches based on fiscal risk-sharing mechanisms). The existence of a public debt limit at the national level also implies the need to use the potential of various institutions to provide supranational debt. These institutions can be regional and international development banks, integration groups, regional financial arrangements or international organisations (such as the IMF, which is often referred to in this function). It also raises the question of how the emergence of digital money, both private and that of central banks, will modify the role and importance of traditional safe assets. Given the evolutionary nature of the safe asset function, it is expected that with the development of financial innovation, including the evolution of forms of money, the current structure of safe assets will be modified.

Given the complexity and multilayered nature of safe asset instruments, as well as the continuing evolution of the international financial and monetary system, it is important to be aware of their evolution and changing paradigms. While acknowledging that safe assets can be used problematically, this book offers a more mature and reflective perspective, offering the potential for further discussion.

> The only real security that a man can have in this world is a reserve of knowledge, experience, and ability.
>
> – Henry Ford

Glossary

ABF	Asian Bond Fund
ABMI	Asia Bond Market Initiative
ABS	Asset-backed securities
AEs	advanced economies
ASEAN	Association of Southeast Asian Nations
BoJ	Bank of Japan
BRICS	acronym of Brazil, Russia, India, China and South Africa
CBDCs	Central Bank Digital Currencies
CBGA	Central Bank Gold Agreements
CD	certificates of deposit
CDS	credit default swap
CE	Credit Easing
CME	comprehensive monetary easing
EBA	European Banking Authority
EBRD	European Bank for Reconstruction and Development
ECB	European Central Bank
EFSF	European Financial Stability Facility
EIB	European Investment Bank
EMEs	emerging market economies
EMU	Economic and Monetary Union
ESM	European Stability Mechanism
ESRB	European Systemic Risk Board
ETFs	Exchange Traded Funds
EU	European Union
FPI	Foreign Portfolio Investor
GDP	Gross domestic product
GEF	geo-economic fragmentation
GFC	Global Financial Crisis
GFSN	Global Financial Safety Net
GG	General government
GIIPS	acronym of Greece, Italy, Ireland, Portugal and Spain
GPFG	Norway's Government Pension Fund Global
GSA	global safe asset

GSE	Government-Sponsored Enterprises
HQLA	high-quality liquid assets
IBC	Insolvency and Bankruptcy Code
IFSWF	International Forum of Sovereign Wealth Funds
IIP	international investment position
IMF	International Monetary Fund
IMS	International Monetary System
LCR	Liquidity Coverage Ratio
LGFVs	Local Government Financing Vehicles
MBS	mortgage-backed securities
MFI	monetary financial institution
MS	Member State
NGEU	Next Generation EU
NQA	No questions asked
OECD	Organisation for Economic Co-operation and Development
OMT	Outright Monetary Transactions
PEPP	Pandemic Emergency Purchase Program
PPP	purchasing power parity
PSPP	Public Sector Purchase Programme
QE	Quantitative Easing
RFAs	Regional Financing Arrangements
RFF	Recovery and Resilience Facility
S&P	Standard & Poor's
SBBS	Sovereign Bond-Backed Securities
SDR	Special Drawing Rights
SGP	Stability and Growth Pact
SIFMA	Securities Industry and Financial Markets Association
SMP	Securities Markets Programme
SOE	state-owned enterprises
SPV	Special Purpose Vehicle
SRM	Single Resolution Mechanism
SSM	Single Supervisory Mechanism
SWFs	sovereign wealth funds
TFUE	Treaty on the Functioning of the European Union
WGC	World Gold Council

Index

Note: Bold page numbers refer to tables; *italic* page numbers refer to figures and page numbers followed by "n" denote endnotes.

ABS *see* asset-backed securities (ABS)
adverse selection 4, 8, 56
Asian 81, 82, 103, 142, 157, 159; Bond Market Initiatives 159, 173n8, 173n23; crisis 59, 90, 111, 125
asset-backed securities (ABS) 50, 51, 58, 59, *60*, 78, 107
asset purchase programme(s) 80, 126, 147

bank(s): commercial 11, 45, 46, 75, 182; debt 44, 61; deposits 10, 43, 109, 114, 121, 142, 149
bonds: central bank 162; corporate 38, 51, 56, 58, 78, 79, 104, 112, 115n5, 124, 143, 161–163, 168; credit 162; financial 161, 162; government 6–9, 14, 24, 39, 41, 43, 48, 51, 57, 58, 62, 63, 66, 67, 69, 75, 77, 80, 81, 98, 104, 106, 107, 109, 110, 115n4, 116n18, 122–124, 142, 143, 154, 158–163, **164**, 165, 166, 168, 174n29, 182; policy bank 161–163, **164**; sovereign 7–9, 38, 48, *50*, 62, 81, 107, 144, 145, *145*, 147, 149, 150, 152, 153, 157, 158, 168, 173n12, 174n28

carry trade 22, 106
CBGA *see* Central Bank Gold Agreement(s) (CBGA)
central bank(s): as lenders of last resort 43, 62, 63, 69, 70n5, 80, 147; money 10, 11, 51, 80; as providers of safe assets 36–39, **37**, *38*, *39*, 56, 63, 134
Central Bank Gold Agreement(s) (CBGA) 92–94, *94*, 96, 97

chartalism 45, 70n3, 136
collateral 6, **12**, 13, **13**, 43, 45, 46, 48–51, 57, 76–81, 84, 115n1, 122, 124, 125, 129, 147, 150, 153, 172
convenience yield 9, 30n2, 58, 114, 115, 124, 181
corporate 108, 166; bonds 38, 51, 56, 58, 78, 79, 104, 112, 115n5, 124, 143, 161–163, 168; debt 10, **11**, **12**, 48, 56, 79, 106, 112, 165, 174n31, 182
covered bonds 48–50, 78, 79, 142
credit rating 4, 8, 10, 41, 48, 51, 56, 57, 59, 63, 83, 104, *146*, 147, **148**, *149*, 152, 156, 158, 172n1, 173n12, 182
cryptocurrencies: bitcoin 15, 24, 25, 169, 170; as safe assets 24–25
currency: digital 24, 160, 169–172, *170*, 174n26, 174n34, 181; EUR **37**, 104, 115n6, 137–139, 154–156; international dominant 3, 36–38, 41–43, 47, 98; reserve 15, 21, 24, 38–40, 43, 59, 65–67, 69, 81, 84, 89, 92, 95, 96, 115n7, 125, 126, 131, 132, *133*, 134, 137–139, 150, 160, 171; RMB **37**, 99, 137–139, 160, 161, 166; USD **17**, 18, *18*, 30n2, **37**, 38, 39, 41–44, 67, 84, 90, 92, 95, 98, 99, 104, 106, 114, 116n9, 126, 135, 137–140, 142, 165, 172, 174n23

debt: excessive 125, 132; government 2, 5, 7, 10, 30, 30n2, 39, 45, 57–59, 65, 67–69, 75, 77–81, 86, 96, 102, 106–108, *108*, 110, 122, 124, 128, 129, **130**, 131, *133*, 134, 143, 145, 165–168; instruments 4, 7, 23–24,

30n5, 36, 42, 43, 46, 49, **53**, 56, 57, 59, 62, 74–78, 101, 102, 106, 110, 121, 125, 134, 141, 143, 150, 152, 154, 163, 172n1, 182; international 38, *38*; overhang 48, 132; private 44, 56–63, *60*, *61*, 172n1; public **12**, 15, 41, 45, 46, 57, 58, 61–69, 81, 96, 110, 117, 122, 123, 125, 130–135, *133*, 141, 143, 159, 182, 183; supranational **11**, **12**, 51, **52**, 56, 142, 154–157, 183
diversifier 15, **15**, 19, 24, **29**, 87

euro area 20, 36, *50*, **54**, 78, 80, 81, 89, **91**, 96, 108, 110, 132, 143, 145–147, 149, 151, 153, 154, 157, 173n12, 174n31, 182; debt crisis **53**, 62, 63, 65, 123, 146; monetary policy of 150
Eurobonds 151–153, **153**
exorbitant 2; duty 66; privilege 38–42, 66

Federal Reserve System (Fed) 3, 18, 75, 80, 92
financial instability 42, 61, 66, 121, 124, 127, 129, 166, 182
financial stability 1–3, 22, **54**, 57, 108, 121–174, 181
fiscal: capacity/space 66–67, 69, 87, 132, 165; constraints 40; expansion 3, 85, 130–132; reduction 140, 183
flight to safety/flight to quality 8, 42, 124, 140, 153
foreign exchange reserves/foreign reserves: accumulation 59, 66, 75, 81–84, 86, 88, 111, 125, 140, 141; currency composition of 135, *137*, 139, 140; holdings 3, 40, 41, 59, *60*, 105, 110, 111, *111*, 112, *112*, **113**, 122, 160, 161, 182; motives of accumulation of 82–84; structure of 21, 112, 137

GEF *see* geo-economic fragmentation (GEF)
geo-economic fragmentation (GEF) 130, 136, 139, 159, 172, 173n3
GFSN *see* Global Financial Safety Net (GFSN)
Global Financial Crisis (GFC) 4, 13, 16, 18, 20–23, 51, 59, 74–76, 78–80, 84–86, 89, 93–95, 97, 99, 105, 111, 113, 125, 126, 129–132, **130**, 138, 140, 144–148, 150, 151, 154, 157, 158, 162, 167, 181
Global Financial Safety Net (GFSN) 83–84, 87, 94, 130
global imbalances 84, 98, 125, 126
global saving glut 126, 163
Global Sovereign Bonds (GloSBies) 141
gold 5, 15–20, **17**, *17*, *20*, 21, **21**, 24, 25, 30, 37, **37**, 44, 46–48, **47**, 56, 67, 87–90, *88–90*, **91**, 92–100, *94*, **95**, **96**, *97*, 115–116n9, 116n11, 168, 173n7, 182
good friend analogy 8, 10, 62

hedge 7, 13–17, **15**, 19, 24, **29**, 30, 77, 87, 103, 129; portfolio hedge **12**, 30

IMS *see* international monetary system (IMS)
information insensitivity 7, 8, 13, 74
instruments: debt 4, 7, 23, 24, 36, 42, 43, 46, 49, **53**, 56, 57, 59, 62, 74–78, 101, 102, 106, 110, 121, 125, 134, 141, 143, 150, 152, 154, 163, 172n1, 182; non-credit 5, 46, 56, 116n19
insurance corporations 107, 108
international monetary system (IMS) 1, 2, 3, 37, **37**, 41, 43, 47, *47*, 67, 69, 70n1, 84, 87, 89, 90, 92, 98, 111, 114, 116n9, 135–141, *137*, 169, 171, 172, 182
investment funds 101, 103, 107, 108, 111, 116n14, 131
investors: foreign 40, 75, 110, 115, 158, 160, 161, 165–168, 174n28; global 41, 106; institutional 48, 75, 87, 101, 160, 173n22, 182

Laffer curve 63–66, *64*, *65*, 125, 131, 134, 182
liquidity 6–11, **12**, 24, 30, 40, 45, 46, 58, 61, *61*, 65, 67, 74, 76–84, 87, 94, 100, 104, 105, 109, 112, 113, 125, 128, 136, 139, 141, 142, 145, 147, 149, 150, 160, 163, 166, 173n2; global 2, 37, **37**, 42, 47, 172; high 5, 13, 22

MBS *see* mortgage-backed securities (MBS)
money market fund shares 7, 10, **12**
moneyness 7, 9, 74, 181
mortgage-backed securities (MBS) 50, 51, 58, 59, 78, 79

no questions asked (NQA) 9, 57, 61, 121, 145

pension funds 5, 106, 107, 109, 116n15
portfolio theory 26, 30, 181

QE *see* quantitative easing (QE)
quantitative easing (QE) 18, 69, 79–81, 95, 107, 115n6, 122

Regional Financial Arrangements (RFA) 56, 87, 183
repurchase agreement (repo) 6, 10, 11, **12**, 45, 51, 57, 58, 76–79, 114
RFA *see* Regional Financial Arrangements (RFA)
risk: aversion 65, 99, 126, 127; credit 5, 10, 11, 51, 56, 59, 61, 98, 99, 113, 141, 172; default 4, 8–10, 56, 68, 116n13, 122, 136, 145, 156; exchange rate 5, 41, 81, 166; inflation/inflationary 5, 11

safe asset(s): demand for 39, 41–43, 46, 58, 59, 67, 74–116, 125, 128, 130, 149; global provider 36–38, **37**, *38*, 41, 56, 66, 110–115, *111–113*, **113**, 130, 136, 182; historical 1, 44–48, **47**, 69, 78, 155; of provision **13**, 43–48, **47**, 56–63, *60*, *61*, 181–182; regional provider of 2–3, 36–38, **37**, *38*, 56, 63, 66, 130, 182; scarcity/shortage 3, 57, 66, 75, 80, 121–174, 181, 182; supply of 36–70, 74, 81, 125–130, **130**, 141, 154, 169–172, *170*; tautology 8–9
safe-haven: asset 8, 13–30, **14**, **15**, *16–18*, **17**, **20**, *20*, **21**, *23*, *25*, *27–29*, **29**, 30n2, 56, 66; commodities 16; currencies 21–23, *23*, 86, 124; strong 14, **15**, 24, 25; weak 14, **15**
safety trap 66, 128, 129, 173n2
sanctions 98, 138, 139; financial sanctions, imposition of 10, 99, 144
SBBS *see* Sovereign Bond-Backed Securities (SBBS)
securitization 8, 10, 11, 45, 48, 50, 59, 142, 182
shadow banking 45, 122
sovereign 5, 7–9, 38, *39*, 41, 45, 46, 48, 49, 67, 75, 78–81, 84, 86, 106–108, 116n14, *123*, 124, 125, 129, 131, 138, 144–148, *145*, *149*, 151–154, 157, 158, 165, 168, 172n1, 173n12, 174n28, 182; creditworthiness 8, 102, 123, 141, 150; debt crisis 20, **53**, 62, 63, 65, 68, 121–123, 130, 146
sovereign-bank nexus/diabolic loop/doom loop 122–123
Sovereign Bond-Backed Securities (SBBS) **153**, 153–154
sovereign wealth fund(s) (SWFs) 5, 86, 100–106, *102*, *104*, *105*, 116n14, 140
store of value 4–6, 13, 42
strategic complementarity 8, 43, 67
SWFs *see* sovereign wealth fund(s) (SWFs)

treasury: bills 5, 30, 106, 107; bonds 5, 9, 24, 106, 122, 162, **164**; US 9, 18, 24, 30, 59, *60*, 78, 106–108, 110–112, *111–113*, 114, 115, 127, 129
Triffin dilemma/Triffin paradox 67, 98, 125, 131, 182

unconventional monetary policy 79, 80

For Product Safety Concerns and Information please contact our EU representative GPSR@taylorandfrancis.com Taylor & Francis Verlag GmbH, Kaufingerstraße 24, 80331 München, Germany